WHERE NEXT FOR CRIMINAL JUSTICE?

David Faulkner and Ros Burnett

First published in Great Britain in 2012 by

The Policy Press
University of Bristol
Fourth Floor
Beacon House
Queen's Road
Bristol BS8 1QU
UK

t: +44 (0)117 331 4054
f: +44 (0)117 331 4093
tpp-info@bristol.ac.uk
www.policypress.org.uk

North America office:
The Policy Press
c/o The University of Chicago Press
1427 East 60th Street
Chicago, IL 60637, USA
t: +1 773 702 7700
f: +1 773 702 9756
e: sales@press.uchicago.edu
www.press.uchicago.edu

British Library Cataloguing in Publication Data
A catalogue record for this book is available from the British Library.

Library of Congress Cataloging-in-Publication Data
A catalog record for this book has been requested.

ISBN 978 1 84742 891 2 paperback
ISBN 978 1 84742 892 9 hardcover

Cover design by Qube Design Associates, Bristol
Front cover: image kindly supplied by iStock.com
Printed and bound in Great Britain by TJ International,
Padstow

The Wind and the Sun

The Wind and the Sun were disputing which was the stronger. Suddenly they saw a traveller coming down the road, and the Sun said: "I see a way to decide our dispute. Whichever of us can cause that traveller to take off his cloak shall be regarded as the stronger. You begin." So the Sun retired behind a cloud, and the Wind began to blow as hard as it could upon the traveller. But the harder he blew the more closely did the traveller wrap his cloak round him, till at last the Wind had to give up in despair. Then the Sun came out and shone in all his glory upon the traveller, who soon found it too hot to walk with his cloak on.

Kindness effects more than severity.

Aesop (sixth century B.C.) *Fables*,
retold by Joseph Jacobs

Contents

Contents

About the authors

David Faulkner has been a senior research associate at the University of Oxford Centre for Criminology since 1992, where he has written and lectured on various aspects of criminal justice and public service reform. He was a Fellow of St John's College Oxford from 1992 until 1999, and he has been a trustee or adviser to several national and local charities. He served in the Home Office from 1959 until 1992, with tours of duty in the Prison and Police Departments, and was seconded to the Cabinet Office in 1978–80. He became Director of Operational Policy in the Prison Department in 1980 and Deputy Secretary in charge of the Criminal and Research and Statistics Departments in 1982, and was involved in most of the reforms of criminal justice during that period. His book *Crime, State and Citizen: A Field Full of Folk* was published in 2001 (second edition 2006), and he has written numerous articles in journals and chapters in edited collections. He was appointed CB in 1985.

Ros Burnett obtained her doctorate in social psychology from the University of Oxford and was a probation officer and a relationship counsellor before entering criminal justice academia. She is a research associate of the University of Oxford's Centre for Criminology where she was Reader in Criminology and contributed to the teaching programme of postgraduate students. Her research has encompassed probation, youth justice and prisons, the unifying theme being processes that support the efforts of ex-offenders to desist from further crime. Her publications include *Accounting for Relationships* (with McGhee and Clarke; Methuen, 1987), *Fitting Supervision to Offenders* (Home Office, 1996), *Joined-up Youth Justice* (with C. Appleton; Russell House, 2004) and *'What Works in Probation and Youth Justice'* (with C. Roberts; Willan, 2004). She is a member of the editorial board of the *International Journal of Offender Therapy and Comparative Criminology*.

Acknowledgements

A book of this scope is an ambitious undertaking. We embarked on it with some trepidation but in the knowledge that we had a rich bank of academic sources on which to draw, as the long list of references will testify, and some very knowledgeable colleagues who generously allowed us to consult them and offered advice.

In particular, we are grateful to Graham Towl, Professor of Psychology and Deputy Warden of Durham University, for his collaboration in drawing up the book proposal submitted to The Policy Press and for his insights and ideas on prisons and public service reform more generally. We are also grateful to John Halliday, whom we consulted in preparing chapters two and three, and John Graham, whom we consulted on chapter six. Other inspirational colleagues whose direct experience as senior managers we drew on were Tim Newell, John Dring and Stephen Pryor, who each provided helpful comments on drafts of chapter eight, and Gerry Marshall, who did so on chapters one, seven and ten.

The book has benefited from our discussions with colleagues and students at the Centre for Criminology at the University of Oxford, from interdisciplinary seminars and from access to the rich electronic and library resources of the University of Oxford. We thank Ian Loader, Director of the Centre for Criminology, and Julian Roberts, Assistant Director, for their enduring support.

The following have helped one or both of us over the years more than they may know whether by their encouragement or by the acuity of their writing , and sometimes both: Catherine Appleton, John Croft, María-Cristina Dorado, David Downes, Mike Hough, Alison Liebling, Shadd Maruna, Rod Morgan, Anne Owers, Andrew Rutherford, Alisa Stevens, Lucia Zedner. Other sources of experience and ideas have included the Thames Valley Partnership and the conferences, seminars and publications of various national voluntary organisations concerned with offenders, victims and their families, too numerous to mention individually.

We thank Alison Shaw, Director of The Policy Press, and Laura Greaves, Production Editor, for their flexibility and guidance, and their colleagues Hilary Brown, Jenny Hinchliffe, Jane Horton and Kathryn King, for their efficiency and helpfulness.

Last but by no means least, we warmly thank our families and friends for their encouragement and some lively debates about crime control and criminal justice. From the second author, special thanks go, as always, to Peter Burnett for his unfailing support. The first author especially thanks Sheila Faulkner for her constant patience and reassurance, and for reading through successive drafts and checking them for mistakes and intelligibility.

Introduction

'[A]t a time when our discourse has become so sharply polarised – at a time when we are far too eager to lay the blame for all that ails the world at the feet of those who happen to think differently than we do – it's important for us to pause for a moment and make sure that we are talking with each other in a way that heals, not in a way that wounds.' (Barack Obama, January 2011)[1]

Criminal justice has become one of those highly politicised issues that arouse strong views and emotions and divide people to the extent that those who disagree seem to be on entirely different wavelengths. They either stop communicating or argue with mutual derision. There seem to be deep divisions about the way in which a modern democratic society should try to prevent crime, deal with it when it occurs, help its victims and respond to those who commit it. Opinion is polarised between those who focus on the direct consequences of crime, for the victim or for society, and argue for offenders to be punished or put where they can do no more harm; and those who focus on the offender as a human being and as a person who may be capable of change – and also on their families, including children, sometimes referred to as hidden victims of crime – and therefore argue for prevention and rehabilitation.

Both opinions are sincerely held and sometimes vehemently expressed, and both are likely to come from the same well-spring of basic decency and concern for a better society. The differences between them and the feelings they arouse can be exploited politically, and commercially by the media, so intensifying the emotions involved and making agreement harder to achieve. The lack of common ground leads to frustration and sometimes to moral indignation on both sides of these arguments.

An exacerbating factor is that the generic category 'crime' covers such a vast range of behaviours – from serial killer to class C drug-user; from white-collar fraudster to homeless shoplifter; from violent child abuser to vulnerable teenager drawn into a gang; and so forth. Those on each side may have their own vivid example in mind that best exemplifies

---

[1] Address to the memorial, called 'Together We Thrive: Tucson and America', held at the University of Arizona on 12 January 2011.

their preconceptions, yet continue to argue in generic terms, resulting in disputes where people are to some extent at cross-purposes. Extreme cases reported in the media, or drawn from personal experiences as a victim, may lead to understandable bias in the generalisations made. The exceptional may come to be seen as ordinary.

In another respect, disagreements may derive from alternative outlooks on human nature and its potential, some people being more typically wary and distrustful in their assumptions while others are generally ready to trust and are optimistic in their assessments. These general perceptions of human nature may contribute to different understandings about the 'causes' of crime, the purpose of the criminal justice system and justice itself. According to one view, people are motivated mainly by self-interest, have minimal genuine concern or goodwill towards others, and might take advantage of or disregard others unless there are deterrents or incentives; if they comply with the law and social obligations that restrict their actions, it is because it is in their interests to do so (instrumental compliance). According to the other view, people are basically decent or have some capacity for good and, although they may sometimes behave badly in reaction to adverse circumstances or temptation, they are usually capable of change and improvement. This more favourable view of people, in general, sees them as complying with the law and their social obligations because they want to and doing so is consistent with their values (normative compliance).

The wider literature contains various accounts of those contrasting visions of human nature, characterising them as the 'tragic' and 'utopian' conceptions of humankind (Pinker, 2002), or as 'constrained' and 'unconstrained' views of human potential (Sowell, 2007). These divergent visions are seen as underpinning the polarisation between liberal/leftwing and conservative/rightwing politics, each with its own moral logic and implications, and help explain the incomprehension that can occur between parties (Lakoff, 2002; Sowell, 2007). In criminal justice, the division is broadly between those who think in terms of a distinct and probably incorrigible 'criminal class',[2] and those who believe that there may be good in everyone[3] if only it can be recognised

---

[2] Such views find strong affirmation of course when there are – so far, very rare – 'outbreaks of lawlessness' such as the riots with looting and large scale criminal damage which took place in London and other cities in early August 2011.

[3] Anne Frank wrote, in her diary (Frank [1947], 2007), '… in spite of everything, I still believe that people are really good at heart'. She further explained that because of this belief she felt able to cling to her ideals during the grim realities that her family and other Jewish people were experiencing. She also believed in the transformative

and nurtured. The former see the solution to crime as the retributive punishment of offenders as well as their incarceration for the protection of others, and the latter see crime as part of the wider problems of a complex modern society and offenders as often victims of social injustice themselves and as able to improve and contribute to society if given the chance. The different visions, or leanings towards them, are likely to influence perspectives on the purpose of sentencing, decisions about appropriate sentences, the prospects for rehabilitation and the trust that can be placed in people who have offended.

Resolving conflict

The quotation that opens this chapter is one of several appeals Barack Obama has made to the shared values that unite people, and calls on citizens 'to expand our moral imaginations, to listen to each other more carefully'. The words were part of a speech that followed the shooting of 19 people, six fatally, at a political rally in Arizona on 8 January 2011. In a different political context, the Prime Minister of Norway, Jens Stoltenberg, made a similar appeal to shared values after the atrocity in that country when scores of people were killed on 23 July, 2011.

In the United States incident, it is poignantly pertinent that the main target, the Democrat representative Gabrielle Giffords, had on the evening before she was shot sent an email to the newly appointed director of Harvard University's Institute of Politics seeking advice about 'how to tone our rhetoric and partisanship down' and finding ways to 'promote centrism and moderation'. While there has been no comparable political feuding situation in Britain in recent times, a jeering and contemptuous tone continues in some public and parliamentary debate, and in some sections of the media, between those who position themselves as being on different sides of a moral divide.

It is a matter for governments and – in criminal justice – courts and practitioners to negotiate that situation and develop policies and practices that acknowledge both sides of the argument and are, as far as possible, acceptable to all sides. Much of the business of democratic politics and government – and, indeed, much of professional and family life – involves making choices and resolving conflict. The conflict may

---

power of generosity of spirit and what we now call pro-social modelling: 'People will always follow a good example; be the one to set a good example, then it won't be long before the others follow [...] How lovely that everyone, great and small, can make their contribution toward introducing justice straightaway... And you can always, always give something, even if it is only kindness!'

be between different interests, attitudes, emotions and opinions; or between communities and individuals, the state and the citizen, the state and the market, equality or competition, long-term investment and immediate relief, security and risk. Sometimes the judgement to be made is practical or economic – what is easier, safer, more affordable, more likely to be successful or bring a better return on investment? Sometimes it involves other people or public opinion – what will they want or expect, what will earn their approval or respect? Sometimes it is a matter of human rights, irrespective of public opinion.[4] Questions of fairness, cost and legality have to be considered, and calculations made about possible consequences and implications. The calculations will often be difficult, especially when – as often happens – the evidence on which to base them is uncertain, incomplete or difficult to interpret. That applies as much to the effects on crime and human behaviour as it does to taxation, interest rates, public debt, the environment or putting public services out to competitive tender.

Perhaps more than any other subject, criminal justice involves a tension between the competing and often conflicting interests of the individual and those of the community, the state or the victim. That applies both at the level of policy and legislation, and in treatment of particular situations and individuals. People are complex beings and so are the situations in which they relate to one another. Neither human beings nor the systems they create can ever be perfect. There will be cases where there is not enough evidence to prosecute or convict a suspect or defendant, or where the sentence is not thought adequate in comparison with what the victim has suffered, or to have sufficient regard to the continuing dangerousness of an individual's pattern of behaviour. The victim may then feel inadequately vindicated or supported, or think that the system is 'on the side of the criminal'. There are situations where people may think the legislation or practice on sentencing is too lenient, or that prisoners' conditions are too comfortable. The judgement may in the end be one of principles or values – is this what I ought to do or really want to do, is this the kind of person I want to be, the kind of job I want to do or the kind of country I want live in? Or is this justice?

---

[4] Most notably, overriding popular opinion, the death penalty has been abolished in most countries on the basis of human rights principles (see Hood and Hoyle, 2008).

Which way from here?

Various moments have been seen as turning points in British politics – obvious examples are the election of Clement Attlee's Labour government in 1945 and of Margaret Thatcher's Conservative government in 1979. The formation of the Conservative–Liberal Democrat coalition government in May 2010 may come to be seen as another. There have also been turning points in criminal justice, but they have not usually coincided with those in politics. The post-war Labour government's 1948 Criminal Justice Act established a radical new framework for sentencing, including the abolition of judicial corporal punishment, but it gave effect to policies decided by a Conservative government in the 1930s. The turning point that had been expected under Margaret Thatcher's Conservative government, arguably, came not in 1979 but in 1992/93, after Margaret Thatcher had resigned and John Major had become Prime Minister (Windlesham 1993, 1996; Bottoms, 1995; Garland, 2001; Faulkner, 2006).

Whether the formation of the coalition government will mark a new departure in criminal justice has not yet become clear. The government took office at a time of frustration that comparatively little seemed to have been achieved from the legislation and the administrative reforms that had consumed so much energy over the previous 20 years, or from the increase in expenditure that had accompanied them – an increase of two thirds since 1997. Promises of 'change' and the argument that 'we cannot go on as before' had been made by all parties during the campaign for the 2010 election, but they were not made as often or as loudly in relation to criminal justice as they were for other areas of government policy, or as loudly as they would have been two or three years previously. That was partly because the election was dominated by the state of the economy, but also because the parties realised that promises of far-reaching new reforms in criminal justice would no longer sound convincing. Too much had been promised before, by both Conservative and Labour governments, and too little had been achieved for any party to claim that it had a new solution.

The first indications of the new government's intentions for criminal justice came in speeches by Kenneth Clarke, the Justice Secretary,[5] and other ministers (Blunt, 2010; Herbert, 2010) who promised a

---

[5] Unpublished speech, 'The Government's vision for criminal justice reform', given at the Centre for Crime and Justice Studies, King's College London on 30 June 2010. No longer available on the Ministry of Justice website. Last accessed at: www.kcl. ac.uk/news/news_details.php?news_id=1402&year=2010.

'revolution' in the rehabilitation of offenders and a serious attempt to limit and if possible to reverse the growth in the use of imprisonment. The government quickly published a consultation paper, *Policing in the Twenty-first Century* (Home Office, 2010), which announced a new set of proposals to reform the police service, including the election of 'police and crime commissioners'. Legislation followed in the Police Reform and Social Responsibility Bill. Later in the year, the government published its proposals on sentencing, prisons and the rehabilitation of offenders in its green paper *Breaking the Cycle: Effective Punishment, Rehabilitation and Sentencing Offenders* (Ministry of Justice, 2010a). The shadow justice secretary Sadiq Khan[6] said that he too would like to see fewer people in prison, achieved through better rehabilitation and intervention, although he criticised the government for acting on economic grounds rather than criminal justice principles, and argued that its plans for rehabilitation were short-sighted.

Those speeches and the green paper suggested that both the government and the opposition might share some of the doubt – which penal reformers and academics had felt for some time – about whether criminal justice should continue to move in the direction of more central control and more effective – which in practice meant more severe – law enforcement and punishment that governments had followed during the previous 20 years. It seemed there might even be some prospect of a political consensus on the main direction that reform should take. Despite inevitable strains, the coalition, by its nature, requires opposing parties to find common ground, though it is right for them, to assert some firmly held differences. The formation of the coalition government brought the possibility of change, and new hope for some, but the summer of 2011, especially after the riots in August of that year, was still one of uncertainty about the direction in which criminal justice might develop in the future.

Financial stringency may provide a stimulus to decisive leadership and to much-needed reforms that might not otherwise take place; necessity may be the parent of invention. Careful judgement will, however, be needed about which sacrifices are and are not to be made, and new ways of doing things may require new money that may not be easy to provide from savings elsewhere. It is essential that reforms should be grounded in a fundamental reassessment of what criminal justice is for, and what it is able realistically to achieve.

---

[6] www.prisonreformtrust.org.uk/PressPolicy/News/vw/1/ItemID/120

Aims and outline

Our aims in writing this book are to review the situation and prospects for criminal justice in England and Wales as the country moves forward in the second decade of the 21st century and to make suggestions for the direction it might take. In the chapters that follow, we address what we see as the underlying issues and principles, and the insights to be gained from the experience of the past 30 years, taking account of empirical and theoretical studies that we have found most relevant to our purpose. We make no claim that our review has been comprehensive or exhaustive, but the lessons from that experience and those studies have too often been overlooked in the processes of policy formation, legislation and the development of professional practice. We are concerned principally with crime and criminal justice, and thus with knowledge drawn from the academic discipline of criminology, but other disciplines, such as politics, philosophy and psychology, can all contribute. Just as crime should not be treated as a self-contained issue separate from other social economic and political issues, so criminology should not be isolated from wider studies of and reflection on social and economic policy, government, public administration and politics.[7]

While our focus is mainly on criminal justice in England and Wales, similar principles and considerations apply to public services more generally as well as to other parts of the United Kingdom and to other developed countries. Scotland in particular provides an example of thinking that is similar to our own, with the McLeish report's recommendations for reducing the prison population and for reforms of prosecution and court processes, of sentencing and the management of offenders, and of community justice, prisons and resettlement (Scottish Prisons Commission, 2008). The recommendations on sentencing became part of the 2010 Criminal Justice and Licensing (Scotland) Act.

Chapter one sets some parameters for the discussion that follows. It asks what people are doing when they talk about justice, and especially criminal justice, and it examines the significance of the related concepts of the rule of law, fairness, procedural justice and the legitimacy of the authority of the state. The chapter continues with a discussion of the – perhaps changing – relationship between the state and the citizen, and the implications of treating criminal justice as a 'system', to be

---

[7] Observations made by Bhikhu Parekh in a discussion of political philosophy and its public role, and its distinction from political science, could apply to the distinction between criminology, as some of us try to understand it, and 'crime science' (see Jahanbegloo and Parekh, 2011, pp 38-64).

managed as if it were a 'business'. It concludes with some reflections on the language in which public discussion of criminal justice often takes place. The theme that emerges from this chapter is that 'justice' cannot be equated with political or managerial objectives such as efficiency or effectiveness, or merely with measurable outcomes in terms of reductions in crime and reoffending or increases in public confidence.

Chapters two and three look back to the origins of the situation that faced the coalition government when it came into office. Many of the issues and considerations that government had to take into account were essentially the same as they had been for the previous 50 years – an increase in crime and concerns about sentencing, prison overcrowding, questions about the effectiveness and credibility of community sentences, loss of public confidence, and uncertainty about the 'causes' of crime, the means of reversing the growth in crime and the part that criminal justice should play in that process. Others, such as the treatment of victims, women and members of minority groups, were beginning to emerge. Today's political context is similar in many respects, with the same contrast between those advocating 'tough' measures and greater use of imprisonment and those who prefer to emphasise prevention and rehabilitation. The contrast does not follow party lines: the difference is to be found more within the political parties than as an issue which separates them from one another. The earlier events in that period are receding from public memory and there is no collective memory of them in government or the criminal justice services. An understanding of the ways in which government and the services approached those issues, the obstacles they had to face, and their success in resolving them, provides a valuable guide for judgements about how they should be dealt with in the future.

Chapter two describes the confidence that existed up to the 1960s; the period of disillusion that followed; and the strategy that the Conservative government developed during the first part of its period in office (corresponding roughly with Margaret Thatcher's time as Prime Minister). That was the period during which the government for the first time began to develop a comprehensive strategy for preventing and reducing crime, for supporting victims and for improving the quality of justice as well as the treatment of those who commit it, and at the same time for coordinating the work of government departments, courts and operational services.

Chapter three describes the abrupt change of direction that occurred in 1992/93 and the approach that the Conservative and Labour governments followed until 2010: the emphasis on criminal justice as the means of controlling and reducing crime; the legislative and managerial reforms that were intended to make criminal justice more effective in doing so; the commitment to evidence-based policy but with selective use of the evidence that was available; the achievements and disappointments and the reasons for them.

Chapter four moves on to discuss the role of civil society, and considers the nature, characteristics and significance of the communities that make up contemporary British society. It explores the concepts of community and local justice, and continues with a discussion of the role of the voluntary and community sector. It concludes with some reflections on what might be called a 'good society', and on the 'Big Society' as it features in the policies of the coalition government.

Chapter five focuses on the roles of the courts and the criminal law. It reflects on the nature of punishment and changing attitudes towards its use, and on the structure and purpose of sentencing. It argues for reliance on criminal penalties and criminal processes to be reduced where possible, for clearer criteria to be established in determining actions and situations where new criminal offences are and are not needed, and for the need for existing offences to be reviewed. It argues that legislation on sentencing should be simplified and indeterminate and mandatory sentences abolished wherever possible. The chapter continues with a section on the position of victims and witnesses, and concludes with a discussion on the role of restorative justice and the scope for its development.

Chapter six considers policing – how the nature of policing and the demands on police have changed and are changing; the significance of the reforms that have already taken place and those that are now proposed; and the implications of elected commissioners for police and crime. It considers the mechanisms by which police are accountable to the public and the importance of their accountability also to the law. It goes on to discuss the government's and the public's expectations of what police should and should not do, and the need to manage those expectations, especially at a time of shortage and austerity. It reflects on the connections between police bureaucracy and culture, and concludes by identifying some of the considerations that will have a critical influence on the future of policing in England and Wales.

Chapter seven focuses on community-based sentences and interventions and on the process of change from involvement in offending to prosocial integration in society. It provides a critical review of the restructuring and recharacterisation of probation and youth justice services during the past three decades. It considers past and present frontline practice in work with offenders and their families; interagency partnerships and voluntary sector contributions to community justice; relationship and self factors in effective interventions to change behaviour; and the revival of 'rehabilitation' through problem-solving, strengths-based approaches and the desistance paradigm.

Chapter eight reviews the social and political context in which the Prison Service now operates, the effect of successive reforms of management and reorganisation, and the culture and attitudes of prison staff. It examines the implications of the new proposals on work and rehabilitation and considers the factors on which their success will depend, including the influences on prisoners' own behaviour and the effect of wider public attitudes towards prisoners and imprisonment.

Chapter nine looks beyond criminal justice to wider reforms in government and public services – the transition from 'old public administration' to 'new public management', the mixed results it achieved, and the areas for improvement. The chapter considers in particular policy making and legislation; the relationship between ministers and public servants; localisation and citizen's empowerment; the management of risk; promoting innovation; the use of research and expert advice; and the implications of outsourcing services to the private and voluntary sectors.

Chapter ten sets out some conclusions; suggests some of the ingredients that future policy and practice should contain; and reviews the government's policies and proposals against those criteria.

We are conscious that, apart from a few relevant considerations and examples, throughout this book we do not give sufficient explicit attention to the issues in relation to women, ethnic and religious minorities, people with disabilities, and other minorities. This will rightly earn the criticism of some readers, but in the limited space available we have chosen to prioritise issues that we believe have general applicability. Our themes are humanity, empathy, caring relationships, and facilitating self-determination and human flourishing; and the practical implications are for policies and approaches that address individual differences, needs and situations, including those that arise for individuals by virtue of their membership of particular groups.

Main arguments

We have three main arguments. One is for a movement away from the recent pattern of unrealistic claims about what can be achieved, from the micro-management of public sector services and from risk-led systems based on cynicism and expecting the worst. The rule of law remains paramount but the time is ripe to break away from the recent trajectory of excessive legislation, reforms of reforms and officious governance to 'fix' criminal justice.

The second is that more responsibility for preventing crime and dealing with its consequences should fall on other parts of government, other public services and civil society. Early work with children (and their parents) who are at an inflated risk of not thriving socially and economically may very well have a positive indirect impact on reducing future crimes, for example violent crime. The need is for better education and mental health services, for substance abuse treatment, for social support and regeneration of poor neighbourhoods – to build up individual capabilities, and to increase social capital in communities, and thereby facilitate natural influence processes in civil society. The best hope for preventing and reducing crime lies in reducing the present wide embrace of the criminal justice system and, within the rule of law, less emphasis on punishment for the sake of retribution or revenge, and more optimism in informal social and psychological processes that nurture human development.

The third is that there should be an agreed set of moral and practical principles, based on reflection and debate, within which criminal justice policies are framed. In addition to their intrinsic necessity, these would enhance the institutional legitimacy of criminal justice governance and administration. Our own proposals are that the principles, and their practical applications, should include:

- integrity, transparency and mutual trust in the governance and administration of criminal justice – in the formation of policy and legislation, in their implementation, and in professional practice;
- humanity, dignity and respect in the treatment of offenders and ex-offenders, as well as victims, and in the administration of justice;
- a shift of emphasis from the 'criminal justice system' to community, relationships, capabilities and positive motivation as the means of preventing and reducing crime;
- strengths-based, problem-solving and restorative approaches to promote reparation, integration and desistance.

We look towards an approach that facilitates a sense of belonging and citizenship with the rights and responsibilities that that implies; that kindles and places trust in people's better nature and ability to improve; and that demonstrates and encourages civility and magnanimity. At the same time, it is realistic about the harms of ordinary crime and the extent to which individuals, no matter how disadvantaged, can be held blameworthy and deserving of communicative retribution and proportional sentencing. While such an approach, as well as being principled, looks forward to an improved outcome in terms of lower crime and recidivism rates, it gives equal emphasis to honesty about the limits to which 'crime', in all its guises, can ever be resolved by criminal justice policies whatever form they take.

Wary of the ambiguity and negative associations of labels, we have resisted affiliating ourselves with any single philosophical or political '-ism', such as liberalism, humanism, centrism, communitarianism, left realism, and so forth, although we find echoes of our own views within most of these. Instead, we draw widely on the most inspiring and encouraging bodies of criminological and socio-legal research that have informed our own work, including desistance theory and positive psychology, therapeutic jurisprudence, procedural justice and legitimacy theory. Less contentiously, our commitments are to humane principles in the prevention and reduction of crime, and what has been described as the 'pursuit of decency' in criminal justice (Rutherford, 1993). We share with Bhikhu Parekh (in Jahanbegloo and Parekh, 2011, p 63) his assertion of the universal importance of:

> ... such liberal values, attitudes, and sensibilities as human dignity, equality, respect for human integrity, an inviolable area in personal privacy, fear of power in all its forms. institutionalized criticism, aversion to coercion, limited government, separation of powers, and constitutionally guaranteed rights.

At the same time we are troubled by some recent directions in liberalism, and the tendency of some liberals to convey – and again we are indebted to Lord Parekh here for his clear and authoritative articulation of this point – 'the kind of moral certainty and dogmatism' that 'denies liberalism the opportunity to engage in a critical dialogue with, and learn what is valuable in, other ways of thought and life' (Jahanbegloo and Parekh, 2011, p 58). For this book, while we may not always succeed, we endeavour to respect different perspectives and seek out common ground.

Our inclination towards a non-partisan position is determined by the principles of inclusiveness and empathy, and by realism about the extent and experience of crime. We aim for inclusiveness because, such is the polarisation in perspectives on criminal justice, that writings on the subject are typically for one audience or the other. Both sides have authentic concerns, however, and this book aims to empathise with the position of those with whom we may sometimes disagree as well as asserting our own normative position. In a civilised debate, the communication of one's perspective should include an attempt to understand and an acknowledgement of the other's moral logic without ridiculing or despising it.

An effort to be non-partisan – or even-handed – is also determined by realism about the pains caused by everyday, ordinary crime. Increasingly, criminologists and others have turned their attention to the crimes of the powerful (see, for example, Coleman et al, 2008; Whyte, 2009), and to more globalised or far-reaching crime, such as organised crime on a large scale and terrorism. Government has been criticised for focusing too narrowly on 'crimes of the powerless' and this extension of horizons is needed. However, ordinary crime mostly affects the powerless and includes seriously harmful deeds of violence, sexual abuse and cruelty, as well as a wide range of acquisitive offences, many of which cause significant distress. Many of those responsible are relatively poor people who are excluded from the advantages of privilege and wealth they see around them (Young, 1999), and many will have been victims of crime themselves. On a large scale, such as in the outbreak of lootings and criminal damage which occurred in August 2011, crime can devastate communities and invoke fear and hate. It is therefore such mainstream offending behaviour which we concentrate on in this book.

To the extent that human behaviour is unpredictable, responses to former offenders can err on the side of optimism or pessimism, in the way described above. There are psychological and moral reasons for erring on the side of optimism. Expectations can have a self-fulfilling effect and a spirit of trust or distrust can be contagious. Scrupulous optimism, however, should be tempered by evidence and suitable precautions rather than blind faith. Therefore, while our perception of human nature is far from utopian, rather than concentrating on punishment for wrongdoing or failure, we believe more will be achieved by nurturing human goodness.

Postscript: This book was in the final stages of preparation when the country was shocked by the riots, arson and looting which took place in London and other English cities in early August 2011, causing damage and distress on a scale which had not been seen for a generation. The riots were universally condemned, but disputes were taking place about the reasons and the action which had been taken or should be taken in future and are likely to continue for some time. We will not attempt to enter into those disputes ourselves, except to say that one-dimensional simplistic explanations are inadequate – just as they are for crime in general – and the most sensible commentaries acknowledge this plurality of causes and motivations. The experience of the riots confirms our belief in the arguments we have put forward and the approach which we describe in the chapters which follow.

ONE

Social justice, legitimacy and criminal justice

When people call out for justice to be done in response to an horrific crime, or when they lament the absence of justice for those who are impoverished in a wealthy world, or when there are outcries against the unjust treatment of one category of people compared with another, each is referring to different ideas of justice. The meaning of 'justice' has been the subject of philosophical debate for millennia and, within such analyses, 'criminal justice' is sometimes scarcely mentioned while for others it is deeply entwined. With its connection to ideas of virtue and moral ethics, there is a marked contrast between the ways in which the word 'justice' has traditionally been used, and the ways in which government, politics and the media now use the expression 'criminal justice'. More recently, the expression is mostly used to refer to the process that leads from the investigation of an alleged offence to the conviction and sentence of an offender, and so to the point at which the sentence has finally been served; or it may be used descriptively for the structures, services or legislation that are involved in that process. 'Justice' is then seen as the outcome of a trial, where the test of whether 'justice has been done' is likely to be whether the verdict and sentence satisfy the victim or public opinion, or whether they will be effective in protecting the public.

The purpose of this chapter is to provide a context and a framework of principles for the discussion of more specific issues that follow in later chapters. It considers, first, different theoretical positions on the meaning and importance of justice, the rule of law, and what are sometimes called 'procedural justice' and 'equality before the law' and their connections with ideas of fairness and legitimacy. These ideas have important practical applications: they are about what gives the law, the criminal justice process and the criminal justice services their authority, why people comply with them, and how that authority can be sustained and protected. The chapter continues with a discussion about the relationship between the state and the citizen, about their respective rights and responsibilities, and about a person's status as a citizen if they become an offender. It concludes with a discussion of the nature of the 'criminal justice system' as the term has now come to be used, and about the language in which policy is made and put into effect.

Changing conceptions of justice

Anything other than the most superficial reading of the philosophical and political literature on justice reveals how multifaceted and unresolved the subject is. It has been joked that there are so many ways of defining justice that not even the lady personified in the various statues of justice knows what it is, and that the blindfold in many versions of the statue is illustrative of this. An attempt to selectively summarise the vast literature on justice within a few paragraphs will inevitably result in oversimplifying it. On the other hand, any discussion of criminal justice has to be grounded within recognition of some key differences and concepts used in that discourse. Also, in looking forward to progress in criminal justice, positioning of one's arguments in relation to theories of justice helps provide the moral compass that is needed to guide the direction.

Philosophical approaches to justice can be divided into the following rough categories: virtue-based and meritocratic (concerned with moral desert and purpose); utilitarian (promoting the greatest happiness for the greatest number); libertarian (concerned with the freedom of choice and autonomy of each individual); egalitarian (justice as fairness, and equal rights and opportunities); communitarian (justice as relational, involving belonging and community norms in regulating conduct). There are significant tensions between some of the underlying assumptions separating these, as well as some overlapping ideas and the most influential studies are often hybrids of two or more of these schools of thought.

From virtues to fairness

The motto attributed to the philosopher and theologian St Thomas Aquinas – '*cuique suum*', roughly meaning 'to everyone his due' – perhaps affords the most accessible definition when looking for one that embraces the range of aspects linked to the concept: fairness, equality, liberty, rights, retribution and redress. Following Aristotle, Aquinas identified justice not only as the highest of all moral virtues, but also as a social virtue. It is practised towards others, and involves exchange and distribution. Some things are owed as part of a contract while the simplest obligations are defined by the natural law and based on the natural inclinations of each person[1] to be socially involved with others and to fulfil their own and shared goals as interdependent human beings.

Immanuel Kant also built on Aristotelian theories of justice but whereas for Aristotle and Aquinas, society and the common good have primacy over the individual, for Kant the reverse applies. Aristotle's notions of virtues and the 'good' have regard to outcomes and human purpose, whereas for Kant moral worth depends on the principle of an action – the focus is on what is intrinsically of value rather than a means to an end.[2] Kant ([1785] 1907) identified goodwill as the only virtue that is truly good in itself, and developed deontological (duty-based) ethics that is concerned with what people do, not with the consequences of their actions. A precept of this philosophy is that all individuals have an intrinsic worth and everyone has a right to be treated as such, and has an obligation to treat others likewise. Although the will is free, people are morally obliged by the duty that arises from the categorical imperative to 'Act only on that maxim whereby thou canst at the same time will that it should become a universal law' (moral rules must apply to everyone) and to 'So act as to treat humanity, whether in thine own person or in that of any other, in every case as an end withal, never as means only' (moral rules must respect human beings) (Kant, [1785] 1907).

A groundbreaking study in advancing the idea that justice has to be seen in terms of the demands of fairness was John Rawls's (1971; 2001) study *A Theory of Justice*. It embraces the Kantian ethic of the categorical imperative, extending it to the social institution of justice. Rawls asks what people would agree to if invited to construct a social contract from a hypothetical, initial situation of equality. To prevent self-serving choices, he hypothesised that everyone should make such a choice as if from behind a 'veil of ignorance' that prevented each from knowing what social status, personal and financial assets, religious and political affiliations they might have in the resulting social order. From this original starting point, two sets of principles were derived: the first, that each person has the same claim to basic liberties (fundamental rights) such as freedom of speech, beliefs, movement and access; and the second, that social and economic inequalities should be subject

---

[1] Lamentably, the Aristotelian world view only related to men. It also excludes slaves. Whether the exclusion of women from this entire scheme completely undermines it or can be seen as an exemplar of the socially situated nature of moral cultures is a matter for continuing debate.

[2] Such a brief comparison of Aristotelian and Kantian theories is a travesty, yet bypassing them altogether would seem remiss because so much literature in justice traces its roots back to Aristotle or Kant.

to conditions – they are to be attached to offices and positions open to all under conditions of fair equality of opportunity, and they are to the greatest benefit of the least-advantaged members of society (the difference principle).

Realisation and capabilities

Amartya Sen's more recent *The Idea of Justice* (2009) is partly a critique of Rawls's analysis and is equally majestic. Sen agrees that the 'pursuit of justice has to be linked to – and in some senses derived from – the idea of fairness' (p 54) and makes clear that this central understanding is important to his own analysis. He is, however, critical of the tradition of invoking a social contract begun by Thomas Hobbes and continued by Enlightenment thinkers of which Rawls's study is an example. Describing this approach, variously, as an 'arrangement-focused view of justice' and as 'transcendental institutionalism' (because it seeks to identify ideal social arrangements that cannot be transcended), he contends that, even if it were possible to come up with ideal arrangements, it is not sufficient to conceptualise justice in terms of getting the institutions and rules right. It is also important to examine what emerges in the society and the way peoples' lives go, because of or in spite of those institutions.

Instead, Sen argues for a 'realisation-focused approach', which goes beyond institutional arrangements to life as lived, and is concerned with the 'identification of redressable injustice' (2009, p vii). For this he draws on 'social choice theory' (Arrow, 1963) and on a different group of political thinkers – including, for example, Adam Smith, Mary Wollstonecraft, John Stuart Mill and Karl Marx – who concentrated on making comparisons between different social arrangements and their realisations, and on identifying manifest injustices. This shift of focus is mirrored in the two classical Sanskrit words for justice that Sen employs: *niti*, concerned with the strict organisational and behavioural rules of justice; and *nyaya*, which stands for how such rules affect lives and the world as it actually emerges.

Another way in which Sen's approach redirects thinking about justice is by proposing '... a fundamental shift in the focus of attention from the *means* of living to the *actual opportunities* a person has' (emphasis in original) (2009, p 253). He names this the 'capability approach' (see also Nussbaum and Sen, 1993). Sen suggests that this is more aligned with Aristotle's concern with the '*ends* of good living' (emphasis in original) (2009, p 254) and therefore more liberating and likely to enhance individual fulfilment than the Rawlsian approach of reliance on primary goods for distributional fairness. For example, an increase in income by itself may do nothing to enhance the recipients' power or ability to choose for themselves the kinds of lives they aspire to lead.

Shared narratives of the human good

After Virtue by Alasdair MacIntyre ([1981] 2007) is another influential work on the philosophy of justice, albeit one that is particularly challenging to theories of justice concerned with utility or rights or autonomy from the perspective of individuals, rather than on the basis of a shared value system and conception of the human good. He contends that Enlightenment thinkers were mistaken in rejecting the Aristotelian notions of human virtues and *telos*. According to this teleological view of human nature, a person can progress to achieve their true end or potential as a human being if, guided by practical reasoning and rational ethics, they lead a virtuous life. MacIntyre sees this tradition as extended and deepened by Aquinas, although a theological dimension was added:

> This scheme is complicated and added to, but not essentially altered, when it is placed within a framework of theistic beliefs, whether Christian as with Aquinas, or Jewish with Maimonides, or Islamic with Ibn Roschd. The precepts of ethics now have to be understood not only as teleological injunctions, but also as expressions of a divinely ordained law. The table of virtues and vices has to be amended and added to and a concept of sin is added to the Aristotelian concept of error. The law of God requires a new kind of respect and awe. The true end of man can no longer be achieved in this world, but only in another. Yet the threefold structure of untutored human-nature-as-it-happens-to-be, human-nature-as-it-could-be-if-it-realized-its-*telos* and the precepts of rational ethics as the means for the transition from one to the other remains central to the theistic understanding of evaluative thought and judgment. (MacIntyre, [1981] 2007, p 53)

The Enlightenment broke with this tradition, resulting in a loss of 'impersonal standards' justified by a shared conception of the human good; and, 'without a teleological framework the whole project of morality becomes unintelligible' (MacIntyre, [1981] 2007, p 56). MacIntyre illustrates the arising confusion in the form of a debate, contrasting two concepts of justice in response to the prospect of rising, distributive taxes. Person A grounds the notion of justice in an account of the *entitlement* of employees to spend their income on meeting the needs of their own family. Person B, who is impoverished, grounds the notion of justice in an account of the *equality of claims* by each person to have the means of meeting their basic needs. Each of these can be matched to corresponding philosophical positions – person A's to Robert Nozick's (1974) appeal to the canons of inviolable rights and entitlements, and person B's to John Rawls's scheme for the fair distribution of primary goods.

What is critical to this comparison, though, is that, whereas the philosophical accounts make no reference to 'desert', ordinary people would typically do so. Person A would say that she deserves the money she worked hard to earn, and person B that she does not deserve to be poor and deprived. Desert was a foundational component of justice in classical and medieval philosophy (Tam, 2003), and justice includes what is owed to people and is practised in 'the constant will to render to each person his right'. In this tradition, justice along with other moral virtues is connected to the social role of the individual as part of a broader community, which collectively strives towards the highest good for man.

Central to MacIntyre's argument is his observation that, while this older, more Aristotelian and Christian, view of virtues and human good and purpose has been lost to philosophy, it continues or gets regenerated by 'plain persons' in their everyday lives (MacIntyre, [1981] 2007, p xiii), as a result of what people inherit from their own cultural backgrounds and the roles and functions people have in relation to others. He links this to the narrative nature of human lives – 'man is ... essentially a story-telling animal' (p 216) – and how people are each part of and to some extent co-authors of each other's stories. In later work (MacIntyre, 1999), he expands his thesis to include biological grounding related to human interdependence as social animals. In this, he proposes that the virtues for human flourishing (realised only in and through relationships with others) require that we acknowledge the bodily dimension of human existence, including vulnerability to many kinds of afflictions, injuries and disabilities, and in developing from infantile dependence to become independent rational thinkers.

Justice in communities

Some of these ideas have resonance with communitarian perspectives on justice. Though there were forerunners, 'communitarianism' as such became known as a public philosophy in the early 1990s under the leadership of Amitai Etzioni, placing emphasis on 'the common good and social bonds … the notion of balance between the communal and the personal, between individual rights and social responsibilities and the notion of pluralism bounded by a core of shared values' (Etzioni, 1996, p 40). The communitarian position on justice is bound up with membership and belonging, with interdependence within families, and with notions of overarching values that are culturally inherited but allow value pluralism within a community of communities. Critics of communitarianism perceive it as a movement that would sacrifice individual liberties for the common good; as aligned with the prescriptive moralism of Tony Blair's 'third way'; and as, anyway, unviable in the pluralistic communities of advanced modernity. But if people acknowledge the teleological and interdependent nature of human lives, it becomes possible to 'see ourselves as situated and yet free' (Sandel, 2009, p 221).

Although Macintyre ([1981] 2007) rejects suggestions that he is a communitarian – and interestingly on the grounds that it is too similar to liberalism, which he also rejects – there are clear parallels between communitarian thinking and MacIntyre's thesis. The effect of communities on their participants of course varies with the nature of community and, as MacIntyre correctly points out, 'many types of community are nastily oppressive' (p xii) and there are difficult issues in how one community gets along with another. Nevertheless, it is in the context of engagement in community that MacIntyre envisages the achievement and embodiment of the best that humans can be:

> [T]he best type of human life, that in which the tradition of the virtues is most adequately embodied, is lived by those engaged in constructing and sustaining forms of community directed toward the shared achievement of those common goods without which the ultimate human good cannot be achieved. ([1981] 2007, p xii)

This is not in conflict with communitarian literature that embraces notions of the common good – based on a core of shared values handed down from generation to generation, allowing pluralism of religious and political beliefs, but providing overarching values that 'help sort out conflicts between two or more subordinate level values' (Etzioni, 1996, p 103) – in 'solid but not overbearing communities' that enable people to 'function fully' and become 'better than we would otherwise be' (Etzioni, 2004, p 28).

Value pluralism and public discussion

Amartya Sen (2009) brought some of the threads together in his book, already mentioned. He draws attention to the 'pervasive plurality' of the ingredients of what people see as justice, and to their importance as part of a civilised society, but also to the difficulty of protecting and reconciling them in some situations and the comparative ease of doing so in others. Sen's argument is that there are different rationalities brought to bear in social arrangements and politics and that each has some merit: reasonable people will sometimes disagree. It is better to recognise the plural perspectives on justice but still to aim for a less unjust world by concentrating on issues of greatest urgency or on which there is some agreement. He argued that their reconciliation has to be found through a democratic process that involves more than ballots – and he might also have said more than opinion polls and online petitions – and that includes 'public reasoning and government by discussion'. Later chapters will consider what that expression might mean in practice when applied to subjects such as sentencing, the nature and purpose of punishment and policing.

The process of justice and a sense of legitimacy

That there is a relationship between criminal justice and social justice perhaps goes without saying. The sense of what is right and wrong in the treatment of people by other people cuts across all the different conceptions of justice, and simple reflection on how and why laws have originated makes clear the link between these two concepts.[3] It might therefore be unsurprising that the adjective 'criminal' is often dropped in criminological and legal texts, while some treatises on justice do not use 'social' as an adjective.[4] Yet there are clear conceptual and practical distinctions between them. Criminal justice is institutionally distinct, with its own legal and organisational apparatus. Moreover, there are many who argue that some policies of criminal justice exacerbate and actually create social injustice (for example, O'Mahony, 2000; Garside, 2009). No one is suggesting that the criminal law is unnecessary or denying the need for sanctions against some behaviours identified as crime, but there are good grounds for a major shift of emphasis

---

[3] Indeed, many animals appear to act in accordance with social rules, and there are consequences if these rules are infringed.

[4] Notably, F.A. Hayek (1960), who in *The Constitution of Liberty* suggested that describing justice as 'social' is unnecessary.

from offending by people who have low incomes or are socially disadvantaged to 'crimes of the powerful' (Whyte, 2009).

In western societies, justice is closely connected with the rule of law, democracy, shared values and human rights. People's sense of justice, about what is fair, or merited, or humane, comes from their socialisation about such values as well as their experiences and observations. It is also, as suggested previously, embedded into our social and biological nature (MacIntyre, 1999; Bekoff and Pierce, 2009). Nevertheless, given the tensions as well as practical complexities in all these issues, the rules and regulations within which governments operate are normally written into legislation and constitutional or other statutory documents.

The United Kingdom is rare among liberal democracies in not having a codified constitution as such; that is, it does not have a single document incorporating key constitutional provisions. Justice is instead protected partly by various Acts of Parliament and more recently the European Convention on Human Rights and now the 1998 Human Rights Act which incorporated the Convention into domestic law. Those statute laws are supported by case law (legal principles and precedents drawn from previous judicial decisions) and documented principles, notably the rule of law. During the last 20 years, there has been debate on whether the United Kingdom would benefit from a national Bill of Rights, for which the Human Rights Act was originally seen as a first step but then as a substitute. The coalition government has revived the issue, but there is at present no agreement on what its purpose would be or what form it would take. At the time of writing, a commission headed by Sir Leigh Lewis was considering whether Britain now needs a Bill of Rights, but whatever its outcome, the important point is that there should be some rules that no government should be free to violate without restraint.

Criminal justice has always been a matter of the resolution of conflict, for example between the offender and the victim, and of reconciliation – between the interests of the individual and those of the state, between those of children and those of their parents, between freedom and security, or between the freedoms of one person and those of another. The tension may become more acute in wartime or at times of social unrest characterised by, for example, demonstrations or industrial action. Acts of terrorism and their direct and indirect effects have in recent years made the tension more conspicuous and more alarming as some principles of justice have been sacrificed in order to protect others. The value of 'public reasoning and government by discussion' (Sen, 2009) becomes even more salient. Insofar as agreement has been reached and set into legislation, the authority of those agreed rules and values are protected by the rule of law.

The rule of law

The expression 'rule of law' signifies that the law of the land is supreme over any other authority, is applicable to all regardless of status, and that behaviour should be regulated and punishment and rights meted out only by the authority of the law and in strict accordance with well-established and clearly defined procedures. It provides predictability and certainty, and is the vehicle for upholding the values and principles of the nation's democratic way of life (Goldsmith, 2006).

Lord Bingham's book on *The Rule of Law* (Bingham, 2010) traces the origin of the principle of the rule of law, perhaps to Aristotle and certainly to jurist and constitutional theorist A.V. Dicey ([1885] 1915). He set out eight principles that should always be followed, namely:

- The law must be accessible and so far as possible intelligible, clear and predictable.
- Questions of legal right should ordinarily be resolved by the application of law and not the exercise of discretion.
- The laws of the land should apply equally to all, save to the extent that objective differences justify differentiation.
- Ministers and public officers at all levels must exercise the power conferred on them in good faith, fairly, for the purpose for which they were conferred, without exceeding the limits of such powers and not unreasonably.
- The law must afford adequate protection of fundamental human rights.[5]
- Means must be provided for resolving, without prohibitive cost or inordinate delay, bona fide civil disputes that the parties themselves are unable to resolve.

---

[5] These include: right to life; freedom from torture and inhuman treatment; right to liberty and security; freedom from slavery and forced labour; right to a fair trial; no punishment without law; respect for your private and family life, home and correspondence; freedom of thought, belief and religion; freedom of expression; freedom of assembly and association; right to marry and start a family; protection from discrimination in respect of these rights and freedoms; right to peaceful enjoyment of your property; right to education; right to participate in free elections (1998 Human Rights Act).

- Adjudicative procedures provided by the state must be fair.[6]
- The rule of law requires compliance by the state with its obligations in international law as well as national law.

He examined the departures from the rule of law, as he saw them, which took place in the United Kingdom and the United States as part of the 'war on terror' that followed the events of 11 September 2001. He concluded:

> ... in a world divided by differences of race, colour, religion and wealth [the rule of law] is one of the greatest unifying factors, perhaps the greatest, the nearest we are likely to approach to a universal secular religion. It remains an ideal, but an ideal worth striving for, in the interests of good government and peace, at home and in the world at large. (Bingham, 2010, p 174)

Other writers have explored the relationship between justice or the rule of law and terrorism and security (Hudson, 2003; Ashworth, 2007; Loader and Walker, 2007; Zedner, 2007a; Loader and Sparks, 2010), but Bingham's eight principles have a wider application that extends to the legal process as a whole and to the principles on which a modern society is governed. Direct appeals are rarely made to such principles in the context of policies or practice in criminal justice (as distinct from the treatment of individuals under the Human Rights Act), but governments and criminal justice services may lose sight of them or ignore them if they are in a hurry or feel they have to 'do something' or be seen to have 'done something' when they are under political pressure.[7]

---

[6] For practical purposes, fairness here refers to procedures conducted according to due process and procedural justice. In some situations, though, people will ground their conceptions of fairness on beliefs or knowledge that may not be available to the legal actors (for example, a rape victim may 'know' that a defendant is guilty, although he may be fairly acquitted according to a point of procedure that breaches due process).

[7] A leading article in *The Times*, commenting on the Supreme Court's judgment on ex-offenders' *right to apply* (emphasis added) to have their names removed from the sex offenders' register, said: 'The court of public opinion will very rarely provide justice for those whom public opinion despises. Democracy plus the rule of law ought to' (*The Times*, 17 February 2011, p 2 [untitled editorial article]).

Procedural justice and legitimacy

Procedural justice is about the formulation and observance of rules and procedures for dealing justly with people and situations. It applies particularly to the exercise of authority and especially the authority of the state and its institutions. It includes due process: the recognised and established rules of fairness, equity, consistency and impartiality that apply generally, and the principles that apply especially to criminal justice, including the presumption of innocence, rules on the admissibility of evidence, prohibition of imprisonment without trial, 'equality of arms', judicial independence, trial by jury, and proportionality of response (Packer, 1968; Sanders and Young, 2007). It would be unreasonable to demand that the detailed implementation of those principles should be set in stone and entrenched in the constitution, even if that were possible in the British parliamentary system. They can and should be exposed to political debate, and change may sometimes be justified. But it should be understood that significant changes need special justification – one that is more than a reaction to an event, a calculation of political advantage, or a response to a campaign in the media.

Procedural justice is, however, about more than due process. It includes treating people with dignity and respect; courtesy; the giving of reasons; neutrality, or the absence of bias, prejudice, favouritism and corruption; and the opportunity to be heard and state a case, together with the values of civility and respect for human dignity (Duff, 2007; Zedner, 2010; Loader and Sparks, 2010, p 9). In public affairs, it includes public deliberation, collective accountability and transparency in the formation of policy and legislation, and good management of services and organisations. Procedural justice is connected with people's sense of what is fair, and it links with liberty, equality and consistency (Rawls, 1971). These are necessary conditions if the authority of the state and its institutions are to be accepted as legitimate, and if people are to have confidence in them.

The rule of law and justice institutions are in a sense legitimate by definition (they are authorised by law), but whether they are perceived as having legitimacy in the sense of deserving compliance and respect will depend on such factors as the integrity of procedures, respectful processes, and fairness of treatment and outcomes. A distinction is made in scholarly literature between empirical legitimacy, where an institutional arrangement is legitimate 'as a matter of fact', and normative conceptions of legitimacy that meet certain substantive requirements of basic justice and rationality (Hinsch, 2010; Jackson et al, 2011). In both respects, there are people who believe the arrangements should regulate their conduct, but the normative concept of legitimacy involves moral approval and commitment. The distinction is important in gaining the compliance and respect of those subject to the institutional arrangement: 'a power relationship is not legitimate because people believe in its legitimacy, but because it can be *justified in terms of* their beliefs' (emphasis in original) (Beetham, 1991, p 11).

Practical implications

The practical implications of procedural justice and perceived legitimacy have been explored in relation to the police (Tyler and Huo, 2002; see also chapter six) and prisons (Sparks et al, 1996; Liebling, 2004; see chapter eight), but they also apply to therapeutic jurisprudence and problem-solving approaches (see chapter seven), to compliance with community orders and to the will of individuals to lead law-abiding lives more generally (Bottoms, 2001; Tyler, 2006a, 2009). They are closely related to the arguments for restorative justice, which provides opportunities for each party to understand each other's experience and perspective and for the offender to offer some reparation to the victim and the community – see chapter five.

Claims of injustice have arisen over the system's treatment of women and minority groups – for example over the sentencing of women, especially those with young families, or the policing of members of minority ethnic groups – and of disregard for the needs of victims and witnesses. Complaints such as these have often been justified and have led to much-needed reforms. They can arise in what may be seen as perverse acquittals; in decisions not to prosecute, perhaps for lack of evidence; or when a householder risks prosecution if they use a weapon or violence to defend their family or their property against an intruder. Given tensions between different needs and ideas of justice, there may, however, come a point at which it is impossible to please everyone and where someone still feels understandably aggrieved. There may in some cases be a conflict between due process for the defendant and the victim's sense of justice, which may give rise to the perception that the law is 'on the side' of the person charged or found guilty of an offence.

Especially difficult are cases where, for example, a person whom the victim knows to be guilty is acquitted on a technicality, or a child has died but the person responsible cannot be found, or receives a sentence that the family feels inadequate when compared with the loss they have suffered. Such an event can become a defining moment in a person's life, with consequences that affect every aspect of day-to-day living – ability to work, family relationships, physical and mental health.[8] It is then important that the process is seen as being as far as possible fair to all those affected by the event and its aftermath, including society as a whole as well as individual offenders and victims. A sense of being heard and properly treated is necessary for the process and the outcome to have authority and legitimacy, especially if the outcome is one that some of those involved would otherwise find difficult to accept. The relationships and dynamics involved in the process are as important a part of justice as the outcome, but 'closure' may not always be possible. See also the discussion of victims and witnesses and of restorative justice in chapter five.

Equality before the law and consistency of treatment

The concept of 'equality before the law' is generally accepted in principle, for example, in terms of who gets arrested and charged, in the protection and treatment that people receive from the police, in the quality of their representation as defendants, in the consideration they receive as witnesses or victims, in the process of trial and sentence, in the treatment they receive while serving a sentence, and in access to justice. It may not always seem to be observed in practice, with the use of powers to 'stop and search' and the disproportionate number of young black men sentenced to imprisonment as the most obvious areas of contention. The coming restrictions on legal aid may be an important issue for the future if it appears that poor people are denied access to legal representation, with the risk that errors may occur in court decisions made.

Most people will argue that standards of service should be consistent across the country as a whole, and any appearance of 'postcode lotteries' in provision of resources and services is always criticised. In criminal justice, there is an expectation that the criteria in decisions to prosecute be applied consistently in all areas, and that similar offences should attract similar penalties wherever they are committed. Lack of consistency in sentencing has engaged government and the judiciary for several years – see chapter five. On the other hand, it is accepted that different police forces may use different methods in different places and on different occasions, for example when dealing with demonstrations or anti-social behaviour; and no one argues that all prisons should have

---

[8] The charity Escaping Victimhood – www.escapingvictimhood.com – aims to help people whose lives have been fragmented in that way to move on from being a victim to being a survivor.

identical regimes. The current coalition government's programme of localisation and greater use of professional discretion (see especially chapters six and nine), if it is followed through, may lead to more local variations in practice; and commissioning from a wider range of providers, including voluntary organisations, may lead to greater diversity of provision. That will inevitably happen if arrangements are to promote innovation and take account of local situations and opportunities. How far government will expect or be expected to impose consistency and standardisation may be one of the issues to be resolved in connection with the coalition's new policies.

Risk, liberty and security

If compromises have to be made, for example in response to terrorism, they must be justified and limited both in their scope and the duration for which they are to apply. Interference with people's lives and liberty must similarly be justified and limited, and procedures for risk assessment and risk management must be proportionate and kept in perspective. It is especially important to recognise the fallibility of risk assessment procedures, whether they are based on actuarial methods or processes based on human judgement (Towl, 2010), following the events of 11 September 2001 and the introduction of legislation to deprive people of their liberty without bringing charges against them.

The state, citizenship and criminal justice

There is an underlying difference of attitude about what citizenship means and what status it confers. On one view, associated with the philosopher Immanuel Kant and with more recent scholars such as Antony Duff (2001, p 36), citizenship is a permanent possession, part of a person's identity. A person should be seen as an 'end', not as an agent or instrument to be used as a means of serving the purposes of the state. Citizenship brings certain rights, benefits and obligations, and a status in which all people are equal and entitled as far as possible to equal consideration, treatment and respect. A person might have some of their rights and benefits suspended or withdrawn if they are abused, and they could be penalised for breaking the law, subject to the rules of due process, but they remain citizens in all other respects.[9]

---

[9] This is the sense of Lord Wilberforce's judgment in *Raymond v Honey* ([1983] 1 AC 1) – that prisoners should be able to function as citizens in the wider community to the extent that they are not prevented by the fact of their imprisonment.

They still have responsibilities to care for their families, and to support themselves and their families and to contribute to society as far as they are able to do so. It would not, according to that view, be acceptable for penalties such as the withdrawal of a passport or driving licence or loss of welfare benefits to be imposed for unrelated offences such as theft or burglary, or for anti-social behaviour. And, on that view, perhaps it would be thought reasonable for prisoners to have the right to vote in parliamentary elections.

Another view regards citizenship in more functional terms. Citizens are seen in terms of their relationship with the state, for example as users or customers of public services, as in the Conservative government's Citizen's Charter; or as producers or consumers of goods or units of economic activity. An example is where education and especially higher education is seen as a commodity to be purchased for its financial benefits to the individual or the economic advantages which can accrue to the state. A person may be seen as less of a citizen if they are thought to be 'risky' or 'not making a contribution'. The state may then try to change their behaviour, using whatever inducements or threats may be at its disposal – loss of benefits or the threat of criminal penalties (for example, for smoking in public places) on the one hand, or rewards or 'nudges' for good citizenship and incentives to take employment or avoid drugs and alcohol on the other.[10] In its more positive sense, this view of citizenship also emphasises the empowerment of individuals to make a social contribution and influence change in their capacity as citizens. As commented by Louis Brandeis, a former Justice of the United States Supreme Court, 'in a democracy, the most important office is the office of citizen' (cited by Obama, 2006, p 236).

A government, a political party or an individual may lean towards one view rather than another, but it does not help to say categorically that one is 'right' and the other is 'wrong'. Both have to be accommodated in day-to-day life. The second view has, however, been foremost in a large part of criminal justice and social policy and of the reforms in public services over the past 20 years, including the 'New Public Management' – see chapters three and nine – and a change of emphasis might now be appropriate.

---

[10] The coalition government set up a Behavioural Insight Team, based in the Cabinet Office, to explore 'nudging' as a possible basis for new social policies, based on theories of behavioural economics (Thaler and Sunstein, 2008). The basic concept underlying this approach is that the citizen retains a sense of personal choice in what they do, but the situation is structured to make the preferred choice of government the most likely 'option' to be taken.

Criminal justice and the duty of the state

Criminal justice is one of the most critical areas in which the duties, responsibilities and functions of the state engage with those of the citizen and civil society (Faulkner, 2006, pp 55-71 and 152-3). In broad terms, it is the duty of the state to preserve the rule of law and protect its citizens; it is the duty of the citizen to obey the law and comply with lawful instructions (for example, from a police officer), and to perform tasks such as jury service and giving evidence in court when required to do so. Their readiness to do that may depend on the perceived legitimacy of what they are being asked, or ordered, to do. The state has a responsibility to provide and maintain the institutions and services needed to perform its necessary functions, including the armed forces and the criminal justice and emergency services; and citizens have a responsibility to pay taxes and cooperate with the state's institutions when necessary.

Further responsibilities of the state include the provision of services such as education, health and welfare. How far those responsibilities extend and how the state should discharge them – for example, directly, by contracting out or by commissioning services from the private or voluntary sector – becomes less a matter of principle and more a question of affordability, accountability and judgement. How that judgement should apply to criminal justice, and what services or activities should be regarded as available for contracting out or commissioning, has been a matter of argument since responsibility for prison escorts was contracted out in the 1980s. No clear boundary has been established; the declared criteria so far seem to be cost and value for money, but the coalition government has also been seen as having an underlying aim of cultivating markets and 'shrinking the state'. The boundary is likely to be the subject of further discussion and possibly disagreement over the coming years – see chapter nine.

Most people would agree that citizens' responsibilities include the care and protection of themselves and their children, considerate behaviour towards others, 'making a contribution' to society or their communities, and taking part in democratic processes such as elections and public consultations. The state must protect its citizens from crime and other harms (for example, threats to health and safety) as far as it can reasonably do so, but there are limits both to what is practicable and to what would be acceptable, and proportionate to the harm, without becoming oppressive interference. Citizens cannot expect the state to protect them from every misfortune or annoyance they might suffer, or from every crime that might be committed against them, and they should take reasonable precautions themselves. In a time of austerity, the state may not be able to afford the degree of protection it has provided in the past, and citizens may have to accept some risks or a lesser degree of protection than they have been used to in the past – see chapters six and nine. Again, there is at present no clear boundary, but Lord Bingham's eight principles provide an important point of reference.

A sense of being accepted and respected as a citizen, and the opportunity to re-establish oneself as a citizen with the responsibilities that implies, can be a powerful element in an offender's rehabilitation (Roberts, 2010). The coalition government seems to recognise that process in its proposal to review the 1974 Rehabilitation of Offenders Act, in order to reduce the obstacle that a conviction can present to an offender's reintegration (Ministry of Justice, 2010a, p 34; 2010b, p 56). Further considerations apply to the nature and status of communities, the different kinds of community to which a person may belong, their influence and responsibilities, and the means of making their voices heard in a complex and diverse society.[11]

Denigrating trends: managerialism and debasing language

The expression 'criminal justice' is often used in connection with what has come to be called the 'criminal justice system', now commonly spelt with capital letters and abbreviated to CJS. The government website www.direct.gov.uk states that:

> The Criminal Justice System (CJS) is one of the major public services in this country. Across the CJS, agencies such as the police, the Crown Prosecution Service, the courts, prisons and probation work together to deliver criminal justice.

The idea of criminal justice as a 'system' is of quite recent origin. Until the 1980s, there was little thought of justice as a 'system' that could be 'managed'. It was even argued within the Home Office that principles such as the independence of the judiciary and the operational independence of chief constables meant that there could not and should not be a system in the sense that has now become accepted. Those objections were overridden when the criminal justice services, like

---

[11] For speculative articles on how the ideas of citizenship might be applied more directly to criminal justice and the treatment of offenders, see Faulkner (2003, 2004).

other services, had to be managed in accordance with the government's Financial Management Initiative and its policies for efficiency, economy and effectiveness in the 1980s. Those demands, and government's expectations of what could be achieved, were set to grow in the years that followed. Even so, as Lucia Zedner (2010, p 85) has said:

> Despite being referred to as a system, it is no more than a series of largely independent organisations with different cultures, professional ethos and practices which come together and interact only insofar as is necessary to pursue their respective goals.

'Managing criminal justice', and managing criminal justice 'as a system', seemed a good idea at the time when it first became part of government policy. Each of the agencies acted as if they believed themselves to be superior to the others and were inclined to look down on them. Some of them could take decisions for which others had to pick up the consequences, and could impose costs that they had no incentive to restrict and that those who had to meet them were unable to control. The lack of communication between the agencies and between the agencies and the judiciary, the conflict of cultures, and in some instances the lack of basic management disciplines, all presented and can still present serious problems.

Much has improved in those respects, although some would argue the improvements were more the result of action by the service managers and practitioners themselves than of any reorganisation imposed by government. The problem of coordinating the work of different agencies and government departments remains, most obviously in sentencing and the demands it makes on the prison and probation services, but also in the processes of investigation, prosecution and trial (Raine and Willson, 1993; James and Raine, 1998), in the enforcement of orders (Ministry of Justice, 2010b), and in the rehabilitation of offenders. It is still important, perhaps more important than ever at a time of financial pressure, to break down the 'silos' in which public services too often continue to operate, to think of and where possible improve the connections between different processes and services, and to consider their collective impact on situations and individuals.

The coalition government's green paper for the reform on criminal justice (Ministry of Justice, 2010a), together with its evidence report (Ministry of Justice 2010b, p 67), indicated a number of promising ways in which 'criminal justice agencies and wider partners can deliver services in a more joined up way in order to increase effectiveness'.

Promoting joint working and improving connections between services, however, is not the same as managing criminal justice as a system. Chapter three will argue that the Labour government's emphasis on treating criminal justice as a unified system and on 'managing it as a business' caused the boundary between criminal justice and other services to become more strongly defended and harder to cross, with damaging consequences.

Another negative development in recent decades has been the adoption of demeaning language in debate about crime. The language of criminal justice is important. The unsuitability and the damage sometimes caused by the language of warfare and of denigration or demonisation has been pointed out many times (Faulkner, 2006, p 144; Roberts et al, 2010; Scraton, 2008). This applies in particular to the tabloid media[12] but also to some government communications. Expressions like the 'war on crime', the 'war on drugs', 'vermin', 'feral' children and 'monsters' create an impression of an enemy who has to be defeated, of creatures of a different species, of people who are worthless and beyond redemption, or of a criminal class that has no place in a civilised society and have to be driven from it. Such dehumanising language serves to put them beyond the considerations normally extended to humans; and the use of such expressions implies a justification of oppressive methods of law enforcement and of punishment, the removal of some of the protection that the criminal justice process is supposed to provide, and arbitrary loss of liberty 'for the protection of the public'.

Such language also undermines efforts to bring about an offender's rehabilitation and reintegration. Even the word 'offender' when continually used to label a person whose offending is in the past, albeit less stigmatising than 'criminal', gives a person a stereotyped identity for something they have done and not for what they might be or might become (Guilfoyle, 2010; Roberts et al, 2010). While the offending behaviour in question may be extreme and should then rightly receive public disapproval, to turn such descriptions into an identity of who they are fixes that behaviour to them as a permanent characteristic such that they may be judged by it for all time.

---

[12] As pointed out by Andrew Bridges, Chief Inspector of Probation (Bridges, 2011, p 5), 'to the tabloid media [people who have offended] are, in the customary two-dimensional language, "thugs, louts and lags", and to show any trust or optimism towards any of them ever is to be regarded as weak or naïve and to be exposed to the most vitriolic criticism. Even our Ministers are lampooned in the tabloid press as "buffoons" if they dare to show even an ounce of decency towards sentenced offenders.'

Less often recognised is the damage that can be done by over-use of political slogans and managerial jargon. Slogans such as 'prison works' may be politically appealing but they have little substantive meaning and may in the end produce frustration and disillusion. The jargon of performance, delivery and effectiveness – the vocabulary of middle management appraisal – may be incomprehensible to those who do not share the same managerial culture and may be a barrier to effective communication. Words such as 'producers', 'customers' and 'service-user' may be useful for making a comparison or illustrating a point, but are misleading if they become part of the ordinary language of the administration of justice.

The Labour government presented its approach to 'managing offenders' in the cold, managerial language of 'delivery' and 'value for money', and in the language of coercion and control. For example, 'Offender management ensures that we have a *firm grip on offenders throughout their entire sentence*, both in custody and in the community' (Ministry of Justice, 2008a; emphasis added).

Conclusion: towards reconciliation

Justice, and especially criminal justice, is very often about resolving conflict – between the interests of the state and those of the individual, or between personal freedom and public protection. At a more practical level, the conflict may be between the offender and the victim, crime control and community relations, security and rehabilitation, retribution and restoration or public expectations and affordability. It is easy to think only in terms of 'balancing' one consideration against another, and especially of balancing the interests of the victim or the community against those of the offender or suspect. That kind of formulation risks an assumption that their interests are naturally opposed to one another and the former are always more 'deserving' than the latter, in a contest where what is good for the offender is seen as bad for the victim and the community, and vice versa. Although it may be difficult in an adversarial system, the situation should not be seen as a direct conflict between 'right' and 'wrong' or where there are 'winners' and 'losers', but as one that calls for resolution and reconciliation (Ashworth, 1996).

The choices that are made to resolve those conflicts, the way in which they are made – by government, by services, by the courts, by individual police, prison or probation officers – and the public's attitude towards those choices influence the kind of country that Britain is or wishes to be. Winston Churchill made essentially the same point in his much-quoted speech in the House of Commons on 10 July 1910 when he said: 'The mood and temper of the public in regard to the treatment of crime and criminals is one of the unfailing tests of the civilisation of any country.'

The public's 'mood and temper' seem to have hardened over the past 20 years – see chapter three. Whether the nation as a whole has become more nervous and less compassionate, or whether that is only the appearance given by reports and comments in the media and political reactions to them, is hard to judge. Throughout this book and especially in chapter ten, consideration is given to whether it could now become more balanced and facilitating.

TWO

What happened in criminal justice: the 1980s

The past 30 years have been a period of renegotiation, adjustment and repositioning in the power structure of Great Britain, in criminal justice and more generally.[1] The social and professional elites that formed the 'establishment' lost their influence during the 1980s and gave way to a different elite with different social values and a stronger orientation towards business methods and individual achievement (Oborne, 2007). At first subtle and later more pronounced changes took place in relationships between government and the judiciary as courts' judgments came to have more political significance, especially as a consequence of the 1998 Human Rights Act and the formation of the Supreme Court in 2009. The civil service became less valued and less respected as a source of wisdom and expertise, or as an institution with any authority or even identity of its own. Governments claimed to be committed to 'evidence-based policy', but they had no great regard for professional judgement or experience. The police and the prison and probation services all came under closer political scrutiny and received closer attention from ministers – a healthy development where it led to greater openness and accountability, but having what proved to be unfortunate consequences when ministers tried to take management into their own hands. The services negotiated their relationships with ministers with different degrees of success, reflecting the differences in the power they were able to exercise – a great deal for the police, quite a lot for the prison service, and less for the probation service.

The relationships in criminal justice, especially between government, the judiciary, the police and the prison and probation services and the civil service are continuing to evolve, and are likely to do so more rapidly as the present coalition government pursues its plans for

---

[1] Where no references are given, this chapter draws on David Faulkner's and John Halliday's personal recollections, on David Faulkner's personal papers, and on a discussion at the Centre for Contemporary British History on 7 May 2010 (Faulkner, 2010). As successive deputy secretaries in charge of the Home Office criminal and research departments they played major parts in the events described in this and the next chapter.

devolution to the private sector and localisation. It is a game played for high stakes (the gambling metaphor is not inappropriate), and the players need to know what they are doing.

The changing scene

Within the criminal justice sector, several new features established themselves on the scene during the 1980s. Government, the judiciary and the criminal justice services began to realise that traditional assumptions and practices could not deal adequately with issues of race and ethnicity, and that minority groups would not receive justice unless changes were made. They also came to acknowledge that victims of crime had been neglected for too long and that the scheme of compensation for criminal injuries introduced in the 1960s was a wholly inadequate response to their needs and legitimate expectations. Drug abuse developed into a major social problem. Crime was increasing and affecting more people, including the politically influential middle class. There were riots in Brixton and Toxteth. The prison population was at crisis level, and disturbances by prisoners and industrial action by prison officers were a constant threat. Research was beginning to cast doubt on the effectiveness of punishment and policing as instruments for preventing and reducing crime. The various actors in criminal justice – government departments, the courts, the Crown Prosecution Service (established in 1984) and the police, prison and probation services – were not well coordinated, and confidence and communication between them left much to be desired. Financial stringency and the demand for efficiency, economy and effectiveness were the order of the day.

The government responded with a range of measures designed both to deal with the immediate problems and to establish a sense of direction for the longer term. One of the aims was to move some of the emphasis in dealing with crime away from the processes of arrest, prosecution and punishment and towards prevention and rehabilitation. Another was to improve the quality of justice, especially with regard to minority groups and victims but also within the criminal justice process itself. A third was to improve communication and understanding within what began to be called 'the criminal justice system'. The government hoped that a political and professional consensus might be built around its proposals, as had happened for the 1948 Criminal Justice Act, but those hopes were later disappointed.

Optimism and complacency

The first two thirds of the 20th century was a period of what can be seen in retrospect as optimism or complacency, according to one's point of view. Considerations of justice and humanity were on the whole more powerful than concerns about public protection and safety. Despite, or perhaps because of, the experience of two world wars, there was a sense of progress towards a more tolerant and compassionate society. Landmarks in criminal justice were the creation of the borstal institutions for the rehabilitation of young offenders on the model of English public schools, the introduction of probation as an alternative to a sentence to give offenders another chance, and the formation of separate juvenile courts, all in the early years of the century. They were followed by the abolition of judicial corporal punishment in 1948, and the suspension and then abolition of capital punishment for murder in 1969. The prison population fell steadily until the end of the Second World War. Leon Radzinowicz (1999, p 111) wrote of the 1948 Criminal Justice Act that it 'gave an official and definitive seal to the most progressive and coherent criminal policy, not simply conceived on paper but pursued in practice, of any major country in the world at that time'. There was a confident sense that British justice and the British penal system were the best in the world.

It would, however, be a mistake to think of that period as any kind of 'golden age'. With the benefit of hindsight and later research, it can be seen that the situation was by no means as good as was often supposed. Crime increased steadily from the end of the First World War onwards, but for many years the total volume was not large enough for small percentage increases to attract attention. The middle class was for the most part sheltered from it. Rates of reconviction did not give much cause for concern, but the information may not have been as reliable as it later became. Sexual offending was rarely acknowledged or discussed in public. Miscarriages of justice were thought to be rare or even impossible, but it would be more accurate to say that they rarely came to light. The barrister Marshall Hall was widely admired for his skill in obtaining acquittals and was a role model for many young lawyers, but they were not much concerned that some of those who benefited from his forensic skills might actually have been guilty of the offences with which they were charged. Conversely, later research and successful appeals against wrongful conviction leave little doubt that many people were wrongly imprisoned.

Early concerns: how can criminal justice be effective?

Concerns about the 'effectiveness' of the penal system in reducing crime began to emerge in the 1950s. It was, however, a period when many people were looking to science to solve the world's problems as they saw them. It was the era of C.P. Snow and the 'two cultures' – science and the humanities (Snow, 1959)[2] – and the government believed that scientific research could show it how to 'cure' crime. The white paper *Penal Practice in a Changing Society* (Home Office, 1959) set out a programme of penal reform based on a medical or treatment model, including research-based policies for the assessment, treatment and rehabilitation of offenders; a programme for building new prisons, including special remand and observation centres and psychiatric prisons; and the refinement and extension of borstal training – still at that time seen as the jewel in the crown of the Prison Commission and depicted as a world leader in applied science. Psychologists were appointed not only to provide clinical services in prisons, but also to bring a more scientific approach to prison policy and practice.

That white paper was the first formal recognition by a government in this country that policy on criminal justice needs to be informed by research:

> ... a fundamental re-examination of penal methods, based on studies of the causes of crime ... in this field, research is as essential as it is in the fields of science and technology....
> (Home Office, 1959, p 29)

The following years saw a similar belief in science and technology for the police – patrol ('panda') cars to replace foot patrols; more use of radios; more sophisticated methods of detection; and developments in forensic science and in police records and intelligence. The aim was to reduce response times, increase detection rates and so reduce crime. There was not much interest in the 'softer' aspects of policing, encompassing issues of race, gender and the culture of the police service itself.

It was a time when the government also looked for wider sources of ideas and advice – through the Law Commission, the Criminal Law Revision Committee, the Advisory Council on the Treatment of

---

[2] Snow's argument was that the British education system had privileged the humanities at the expense of the sciences and that the British elite, educated mostly in the humanities, were inadequately prepared to manage the modern scientific world.

Offenders (later the Advisory Council on the Penal System) and the Advisory Council on Probation and After-Care. The Conservative government appointed Royal Commissions on the police and on the penal system, although the latter was abandoned after the change of government in 1964. All were composed of people with national reputations in their fields and were thought to represent the best available source of wisdom and advice on the subjects concerned. New ideas and new methods were being proposed and tested, but there was a sense of continuity with the past, including the Liberal government's reforms 50 years earlier. The post-war liberal consensus applied as much to criminal justice as it did to social and economic policy. The 'old' public administration was still in the ascendant (Loader and Sparks, 2010, pp 87, 137; see also chapter nine).

Disillusion sets in

The Home Office in 1959 was still a confident place. But disillusion came quite quickly. Its seeds were already present in the Mannheim-Wilkins study of prediction methods in borstal training (Mannheim and Wilkins, 1955), which suggested that an offender's progress could be accurately predicted at the time of sentence by reference to their history and personality regardless of any training or treatment they might subsequently receive. A study of intensive treatment by the probation and after-care services had disappointing results (Folkard et al, 1976). The escape of George Blake from Wormwood Scrubs and the subsequent Mountbatten inquiry turned the attention of the prison service sharply from research-based treatment and rehabilitation to security and control. The new remand and observation at Risley proved unworkable in its intended form, and the new, medically oriented Holloway came to be seen as having been a mistake (Rock, 1996; Player, 2010).[3]

Martinson (1974) produced his article, often cited but frequently misunderstood or misrepresented (wilfully or otherwise), in which he claimed that 'nothing works'. A study by Stephen Brody (1976), later reinforced by work at the Cambridge Institute of Criminology (von Hirsch et al, 1999), raised doubts about the effectiveness of sentencing in reducing crime. Other research questioned the effectiveness of police patrols in preventing crime (Clarke and Hough, 1984), and the

---

[3] The psychiatric, therapeutic prison at Grendon was, and still is, regarded as an effective – perhaps the *most* effective – way of rehabilitating violent and sexual offenders (Stevens, forthcoming).

advances in supposedly 'scientific' methods of policing had the effect of withdrawing officers from streets and communities and of alienating the police from the public. All this was taking place against a background of financial crisis and the cancellation of prison building. It was no surprise that the Home Office was much less confident in the 1970s than it had been in the early 1960s, and that the Home Office (1977) review of criminal justice policy was much less ambitious than the White Paper it had produced in 1959.

The Conservative government takes office

The Conservative government that came into office in 1979[4] did so after an election in which crime and criminal justice had featured more prominently than ever before, but its manifesto had given few specific commitments. A series of Home Office internal seminars provided a starting point for what would now be called a 'direction of travel', which successive Home Secretaries accepted for the next 12 years. The main response to crime would be through situational and social methods – improved physical security, better management and design of housing estates, and more opportunities for young people. Within criminal justice, the emphasis would be on efficiency, economy and effectiveness in accordance with the government's Financial Management Initiative, and on the first attempts to achieve better coordination across the system. Attempts to 'manage' the system as a whole were a later development, the emphasis at that stage being on better consultation, coordination and communication.

An immediate task was to restore stability in prisons, after the disturbances by prisoners and the industrial action by prison officers that had taken place during the previous two or three years.[5] That was seen as mainly a matter of administrative action to implement the report of the May Committee's inquiry into the United Kingdom prison services (Home Office, 1979), but ministers also saw the need to deal with the problem of sentencing and to find a better alignment between sentencing practice and prison capacity. In 1980, the Lord Chief Justice, Lord Lane, in his judgments in the case of *Upton*,[6] had himself

---

[4] For other, more detailed accounts of events during this period, see Windlesham (1993), Dunbar and Langdon (1998) and Faulkner, 2006.

[5] The most serious disturbances were at Gartree (1978) and Wormwood Scrubs (1979). As part of their industrial action in 1980, prison officers refused to admit prisoners to prisons that were overcrowded and two temporary prisons were opened and run by members of the armed forces, especially the Royal Military Police.

[6] *Upton* (1980) 71 Cr App R 102.

acknowledged that the shortage of space in prisons could legitimately be taken into account in sentencing. Later, in the case of *Aramah*,[7] he introduced the first of the Court of Appeal's guideline judgments (on the importation of Class A drugs) that were to be the forerunner of the sentencing guidelines later issued by the Sentencing Advisory Panel, and subsequently by the Sentencing Guidelines Council, and now the Sentencing Council.

Those judgments gave some grounds for hope that a dialogue might be established between the Home Office and the higher judiciary, especially with a view to achieving a better alignment between sentencing practice and prison capacity but also to establishing a better mutual understanding of more general issues affecting sentencing and criminal procedure on both sides. An attempt was made to arrange a series of buffet suppers where judges and Home Office officials could meet and talk informally, but judges viewed them with suspicion and they were soon abandoned. More damage was caused by an inaccurate newspaper report that a scheme for 'supervised early release' had the support of the Lord Chief Justice. It seemed inevitable that progress would be slow and more drastic, possibly legislative, steps might have to be taken.

Towards a long-term strategy

Douglas Hurd became Home Secretary in 1985. With the Prime Minister's support and the help of John Patten as his newly appointed Minister of State, he set about preparing a comprehensive long-term strategy that was intended to continue for the length of the Parliament and, he hoped, beyond. Acknowledging the limited impact the criminal justice system can on its own have on the general level of crime, other programmes were to be developed to prevent and reduce crime and its impact and to promote public confidence.

Among those programmes were improved services and greater recognition for victims, including greater funding for Victim Support and later the Victim's Charter; more attention to problems of racial discrimination and disadvantage; and a new emphasis on crime prevention, including the creation of a national voluntary organisation, Crime Concern – see chapter four. The government and the criminal justice services began to think of criminal justice as 'a system', but their emphasis was on cooperation and communication, and on lateral thinking, and not at that stage on central direction and management.

---

[7] *Aramah* (1982) 4 Cr App R (S) 407.

The 1980s were also the period when government, police and sentencers came to see the abuse of drugs as a problem of crime and law enforcement and not, as previously, one of public health. This different perspective was related to a major expansion around that time in the availability and use of 'hard' drugs leading to addiction and persistent offending to finance the habit. The significance of this change in attitude for policing and sentencing was hardly debated at the time and its consequences for increased use of imprisonment and, arguably, the exacerbation of criminality, were not foreseen.

Influenced by Hurd and his political adviser Edward Bickham, the Conservative Party manifesto for the 1987 election articulated a quite limited role for government in criminal justice and in dealing with crime. It was to:

> ... give a lead by backing ... the police; by providing a tough legal framework for sentencing; by building prisons in which to take those who pose a threat to society – and by keeping out those who do not; and by encouraging local communities to prevent crime and help the police to detect it. (Cited in Windlesham, 1993, p 221)

That cautious commitment was consistent with the evidence on 'effectiveness' that was becoming available and the approach that was becoming more firmly established in the government. It was not sufficient for the manifestos that all the main parties issued for subsequent elections, but it was arguably a more accurate statement of what a government could realistically promise to achieve.

Immediate decisions

The most serious strategic issues facing the Conservative government after the election in 1987 were still seen as sentencing, prison accommodation and the relationship between them. Sentencing had become more severe since 1979 and especially since 1983: the Criminal Statistics showed that 63,000 custodial sentences were passed in 1979 compared with 83,999 in 1985, and the proportion of custodial sentences passed by the Crown Court had risen from 52% to 55% in the previous two years. There had been a surge in the prison population, which was now almost 50,000 compared with 43,300 in 1984 (it reached almost 51,000 in July 1987); prisoners were being held in police cells; and the projections showed that the population might reach 54,000 by 1991. Northeye prison had been burnt to the ground in a disturbance the previous year. New prisons were being built, but the projected shortfall in accommodation was 6,800 places.

Ministers took an immediate decision to increase remission from one third to one half of the sentence, so reducing the population by about 3,000 and resolving the situation in the short term. A committee to review the parole system was set up in 1988 under the chairmanship of Lord Carlisle (Home Office, 1988a). Looking further ahead, they believed that although the money for yet more prisons might be forthcoming in the short term, the Treasury could point out with some justification that the present commitment appeared open-ended. The time might well come when it would no longer be possible to provide an ever-increasing number of prison places for an ever-expanding prison population. They had to consider whether there was any way, acceptable both to the judiciary and public opinion, of easing the pressure on the prison system.

The questions that officials put to ministers were whether they should:

- take no special position on sentencing and continue to handle situations as they arise;
- expand prison capacity as necessary to match public and judicial demand for more severe sentencing;
- exert some downward pressure on the rise in the prison population, and therefore on the sentencing of those not regarded as a threat to society.

Officials offered no advice on the choice between them, regarding it as an essentially political decision.

The policy emerges

Ministers decided on the third option. The plan that emerged from the meeting was for legislation to reduce maximum sentences for some non-violent offences such as domestic burglary and to introduce procedural restrictions on custodial sentences such as persistent petty offenders or those facing the possibility of their first custodial sentence. A system of unit fines, relating the amount of a fine more directly to the offender's income, would be tested in local experiments and might be introduced nationally if it proved successful. Community service would be given a higher profile and made more demanding. The plan would need strong political commitment and judicial support. Language would be important – offenders on probation should no longer be referred to as 'clients', but the government would sensibly avoid expressions such as 'the war on crime'.

Intensive discussions then took place – between John Patten and Edward Bickham and Conservative Members of Parliament, between ministers and officials and the judiciary, with the probation service, and with academic criminologists. They took several forms – informal meetings, attendance and talks at conferences or at regular meetings of bodies such as the Judicial Studies Board or the Magistrates' Association. More formal consultation followed the traditional pattern of the green paper *Punishment, Custody and the Community* (Home Office, 1988b), followed by a white paper entitled *Crime, Justice and Protecting the Public* (Home Office, 1990a), which was accompanied by a further green paper *Supervision and Punishment in the Community* (Home Office, 1990b) and a discussion paper *Partnership in Dealing with Offenders in the Community* (Home Office, 1990c).

It is hard to say how far the proposals as they eventually appeared in the white paper grew out of those consultations, as distinct from any preconceived ideas held by the department or by ministers. But the process was certainly different from the one that became more usual in later years, when proposals were formulated in departments, political advisers' offices or No. 10 Downing Street and the purpose of the consultation was more to obtain consent (or some might say compliance), support and publicity than it was to gather ideas.

Consultation with the judiciary

The green paper described the work already in hand and drew attention to the disadvantages and cost of custody for those who were not serious offenders. It then posed a series of questions about the use of imprisonment, including a reduction in the use of custody for thieves and burglars; the components of punishment in the community, including the use of community service, day centres, curfews and electronic monitoring; a possible new community order with a wide range of requirements that might include reviews by judges or magistrates of an offender's progress; and an increase in the age limit for the juvenile court from 17 to 18. It introduced the principle of proportionality – that the sentence should be proportionate to the seriousness of the offence and the culpability of the offender (Ashworth, 2010, and see also chapter five) – which was later developed as 'just deserts' in the subsequent white paper. Anticipating the work of Tom Tyler and others a few years later (see chapters one and seven), it said:

It is better that people should exercise self-control than
have controls imposed upon them.... If they can develop
the skills necessary for life and work, this should encourage
greater self-reliance and respect for others; there should be
less incentive to offend again. (Home Office, 1990b, p 1)

The green paper provided the basis for an unprecedented and never-
repeated conference held at Ditchley Park in September 1989. It brought
together the most powerful figures in criminal justice in England and
Wales, including the Home Secretary, the Lord Chancellor, the Attorney
General, the Lord Chief Justice and Deputy Chief Justice, the Chairman
of the Magistrates' Association, the Director of Public Prosecutions
and the most senior figures in the criminal justice services. No similar
conference has been held since then, but a National Criminal Justice
Consultative Council, with similar membership, and local criminal
justice boards were established following the Woolf report – see below.

Speaking at the conference, John Patten described the government's
proposals as having two aims:

> 'One is to establish firmly those principles of sufficiency and
> proportionality of response. The other is to reinforce the links
> between offenders and society and emphasise the importance
> of social responsibility. Our objective is better justice, with
> greater consistency and emphasis on the offender in society.'

He went on to give a carefully considered statement of the relationship
between the government and the judiciary in respect of sentencing, as
the government saw it at the time.

> 'We have tried to interfere as little as possible with the
> independence and the discretion of sentencers. We are not
> proposing mandatory sentencing guidelines or a sentencing
> commission....We prefer sentencers to be free to consider all
> relevant circumstances: but we do believe that their discretion
> should be properly limited so that it does not frustrate policy
> principles.'[8]

---

[8] That was intended as a statement of policy, not an interpretation of the principle
of judicial independence as it applies to sentencing. The Conservative government,
and later the Labour government, adopted a more assertive stance in later years but
neither breached the principle as it is generally understood (Ashworth, 2010, pp
54-5); see chapters three and five.

The conference seemed to give broad approval to the approach that the government had proposed, although the judges' undoubted goodwill may have been mistaken for agreement to the policy and there may have been some wishful thinking. However that may have been, the white paper *Crime, Justice and Protecting the Public* followed early in 1990 (Home Office, 1990a). Douglas Hurd had by then left the Home Office to become Foreign Secretary and David Waddington had taken his place.

The 1991 Criminal Justice Act

The white paper argued that its proposals would provide for better justice through greater consistency and clarity in sentencing and in the use of parole, and better protection of the public through more effective rehabilitation of offenders. Custody was necessary for serious and especially violent and sexual offenders, but its effect on crime should not be overestimated. It was also expensive – in the white paper's much-quoted words, 'an expensive way of making bad people worse'. Crime could be more effectively prevented by the measures the government was taking outside the criminal justice process. The proposals formed the basis for the provisions on sentencing that became part of the 1991 Criminal Justice Act. The main proposals were that:

- Custodial sentences should only be imposed if they were justified by the seriousness of the offence (or the combination of the offence with one other); or – a late addition to the draft – for an offender found guilty of a serious violent or sexual offence, to protect the public from serious harm 'from him'.
- A similar test of seriousness should be applied to the length of both prison and community sentences.
- Suspended sentences should only be used in exceptional circumstances.
- The probation order was to become a sentence in its own right, and no longer an alternative to a sentence.
- Requirements had to be observed about giving reasons for the sentence and for obtaining pre-sentence reports.
- Fines were to be calculated in units relating to an offender's means.
- An offence was not to be regarded as automatically 'more serious' by reason of any previous conviction or failure to respond to an order, but aggravating factors disclosed by other offences could be taken into account.

A late addition to the draft of the white paper was a new power for the Crown Court 'to impose longer sentences for violent and sexual offences, if this is necessary to protect the public from serious harm' (p 14). The addition attracted little attention at the time, but it was a significant departure from the principle of proportionality on which the policy for the Bill had originally been framed. It began the movement towards preventive sentencing, without regard for proportionality, which culminated in the indeterminate sentences for public protection introduced by the 2003 Criminal Justice Act (see chapter five).

The Woolf report

Soon after the white paper was published, the disturbances at Manchester and other prisons reminded the country that the prison system was still in a precarious state. The consequences might have been even more serious if the prison population had still been at the level it reached in the summer of 1987. The disturbances led to Lord Justice Woolf's inquiry, whose report (Woolf, 1991) was published while the Bill for the Criminal Justice Act was still before Parliament. The report's recommendations broadly supported the direction in which the government was hoping to move. Many of them were on matters of prison administration but they also included closer cooperation between the different parts of the criminal justice system, closer links between prisons and their communities and improved standards of justice for prisoners themselves. The latter anticipated later work by Sparks and colleagues (1996) on legitimacy and order in prisons – see chapters one and eight.

The reaction begins

Officials and perhaps also ministers in the three criminal justice departments – the Home Office, the Lord Chancellor's Department, and the Law Officers' Department (responsible for the Crown Prosecution Service) – believed that a political and professional consensus was beginning to be formed around the plans for the 1991 Criminal Justice Act and the policies associated with them. They certainly tried to achieve that consensus. Ministers and especially John Patten as Minister of State at the Home Office and their political advisers had regular talks with Members of Parliament; residential conferences at national and regional level brought together practitioners in the various operational services, and judges wherever possible; and regular meetings and conversations kept government departments closely in touch with what each of them was doing. There were frequent contributions from the academic community, in a relationship that was generally one of mutual respect.

No one had any illusions about the stability of any political consensus that might have been achieved, and there was some relief that it was not seriously challenged during the 1992 general election. The judges were, however, an unknown quantity: they seemed in conversation to be favourably disposed, but sensitivity over judicial independence prevented any real meeting of minds and officials may have underestimated their underlying suspicion of what was being proposed and their hostility towards it. Their dislike of the sentencing provisions began to be voiced soon after the Bill was published, and became evident in a vehement speech by Lord Ackner during the Bill's final stages in the House of Lords. The first open confrontation came in a speech by Lord Taylor, newly appointed as Lord Chief Justice, in March 1993 when he described the Act's sentencing provisions as 'forcing the judge into an ill-fitting straightjacket'.

A series of judgments by the Court of Appeal,[9] delivered together at about the same time, had the effect of reinterpreting (some critics said undermining) the intentions of the Act, for example by restoring deterrence and prevalence as criteria for judging the seriousness of an offence (Windlesham, 1996, p 20; Dunbar and Langdon, 1998, p 113; Faulkner, 2006, p 125; Ashworth, 2010, pp 101-2). Legislation was hastily prepared to meet the judges' and magistrates' most serious criticisms, on previous and related offences and means-related fines, and was duly enacted as part of the 1993 Criminal Justice Act. The judges' hostility might have subsided once the amendments to the 1991 Act were in place, but no action by officials could have anticipated or prevented the government's own change of direction in 1993 – see chapter three.

Conclusion: learning from history

It has sometimes been thought surprising that Margaret Thatcher's Conservative government, with its commitment to 'law and order', should have pursued criminal justice policies that would now be regarded, and by some people condemned, as 'liberal' in a prejudicial sense. Of course those policies could equally be seen as part of a long-standing Conservative tradition of justice and humanity that went back through R.A. Butler and Winston Churchill (although a Liberal at the

---

[9] For example *Cunningham* (1993) 14 Cr App R (S) 444.

time when he was Home Secretary) to Robert Peel, to whom Douglas Hurd paid tribute in a speech delivered in Tamworth to celebrate the bicentenary of his birth on 5 February 1788. On that view, the policies of Michael Howard after 1993 (see chapter three) could be seen as a departure from a long-standing Conservative tradition. Whether the coalition or a future Conservative government could return to it may be made clear in the months and years to come.

Policy making in criminal justice is a precarious business. It needs a long-term vision and a sense of continuity and confidence that is hard to sustain in a situation of political turbulence. It needs an understanding with the judiciary that does not compromise their independence but allows a constructive dialogue to take place. Patient and persistent endeavour may begin to create a consensus, but it will still be vulnerable to events or to changes in the public mood or to real or perceived threats to the public's sense of safety and security. Policies need to be informed by the evidence that may be hard to find or equivocal, but also by the wisdom and confidence that come from experience.

THREE

A change of direction: the 1990s

During 1992–93, the public and political mood changed dramatically. Criminal justice has always, and rightly, been political, but political parties did not make it part of their appeal to the electorate until 1979 (Downes and Morgan, 2007), and political parties did not seriously contend with one another over criminal justice issues until 1992/93 (Loader and Sparks, 2010). Even then, the difference between the parties was more about the scale on which they could promise more prison places, more police officers and more punitive legislation than about differences of approach. Arguments were driven more by considerations of political advantage than by appeals to evidence or to political or social values (Blair, 2010, pp 54–7).

The reasons included the fact that rising crime meant that more people (and more middle-class people) had direct experience of offences such as burglary and car crime, and communicated their feelings to MPs in their constituencies. Police and local communities complained of children being out of control, and of anti-social behaviour that they seemed powerless to prevent or punish. Anger reached a climax in the reaction to the murder of Jamie Bulger by two young boys in 1993,[1] revived 17 years later in some newspapers' reporting of the arrest of one of those convicted of the murder for a breach of his parole licence. Other factors may have included the fragmented state of the Conservative Party at the time and the need to unite it around a subject on which the government could find general support. It is difficult to tell how far the media, and some politicians, were reporting and responding to a genuine crisis of public confidence, or how far they themselves contributed to it. Older people recalled an earlier time when they could leave the doors unlocked and feel safer on the streets. Increased fear of crime was fuelled by publicity given to rare but extremely serious offences or instances of persistent offending, and fears over the effects of drug and alcohol abuse.

All this was taking place in a wider context of what has been called 'late modernity' – the fragmentation of communities and relationships; shifting boundaries between the public and private spheres; changing

---

[1] Retrospective reports may have been inclined to exaggerate the extent to which it was Jamie Bulger's murder per se that was the watershed event.

attitudes and expectations towards the role and capacity of the state; globalisation; neoliberal economics; and the increasing significance of race, ethnicity and gender. In criminal justice, its features included changing attitudes to risk; increasing public sensibilities towards crime and the way offenders are treated; and the 'culture of control' and the 'criminal justice state' described by Bottoms (1995), Garland (2001), Wacquant (2009) and Loader and Sparks (2010), among others.

The revival of punishment

Michael Howard became Home Secretary in 1993 (the fifth Home Secretary in four years[2]). His statement at that year's Conservative Party conference that 'prison works' symbolised the rejection of all the thinking and all the evidence on which the Criminal Justice Act, 1991 had been founded. It was a far cry from the efforts made at the start of the decade to limit the use of custody, and that prison was 'an expensive way of making bad people worse'. The 1994 Criminal Justice and Public Order Act introduced not only a new secure training order for persistent juvenile offenders, but also new absolute offences to make it easier to convict and punish troublemakers of various kinds; increased penalties for a range of offences and increased maximum periods of custody for children and young offenders; and placed new restrictions on the granting of bail. By this time, criminal justice practitioners were already complaining about the pressures caused by new legislation and administrative reform, but the process had only just begun. The 1997 Crime (Sentences) Act provided for mandatory minimum sentences for certain types of repeat offender (the so-called 'three strikes' provisions) and disregarded the judges' opposition to what they saw as unwarranted and undesirable interference with their discretion. The Labour Party agreed to their enactment during the negotiations immediately before the dissolution of Parliament, and the Labour government brought them into effect soon after it came into office.

In parallel with its legislation on sentencing, the Conservative government introduced the 1994 Police and Magistrates' Courts Act, the 1996 Police Act and the 1997 Police Act, which made changes in the organisation of police forces, created a new form of police authority, and established a new (but in its original form short-lived) Police Complaints Authority. Most significantly of all, the 1994 Act gave the Home Secretary new powers of direction and control including the

---

[2] Lord Windlesham (1993, p 408) drew attention to the destabilising effect of frequent changes of Home Office ministers. See also chapter nine.

---

power to set targets and objectives – powers that the subsequent Labour government exploited to the full. See chapter six for further discussion.

Taking up the baton

The Labour government that came into office in 1997 regarded the system as failing in several respects:

- Sentencing was inconsistent and too many sentences were inadequate to protect the public or satisfy public opinion.
- Sentences were administered ineffectively, with too little attention to punishment or to the enforcement of conditions and the prevention of reoffending.
- Too many crimes remained undetected or unsolved and too many people were escaping conviction.
- Juvenile crime in particular was out of control, and children needed to be brought more firmly within the scope of the criminal law and punished accordingly.
- Anti-social behaviour was a similarly serious problem and should be dealt with through the criminal rather than the civil justice system, using civil rather than criminal standards of proof to simplify the process and avoid the need for a formal conviction.

Like the previous Conservative government, it believed that much of the system was 'infected' by a dangerous 'liberal' or 'metropolitan' elite that favoured the offender above the victim and the public. The system had to be radically rebalanced 'in favour of the victim', with a much stronger emphasis on protecting the public (Blair, 2006). Like other public services, criminal justice was to be run in accordance with the principles of modern public management (the New Public Management) based on targets, markets, competition and contracts (Prime Minister's Strategy Unit, 2006; Blair, 2010, pp 273-5; see also chapter nine). Those criticisms did not for the most part reflect any actual deterioration in the performance of the criminal justice system, but higher expectations of what it can or should achieve.

Labour's policies on criminal justice

The most prominent features of the Labour government's policies for criminal justice proved to be:

- An overhaul of the system for youth justice, including the creation of the Youth Justice Board and youth offending teams, with a new structure of penalties and more opportunities for restorative justice.
- Further legislation to increase the severity of sentencing and to improve rates of conviction (to 'close the justice gap'), especially in the 2003 Criminal Justice Act.
- Further legislation on policing, especially to increase police powers including 'on-the-spot' fines, the introduction of police community support officers and other civilian staff, the creation of new police structures at national level (the Serious Organised Crime Agency, the National Crime Squad, the National Criminal Intelligence System and the National Police Improvement Agency), and full use of the powers inherited from the previous government to 'micro-manage' the service; see chapter six.
- A long-drawn-out, disruptive and demoralising process of reorganisation for the prison and especially the probation service, including the creation of the National Offender Management Service; see chapters seven and eight.
- Programmes to promote community safety, based on a statutory duty for local authorities and chief constables to work together in formulating and implementing strategies to reduce crime and disorder in their areas; see chapter four.
- A major campaign to reduce anti-social behaviour, through the use of anti-social behaviour orders (known as ASBOs) and the related 'respect agenda' to empower communities to tackle anti-social behaviour, coordinated by a Respect Task Force.

All these measures had the effect of increasing central government's control of the operational services and its influence on courts and sentencing, and reflected the Labour government's lack of confidence in the services concerned. Perhaps the most successful, and the one that had been most fully thought out, was the reform of youth justice, for which the Audit Commission (1996) had provided the foundation in its report *Misspent Youth, Young People and Crime*. Few of the others responded to any coherent public demand except for 'more to be done' about crime, which the government believed – in the absence of reliable empirical evidence – could be achieved by the measures it had chosen.

The government also introduced the 1998 Human Rights Act, which has been a source of contention since coming into effect. It has frequently been criticised and often misrepresented, sometimes as a 'criminals' charter', sometimes because it is 'European' (although the European Convention it incorporates was largely based on English common law), and sometimes because it gives too much power to 'unelected judges'. Its intentions and content are, however, entirely consistent with the arguments in this book. A full discussion of the Act is outside our scope here, but the Act or an equivalent provision is essential in a modern democratic state. Similar provisions are to be found in the constitutions of most western democratic states.

For a discussion of the Labour government's wider social policies and their relevance to crime and criminal justice, see chapter four.

Review of the sentencing framework

Early in the life of the Labour government, the then Home Secretary Jack Straw commissioned a review of the sentencing framework in England and Wales and assigned it to John Halliday, who at the time was a serving civil servant in the Home Office. Announcing the review, Straw said that:

> 'The legal framework established in the Criminal Justice Act 1991 ... appears now to be a contributory factor to the inherent problems in sentencing, based as it is on "just deserts" by which the sentence imposed is tied to the seriousness of the offence, taking little account of the offender's propensity to re-offend. [He would like to see] a different framework ... that is based on evidence as well as principles.'

In that statement, he, too, dismissed the evidence on the effectiveness of sentencing on which the 1991 Act had been based, and returned to the earlier assumption that research could provide a scientific foundation for an instrumental sentencing policy that would produce measurable reductions in crime. The assumption seemed to be that systems, processes and 'interventions' either 'worked' or they did not and that 'what counts' is 'what works'. The empirical basis for that assumption was inconclusive and the assumptions neglected the broader context of the person's – often volatile – situation, opportunities and relationships.

The report (Halliday, 2001) found several flaws that made a case for reform. But from a careful review of the evidence it still concluded that reform should not be based on any supposed deterrent effect of sentencing, or on any supposed 'containment' effect of imprisonment. Rather, a new framework should keep to the principle of proportionality in sentencing, while including a more structured and explicit way of taking previous convictions into account, and doing more to support work aimed at diverting offenders from crime, and enabling them to make reparation to victims and communities. Within a modified 'desert' framework, the report argued for investment in programmes shown to be able to divert at least some offenders from crime, and for a sentence structure that maximised the chances of such programmes succeeding, through coordinated work by the prison and probation services. It advocated a new approach to short prison sentences, which in their existing form offered the lowest chance of doing useful work to alter criminal careers. It also emphasised, however, that even the best programmes offered a prospect of reducing reoffending by only relatively small amounts, at the margin. This argument was intended to point to the need to view sentencing in the context of wider crime reduction strategies.

In a key finding, the report showed that the increased use and length of custodial sentences during the 1990s could not be attributed to a larger number of convicted offenders going through the system. Nor could it be attributed to any apparent increase in the general seriousness of the offences committed by those appearing for sentence. The apparent explanation for the larger number of custodial sentences, and their increased length, was that sentencers had responded to their perception of what the public, Parliament or government expected of them.

The report pointed out that there was no necessary connection between a sentencing framework and the number or length of custodial sentences passed within it. The number and length of custodial sentences would depend on how judges determined the seriousness of offences, and what 'tariff' or 'going rate' they set for the threshold for a custodial sentence, and its length. Building on the work already done to build up sentencing guidelines, the report advocated moves towards a Sentencing Council, the underlying rationale being that a more structured dialogue between government and Parliament on the one hand, and the judiciary on the other, could be used to develop clearer understandings about how the crucial question of 'tariff' was to be determined, so that the consequences could be more accurately foreseen and anticipated and preparations made for them.

The government welcomed the Halliday report in enthusiastic terms, but then departed from it in several significant ways. It announced its conclusions in the white paper *Justice for All* (Home Office, 2002), which then formed the basis of the 2003 Criminal Justice Act. On sentencing, it followed the report's recommendations on community sentences. It proposed a new set of short prison sentences – 'custody plus', which included supervision and practical support after sentence (broadly the sentence Halliday had proposed); suspended sentences with requirements and conditions ('custody minus') and intermittent (day or weekend) custody. But the proposals for violent and sexual offenders went further than Halliday had proposed, with new forms of life, indeterminate and extended sentences for the protection of the public. The white paper also included a range of proposals for changes in procedure and the rules of evidence with the aim of 'bringing more offenders to justice'.

After a perfunctory process of consultation, the white paper formed the basis for the 2003 Criminal Justice Act. The proposal for 'custody plus' was not implemented. No evaluation of the Act has been carried out, and it is not possible to determine what difference its sentencing provisions have made except to complicate the sentencing process, increase the number of people sent to prison and the time they spend there, and add to the pressures on the penal system.

Achievements and disappointments

Some success was achieved. The structural reforms of youth justice worked well for the most part, especially the connection between youth offending teams and local authorities, but there were serious concerns about some of the practices that were followed, especially the increase in the number of children sentenced to custody and the treatment which some children received in custodial institutions (Soloman and Garside, 2008). Prisons were on the whole safer and more secure than they had been 15 years before; they had become more 'decent' as a result of the campaigns of successive directors-general (HM Chief Inspector of Prisons in England and Wales, 2010), and their 'moral performance' had arguably improved in some areas (Liebling, 2004).[3] The police were more responsive and sensitive to the public, and neighbourhood policing had made them more visible and had contributed to reductions in crime and improvements in public confidence. Significant changes in attitude and culture followed the Stephen Lawrence inquiry (Macpherson, 1999; Waddington, 2010), although there was debate about the effect of the inquiry itself (Hall et al, 2009) and about the extent to which police culture has actually changed (Loftus, 2008, 2010; see also chapter six).

---

[3] Note, however, that Ben Crewe and Alison Liebling have subsequently written: 'Most prisoners now face a deeper, heavier, "tighter" and less liberal version of imprisonment than their predecessors, with some Victorian notions of individual responsibility and less eligibility returning in new guises' (Crewe and Liebling, 2011, p 177).

Racially motivated violence and discrimination against minorities were less common, although disproportionate numbers of black people were still caught up in the criminal justice system, and conflicts of culture or religion may become an increasing concern in the future.

The government was more ready to consult and to respond to consultation, although the impression remained that it was sometimes more ready to tell than to listen. The needs of victims were better understood and more often met, although there was more to be done, especially for families affected by homicide or disabling injury and for children who had experienced sexual abuse. The volume of crime, whether uncovered by the British Crime Survey or recorded by the police, fell substantially after 1996,[4] although the facts and the explanation are open to argument (see below).

Some of the reforms of management and organisation can also be regarded as successful. As well as the new structures for youth justice, examples include the reforms of the Crown Prosecution Service and the Court Service, and the arrangements for strategic management at national and regional level, including cross–departmental Public Service Agreements.[5] The independent commission for judicial appointments, the Sentencing Guidelines Council and now the Sentencing Council were improvements on the arrangements that existed previously. Many people considered the creation of the Supreme Court to have been long overdue, although others expressed concerns about its implications for the relationship between the judiciary and Parliament. The formation of a Ministry of Justice had been talked about at intervals over the previous 150 years (Faulkner, 2006, pp 339-42), although the way in which it was announced, with no notice or consultation, caused confusion at the time. The balance of power and influence between the Home Office, responsible for public protection and security, and the Ministry of Justice responsible for justice and human rights, may come to be an important issue.

There were also, however, failures and disappointments. Some of the reforms of structure and process, especially the creation of the National Offender Management Service (NOMS), were badly managed and produced confusion and frustration (Hough et al, 2006). The Carter reports (2003, 2007) on which it was based were poorly conceived and lacked intellectual and policy coherence. The recommendations

---

[4] Crime reported to the British Crime Survey fell by 42% overall between 1995 and 2006/07. The fall was greatest for burglary (59%) and vehicle thefts (61%) (Home Office, 2007a).

[5] The coalition government replaced them with departmental business plans.

contained inherent tensions, for example between 'seamlessness' in offender management and the fragmentation created by separating management from supervision and 'interventions' for purposes of 'contestability' (Nellis, 2006). The report emphasised the introduction of 'markets' where prisons would be treated as 'public goods'; the private sector would be able to choose which services it suited them to provide and stop providing them if they wished, while public sector prisons would have to ensure that the services were always maintained. NOMS would set the terms of the contracts for private sector providers while competing for the same 'business' itself. Added to those difficulties, ministers' perspectives on what precisely 'offender management' was or should be were subject to constant change.

Performance indicators provide an important source of management and public information and can be a key part of a service's accountability, but when combined with targets and league tables they sometimes had perverse consequences. The effect of police targets in criminalising young people was the most notorious example. The array of targets for the police was eventually replaced by a single target to 'improve public confidence in whether local crime and community safety priorities are being identified and addressed' (Home Office, 2008), and those for the probation service are being greatly reduced. These developments were generally welcomed. Services will still need mechanisms to show 'how well they are doing', whether things that should be done are being done, and whether what they set out to do has been completed on time and within budget. But those mechanisms should be applied as a constructive discipline, and not in an aggressive spirit of competition or of punishment for failure.

Legislation and sentencing

Legislation introduced by the Labour government included 60 or 70 criminal justice Acts, some of them running to hundreds of sections, and hundreds of new criminal offences were created (see chapter five). The volume and complexity of legislation caused confusion for the courts, the police, victims and the country as a whole. The Lord Chief Justice, Lord Phillips, criticised the sentencing structure that emerged in the 2003 Criminal Justice Act as 'restrictive, complex and difficult for the courts to administer or the public to understand' (Court of Appeal, 2009). Parts of the 2003 Criminal Justice Act that might have moderated the use of imprisonment – those for 'custody plus' and for intermittent and suspended sentences – were not brought into effect, whether for lack of resources, fear of criticism of the restrictions they would place on the courts' ability to impose short sentences of imprisonment, or (for intermittent custody) because they were unworkable in the first place.

Indeterminate sentences of imprisonment for public protection (IPP) proved to be a special problem, both in the demands they made on prison capacity and in the injustice that their application could cause to those who received them (HM Chief Inspectors of Prisons and Probation, 2008; House of Commons Justice Committee, 2008; Jacobson and Hough, 2010). There were serious ethical issues about the continued detention of individuals beyond their 'tariff dates' (when the term of imprisonment judged by the court to reflect their culpability and the seriousness of the offence comes to an end), especially when it was linked to the inability or unwillingness of the prison to carry out the appropriate risk assessment, or to provide the courses needed for the person to be assessed as no longer a 'threat to the public' – see chapter four. Again, such approaches were based on very restrictive views of 'risk assessment' and 'risk management'.

Successive governments' policies, combined with the courts' greater sensitivity to criticism in the media, resulted in more severe sentencing by the courts, more recalls to prison for breaches of conditions and more restrictive use of parole, so that the prison population in England and Wales doubled between 1992 and 2010, reaching 85,000 at the time of the election in May of that year.[6] The penal system had for some years been in a state of chronic overcrowding and pressure on its capacity, which prevented it from functioning at more than a basic level of performance. Prisoners who had mental health problems and those serving indeterminate sentences were among those most seriously affected.

Managing criminal justice

The emphasis on the criminal justice 'system' and its management intensified under the Labour government. It caused an increasing range of issues to become seen as 'criminal justice problems', with solutions to be found by the criminal justices services and through the criminal justice process. Anti-social behaviour and the misuse of drugs were the most obvious examples, but the proliferation of new criminal offences drew many other types of behaviour into the ambit of the criminal justice system and process. Those who become involved in it can suffer the disabling stigma of a criminal conviction, which can then affect not only offenders themselves but also their families.

---

[6] It reached over 87,000 after the riots in August, 2011.

Objectives, targets and budgets were set for services or functions, rather than the purposes for which different services and other organisations have to work together if progress is to be made. The resulting 'silos' and the consequent competition have made cooperation between health (especially mental health), education, housing and employment services more difficult to achieve at a time when the need for cooperation was becoming greater and more clearly recognised. Despite good intentions, the boundary between criminal justice and other services became more strongly defended and harder to cross.

Effects on crime

Some people, including some former ministers, connected the increase in punishment, and especially in the use of imprisonment, with the fall in crime that took place after 1996 (Pease, 2010). The increase will have had some effect, but the greatest reductions were in offences of burglary and vehicle theft (see footnote 4), where considerable effort had been devoted to improving the security of premises and vehicles from the 1980s onwards. Innovations in engineering had also contributed to the decline in car crime. Rising prosperity during the 1990s and the loss of the market for stolen electrical equipment will also have helped. It is an open question as to how far the 'real' level of crime had actually fallen, and how far offences such as burglary had been displaced by newer forms of crime such as 'doorstep' or credit card fraud, much of which is not recorded.

Use of research

Research over many years has shown that the reasons for which people commit crime are more complex than governments or some newspapers have been willing to admit. People react to different situations in different ways that cannot easily be predicted. Studies during the 1970s and 1980s showed that changes in criminal justice are by themselves unlikely to have more than a marginal effect on the general level of crime. Police resources and methods have only a tenuous relationship with levels of crime or clear-up rates (Clarke and Hough, 1984).[7] Sentencing does not have much deterrent effect

---

[7] A rapid review of the evidence more recently reached a heavily-qualified conclusion that higher levels of policing are linked to lower levels of property crime, so that a 10 per cent increase in officers might lead to a reduction in crime of around 3 per cent. Evidence for an association with violent crime is weaker (Bradford, 2011).

(von Hirsch et al, 1999), and sending more people to prison has only a limited impact on the general level of crime: an increase of 15% in the prison population might reduce crime by 1% (Halliday, 2001, Appendix 6; see also Ministry of Justice, 2010b, p 64). That view is generally accepted by government and most criminal justice scholars, and is broadly consistent with findings from studies in other countries (Lappi-Seppälä, 2011), but the evidence can be interpreted in other ways (Howard, 2010; Pease, 2010).

A large proportion of the male population has criminal convictions or admits to having committed criminal offences, many victims are or have been offenders, and most offenders have been victims (see British Crime Survey and related statistics).[8] It is therefore oversimplistic to make a binary distinction between the 'law-abiding majority' on the one hand and 'criminals' on the other.[9] Even so, police and probation officers are likely to agree that a large proportion of the crime in their area is committed by a relatively small number of individuals who are often known to them, are often connected through family relationships, and whose children are at risk of becoming the offenders of the future. They are likely to have problems in other aspects of their lives and to be known to several different agencies, including education, health and housing. How to divert those people from crime, especially the children, without alienating them from the support they need, unjustly stigmatising them or giving them what others will see as unfairly preferential treatment, is a perpetual dilemma for criminal justice and social agencies.

Attitudes and assumptions

The separation of crime from its wider social context, and the belief that problems of crime can be solved by criminal justice measures taken in isolation, have always been unrealistic, as the Home Office came to acknowledge 30 years ago (Home Office, 1977). Chapter two has shown how policies to reduce crime during the 1980s were focused more on improving security and on situational and social measures to reduce crime than on arrest, prosecution and punishment. Legislation on sentencing, such as the 1991 Criminal Justice Act, was designed

---

[8] Now published online with police recorded crime. See: www.esds.ac.uk/findingData/bcrs.asp

[9] This is a distinction that is sometimes assumed by critics of the Human Rights Act, who argue that 'rights' should only be held by those who 'deserve' them, having 'earned' them by responsible behaviour.

more to improve consistency, remove anomalies and reduce what was thought to be the unnecessary use of custody than to reduce crime. Nicola Lacey (1994) saw the Act as the start of the movement towards the more pervasive managerialism in criminal justice which gathered momentum in later years.

Governments since the early 1990s implicitly shared the classical economist's view that most human behaviour was a matter of deliberate choice, based on a rational judgement of the risks, benefits and costs. Governments supposed that they could influence that choice by providing incentives and deterrents, and in particular they had assumed that it could reduce crime by insisting on rigorous enforcement of the law, certainty and severity of punishment, the incapacitating effect of imprisonment, 'interventions' to prevent an offender from reoffending, and the use of the latest technology. Instead of recognising that the 'attrition rate' (which shows that only two or three per cent of surveyed crime is 'brought to justice') is an indication of the limited effect the criminal justice process can have on the general level of crime, they supposed that it could be made more effective by better management and stronger direction from the centre.

Those assumptions seemed to many people to be no more than common sense. They provided governments with a politically promising framework for policy and legislation that responded to public opinion and the public's increasing aversion to risks of all kinds that appeared during the 1980s. They gave the impression of being 'tough' and realistic, and were hard to challenge from a 'liberal' perspective, but a government's criminal justice policy needs to be founded on a more considered analysis, one which is more differentiated and holistic.

All this was well known to many of those who work in or are familiar with the criminal justice system, but it was rarely acknowledged by government or the political parties and not well understood by the general public. The prospect seemed to be one of increasing investment in ineffective law enforcement, further pressure on the penal system, and an indefinite need for new prison building, with little impact on people's experience of crime or on their safety or wellbeing more generally (Hough et al, 2008). The House of Commons Justice Committee reached similar conclusions in its comprehensive and radical report *Cutting Crime: The Case for Justice Re-investment* (House of Commons Justice Committee, 2009). The formation of the Conservative–Liberal Democrat coalition government in 2010 seemed to provide the opportunity and the prospect of a more promising approach – see chapter ten.

The revival of rehabilitation

A 'new model of rehabilitation', sometimes referred to as the 'What Works?' movement,[10] emerged at the end of the 20th century (McGuire, 1995; Raynor and Robinson, 2005). This was largely in response to positive findings reported in statistical reviews of previous studies (meta-analyses) which shed new light on the outcomes of interventions to reduce reoffending, and because of growing enthusiasm for approaches using social skills and problem-solving techniques (informed by social learning theory – see Andrews and Bonta, 2010). Reviews using the statistical technique of meta-analysis, which combines results across numerous studies, challenged the negative conclusions of earlier decades. These found that, while punitive correctional sanctions are generally ineffective, rehabilitative treatment is associated with lower recidivism rates (for example, McGuire, 2002; Lipsey and Cullen, 2007).

The concept of 'rehabilitation' is problematic because 'there appears to be no universally agreed definition of rehabilitation in the context of offending' (Raynor and Robinson, 2005, p 14). A recent review defines rehabilitative treatment as that which is 'aimed at motivating, guiding, and supporting constructive change in whatever characteristics or circumstances engender their criminal behavior or subvert their pro-social behavior' (Lipsey and Cullen, 2007, p 302) and contrasts it with punitive and deterrent sanctions associated with, at best, modest reductions in recidivism and, in some instances, increases in recidivism (p 314). Positive outcomes are associated with cognitive behavioural interventions in particular, but this is possibly because they have been more systematically implemented and researched.

Subsequent rigorous reviews have continued to find that the recidivism rates for those engaged in rehabilitative treatment compare favourably against corresponding measures for control groups. Given that consistency, 'the extreme scepticism still shown by some commentators ... seems unfounded' (Raynor and Robinson, 2005, p 107).

That there are limitations to the applicability of such findings is, however, acknowledged by the researchers involved. Behind the overall result is wide variability in the effects at different times and places, and

---

[10] The 'What Works?' movement initially had a question mark, while the movement was primarily concerned with research and evaluation; it was dropped when government decided that it knew 'what works', often still on doubtful evidence, and the emphasis came to be on imposing programmes and practices which conformed to the government's view.

for different categories of participant. The best-designed evaluations meet the criteria for reliable findings: that is, they have 'internal validity', but because they are carried out under experimental conditions they lack 'external validity'. Implementing such 'demonstration' projects into routine practice therefore presents a significant challenge (Lipsey and Cullen, 2007).

When the Home Office implemented the What Works agenda, also termed the 'effective practice initiative', the distilled messages from those systematic reviews were overgeneralised and operationalised through accredited programmes as if they were 'the only or the entire solution' (Stanley, 2009, p 170). Another criticism of the movement was that it did not do enough to address the needs of particular populations with different or additional needs, notably female offenders and those from different ethnic or racial backgrounds (Kemshall et al, 2004). Mistakes were made and improvements were needed. Many regard the vast investment in programmes and the application of an evidence-based approach to the testing and development of 'programmes' as poor value for public money (Crighton and Towl, 2008).

It would be rash, though, to ignore the contribution that has been made. Although 'We have still not moved much beyond the stage of "promising leads", [there are] positive results associated with the completion of programmes [which] cannot be dismissed out of hand' (Stanley, 2009, p 170). Similarly with regard to the adoption of the Campbell approach[11] for evaluating programmes, as Hough (2010, p 12) has noted, 'there is a place for experimental methods in this field. They constitute one form of evidence about what works in reducing reoffending, and in some circumstances this can be very important evidence.' Like other critics, though, he has also pointed to the disadvantages of relying solely on such an approach (Hough, 2010, p 14):

> Work with offenders is a highly reflexive process in the sense that the meanings attributed to the process by those involved in it will affect the outcomes. This means that the effectiveness of interventions will be highly context-specific. What works in one culture at one time may well be ineffective in other settings and at other times.

---

[11] The Campbell Collaboration is modelled on the Cochrane Collaboration in the healthcare field, which collates and provides guidelines for reviews of research evidence, admitting only those studies that achieve acceptable methodological standards.

Research, combined with shared insights from the main participants, is therefore needed to explain the differences observed and to identify underlying social and psychological mechanisms. Desistance theory, therapeutic jurisprudence and procedural justice theory are contributing to the understanding of the dynamic processes involved in changing lives – see chapter six.

Conclusion: sadder and wiser

It is a sad reflection that so much energy, and so much money, was spent for what were often disappointing results. The real successes of that period should not be underestimated, but they owed more to the efforts of the people working in public services themselves than to government. Lessons are that government should not overregulate or overprescribe, and legislation should be kept as simple as possible. Criminal justice should not be treated as if it were a business, or a commodity to be produced, traded and sold to consumers. Government should pay full attention to the whole range of evidence and base its policies on the best evidence that is available, but it should acknowledge its limitations and not try to construct evidence to support what it has already decided. It should not make unrealistic claims or raise false expectations, and it should correct public misunderstandings and mistaken assumptions whenever possible, however politically inconvenient it may be to do so. A sense of justice and common humanity may in the long run count for more than ad hoc initiatives to deal with immediate situations.

FOUR

Crime prevention, civil society and communities

One of the themes to emerge from the previous chapters is the weakness of relying too exclusively on criminal justice as the country's main instrument for preventing and reducing crime or for maintaining public confidence, and conversely the importance of social responsibility, the support of communities to which people belong and the informal influences of family and other attachments. A successful approach to preventing crime and reducing reoffending and to providing support for victims depends not only on the work of the courts and statutory services, but also on the goodwill and effectiveness of civil society. All sections of society can play a vital part in diverting those at risk, especially young people, from turning to crime; in making sure that victims' concerns are heard and in responding to them; and in supporting vulnerable people such as the families of victims and offenders, those with problems of mental health or addiction, and minorities who are likely to be neglected or overlooked.

Preventing and reducing crime

The Conservative government in the 1980s recognised that the situations in which crime has to be prevented and reoffending reduced were more complex than had often been supposed. Alongside its criminal justice legislation and its measures to increase efficiency in the police, prisons and probation, it pursued a range of initiatives to improve support for victims, to reduce discrimination against minorities, and to prevent and reduce crime. Many of those involved civil society and especially voluntary organisations such as Nacro, Victim Support, children's charities and the then new charity Crime Concern.[1] Crime prevention came to have a higher profile, and was seen as taking three forms. 'Primary' prevention included improved physical security, surveillance by CCTV, neighbourhood watch and 'situational' measures such as the design and management of housing estates and public spaces and the design of motor vehicles. It was founded on considerable

---

[1] Now merged with the Rainer Foundation and renamed Catch22.

research in the United States and Great Britain (Jacobs, 1962; Newman, 1972; Clarke and Mayhew, 1980; Wilson and Kelling, 1982).

'Secondary' prevention had its origin in work by David Farrington and others that showed that people are more or less likely to commit or to become victims of crime according to the 'risk' and 'resilience' factors present in their situation and background (Farrington and Welsh, 2007). Schemes for early intervention and for targeting people known to be 'at risk' reflect that approach. 'Tertiary' prevention was concerned with the supervision and reform of known offenders. The Safer Cities programme, introduced in 1988 as part of the Conservative government's wider plan, Action for Cities, aimed to bring together the various forms of prevention in a number of practical schemes based in local authority areas.[2] It seems likely that initiatives begun during that period were among the influences that brought about the reduction in offences of burglary and vehicle crime in the mid-1990s, but the evaluations undertaken at the time were too short term for that to be clearly established.

The Labour government's approach

Those policies were at first restricted by the Conservative government's resistance to any proposal that would give new functions or greater authority or influence to local authorities. The Labour government took a broader view, and was from the beginning committed to promoting what came to be called community safety. The 1998 Crime and Disorder Act placed a statutory duty on local councils and chief officers of police to cooperate with each other and with other agencies in formulating, publishing, implementing and reviewing strategies for the reduction of crime and disorder in their areas. There was an emphasis on local consultation and the importance of responding to groups that were hard to reach.

Primary prevention and its methods have now been absorbed into normal practice, for example in town planning and the design of buildings, shopping malls, residential estates and motor vehicles. The ideas can be related to the present government's interest in 'nudging' and behavioural economics (Thaler and Sunstein, 2008), and its decision

---

[2] Safer Cities schemes took a 'partnership' approach, with the aim of tackling a range of crime problems – domestic and commercial burglary, domestic violence, vehicle crime, theft from shops, anti-social behaviour – according to the priorities as they were seen locally. Each was guided by a multi-agency steering committee (Ekblom, 1996; Faulkner, 2006, p 279).

to set up a Behavioural Insights Team, as part of the Cabinet Office. The evidence for secondary prevention has never been easy to apply to criminal justice because it impinges on social and economic policies and considerations not usually associated with crime or criminal justice, which have their own priorities, champions and interest groups, and which are the business of different government departments. Governments have been understandably reluctant to make adjustments to their policies on subjects such as education, housing or welfare in a way that would specifically benefit those at risk of committing crime, partly because they do not wish disadvantage to appear as an 'excuse' for crime, and partly because it would seem unfair to give benefits to such people that are not available to others. Tertiary prevention became the foundation of the programmes and interventions to reduce reoffending that became a major feature of the Labour government's policies.

The Labour government later developed a more comprehensive strategy in its *National Community Safety Plan, 2008-2011* (Home Office, 2007b; Prior, 2011). This brought together a number of the government's Public Service Agreements – those concerned with improving children's safety and prospects, increasing the number of socially excluded people in more settled situations, reducing the harm caused by drugs and alcohol and building safer, more cohesive, empowered and active communities – and linked them to Local Area Agreements. The plan was essentially a 'top-down' initiative, with a large number of nationally prescribed indicators, but emphasised that the activities to be pursued at local level should promote the involvement and empowerment of local communities and should be related to local issues. For fuller accounts of the development of crime prevention over the past 30 years, see von Hirsch et al (2000), Faulkner (2006, pp 275-93), Gilling (2007) and Prior (2011).

Wider social policies

The Labour government also took a number of initiatives that were intended to improve social conditions more generally, to help those who were socially excluded and to reduce the number of children growing up in poverty. Examples included Sure Start; the New Deal for helping young people into employment; Action Zones for special action in health, education and employment; and the programme for 'active citizenship' and civil renewal (Blunkett, 2003; DCLG, 2008). The Social Exclusion Unit (later the Social Exclusion Task Force) and its Policy Action Teams produced a series of reports on a range of social issues, and other policy papers included the National Strategy for

Neighbourhood Renewal (DCLG, 2010); *Every Child Matters* (DCSF, 2003); and Lord Bradley's report on mental health (Bradley, 2009). The government did not promote them as initiatives intended to reduce crime, but they probably made a contribution to the fall in crime that began in the mid-1990s and continued during the government's period in office.

What the Labour government's initiatives achieved is hard to judge. Schemes were always vulnerable to frequent changes of emphasis as new demands and priorities appeared and took precedence for people's time and energy. Frequent changes of personalities – ministers or managers – made continuity difficult, especially if new arrivals wanted to make their mark by changing what had been done before. The search for 'quick wins', for immediately visible results and short-term political advantage diverted attention from long-term, sustainable change. It was sometimes all too easy for the focus to slip away from situations and contexts and back to individuals who could be demonised and stigmatised through anti-social behaviour orders and 'naming and shaming'. The government's own evaluations and reviews themselves often referred to concerns such as the need for initiatives to take account of their wider context; to reflect local circumstances; to take a long-term view; and to target resources to places where they were most needed (Bradley, 2009; DCLG, 2010). The ideas on which those initiatives were based were difficult to accommodate in the conventional structures of government and government departments as they were at that time, often working in isolation from one another (or in 'silos', as they came to be called), towards objectives and public service agreements. It could, however, be claimed that government's involvement probably helped to prevent wasteful and uncoordinated activity, to encourage cooperation and mutual support, to improve procedures and relationships, and to demonstrate its support. It also attracted practical support from the wider public, and gave encouragement to the organisations, staff and volunteers themselves.

Civil society, social capital and active communities

The Conservative government of 1979-97 for the most part avoided attaching its policies to any kind of social theory, but the Labour government took more interest in ideas such as active citizenship and social exclusion, as already mentioned, and also in civil society, communitarianism, social capital and social cohesion.

Civil society

Civil society is a term used to denote those parts of society that are distinct from the state and from the public and private sectors. There is no generally accepted definition, but it includes voluntary, community and faith-based organisations, together with a range of self-help and interest groups and individuals acting on their own initiative and in a private capacity (Deakin, 2002). Civil society has a long history of involvement in criminal justice, for example in prison visiting and prisoners' after-care, and a longer history of helping children in need. There is no clearly defined boundary between functions that are appropriate for civil society and those that should be performed by statutory services or commercial organisations on behalf of the state, or any definition of the duties or acts of good citizenship or charity that civil society could be expected to perform. The role of civil society has, however, attracted the interest of both the Labour and the coalition governments, which have seen scope for it to perform functions they have considered to be necessary or desirable but have not wished to perform themselves. Their reasons have been mixed – a general view that a strong civil society is a mark of a strong and healthy society more generally; a belief that it will exercise social control and encourage compliant behaviour; a hope that civil society will work in support of government and help it achieve its political objectives; or an attempt to save public expenditure. The mixture of motives may have detracted from the credibility of the efforts that were made.

Communities

Closely related to civil society is the notion of 'the community' or 'communities'. The term can be used in several different ways (Duff, 2001, p 40). The word is often used to mean simply 'not in an institution' such as a prison or a hospital, especially in the context of 'community sentences' or 'care in the community'. At other times it refers to citizens acting collectively or individually in relation to the agencies of the state – as in 'community empowerment' or 'community policing' – or to the community as a recipient of a service's 'responsiveness' or 'accountability'. The community then takes on an identity – it becomes an actor – with characteristics such as 'cohesion' or 'inclusiveness' (or not) that may have social or political significance.

For practical purposes, the 'community' or 'communities' will usually be related to geographical areas or neighbourhoods. General and local elections, for example, are necessarily based on constituency or ward boundaries. But many people will more readily identify themselves with another kind of community that may be based on ethnic origin, religious affiliation, occupation, interests or social class. People will often be members of several such communities; they will relate to them and be influenced by them in various ways, and their combination will give them their sense of identity and 'who we are'. New forms of 'virtual' or 'cyber' communities are being formed through the internet, for example through mailgroups, blogs and social networks such as Facebook. In criminal justice, 'community' may be used positively to promote non-custodial sentences, and to stress that offenders are still members of the community whose laws they have broken and that they are both entitled to its rights and benefits and subject to its obligations – which includes making reparation for their offences – as far as that is compatible with the conditions of any sentence they have received. Or the interests of the 'community' can be used negatively, to impose restrictive or intrusive conditions on people's behaviour, or to exclude those who do not 'fit' or who have 'forfeited' or do not 'deserve' their right to membership.

Communities may have positive characteristics such as resilience, self-reliance and a sense of loyalty between its members. They may generate 'social capital'. These aspects have been explored by writers such as Amitai Etzioni (1996) and Robert Putnam (2000) who see communities as providing solutions to some of the problems of social isolation that are to be found in modern society. Etzioni's main idea is that individual rights and aspirations should be protected but that they should be inserted into a sense of the community (hence the name of the 'communitarianism' movement, which is especially associated with his work). Within the movement, communitarian thinking developed in reaction to the 'me-first' attitude of the 1980s, and also sought to establish common ground between 'liberal' and 'conservative' points of view. The movement works to strengthen the ability of all aspects of the community, including families and schools, in order to introduce more positive values. Putnam makes a distinction between two kinds of social capital: bonding capital and bridging capital. Bonding occurs when people socialise with others like themselves: same age, same race, same religion and so on. But peaceful societies in a diverse multi-ethnic country need to have a second kind of social capital: bridging. Bridging takes place when people make friends with people who are not like themselves, typically when they join together in pursuit of some shared enterprise. Putnam argues that those two kinds of social capital act to strengthen each other, so that a decline in bonding capital brings a decline in bridging capital and with it greater ethnic tensions.

Different communities and individuals will inevitably and rightly have different identities and interests. They will behave and expect to be treated in different ways. Their interests will sometimes compete or conflict. How they can make themselves heard in national or local consultations – for example through elected members, representative organisations, pressure groups or public demonstrations, or whether they want to make themselves heard at all – will depend on a combination of personal and situational factors which attempts to involve or empower communities will have to take into account. Communities and individuals should be encouraged to see themselves as part of a larger, inclusive community of all those who are bound by the laws of the land (Duff, 2001, p 195), or of a nation that should be regarded as a 'community of communities', as the Commission on the Future of Multi-Ethnic Britain argued in its report 11 years ago (Parekh, 2000).

Community cohesion

The term 'community cohesion' came into use after disturbances in a number of northern towns in 2001. Its ideas had much in common with communitarianism, but they were related especially to the position of ethnic and religious minorities. They marked a shift from the 'multicultural' approach to community relations that was seen to have 'failed' because it encouraged minority groups not only to value and preserve their own culture, but also to stay within it and within their own ethnic communities and not to associate with other communities or take part in a wider society. The debate about cultural diversity has been confused by misrepresentation and the pejorative use of expressions such as 'multiculturalism' and 'political correctness', and by attempts to assert or construct a British national identity. A discussion of those attempts are beyond the scope of this volume; the important point here is that the situation can become dangerous if members of particular groups are collectively seen as 'not belonging' or as potentially subversive or dangerous, for example Irish Catholics in the 1970s or members of Muslim communities in more recent times (Hickman et al, 2011). It could become potentially disastrous if those attitudes and the stereotyping that goes with them were routinely carried into their treatment by criminal justice services such as police or prisons (see chapters six and eight).

Community and local justice

The expression 'community justice' is also used in several ways. It includes, but is more than, 'local justice' in the sense that it is usually associated with lay magistrates drawn from local communities sitting in local courthouses (see the next section). It is usually a general expression used to refer to sentences served in the community, as distinct from sentences of imprisonment, or to statutory or voluntary criminal justice agencies that work in the community. That is the sense in which it is used, for example, in the *British Journal of Community Justice*, and in Scotland for the statutory Community Justice Authorities set up under the 2005 Management of Offenders etc (Scotland) Act, as strategic planning and monitoring authorities for the provision of community justice. In Scotland, primary responsibility for supervising offenders lies with criminal justice social work services, the equivalent of the probation and youth offending services in England and Wales, but they are part of local authorities and all relevant local services are required to work in partnership with the relevant statutory and non-statutory bodies. No similar structure exists in England.

Community justice is beginning to acquire more ambitious connotations in England, where it is associated with programmes where offenders do work that is of benefit to the community, often of a kind that has been proposed by the community itself. The government website www.direct.gov.uk[3] states that 'the aim of community justice is to improve the local quality of life. It lets people get involved in making their area a better place to live' and notes that 'community justice is about making sure that people who are affected by bad behaviour and crime have a say in how things are sorted out in their community'.

An obvious and long-standing example of work by offenders that benefits communities is community service, now called community payback. It has always had great potential to benefit both offenders, as part of their rehabilitation, and communities both practically and symbolically as a form of reparation. It is a pity that the expression 'community service' was thought too dignified for an activity that the Labour government wanted to downgrade to become simply a form of punishment. Work done by offenders should be intended and seen as an opportunity for them to do work that is useful to their communities, and to be valued as such, and as a stage towards their own rehabilitation and reintegration into those communities. It should not be seen as compulsion to do demanding and degrading work where offenders

---

[3] www.direct.gov.uk/en/CrimeJusticeAndTheLaw/CrimePrevention/DG_072139

can be pointed at, and perhaps sneered at, as 'criminals paying the price for what they have done'.

Community justice centres

Another example of community justice is the North Liverpool Community Justice Centre, which was set up as an experiment in North Liverpool in 2005. It was based on a combined magistrates' court and crown court centre and was presided over by a single judge. The intention was for the court to be closer and more in touch with its local community and its social concerns, such as addiction, unemployment, poor housing and mental health, and to involve the local community much more closely in the work of the court. In that way the 'community' would gain a sense of ownership and empowerment and efficiency would be improved. An evaluation of its work (Ministry of Justice, 2007) showed improvements in efficiency but not much impact in terms of community engagement, and the need to build dedicated premises for it had made the centre an expensive undertaking.[4]

Community justice centres, as such, are unlikely to be developed any further in the foreseeable future, but the underlying ideas of community involvement should still be taken forward. This seems to be the intention of the coalition government (Ministry of Justice, 2010a, p 81), as evidenced by the establishment of two one-stop justice centres (one in Nuneaton, one in Leamington Spa) that house the police, courts, the Crown Prosecution Service, victim and witness support services, and probation and youth offending services under one roof, and claim to improve access and integrate services for the local community.[5] Community justice is also sometimes associated with restorative justice – see chapter five.

The promotion of community justice in the sense in which the government now uses the expression has great potential for realising wider and longer-term social and perhaps political benefits for which the government hopes and for which this volume argues. It is not, however, obvious how far such a vision can be reconciled with a competitive market in the supervision and rehabilitation of offenders or with payment by results, and political commitment and strong

---

[4] For an account of the centre's achievements and disappointments, see Raine (2011) and the brief summary in the *Green Paper Evidence Report* (Ministry of Justice, 2010b, p 68).

[5] www.crimeandjustice.org.uk/doingjusticelocallypr.html

professional leadership will be needed to give a sustained sense of direction. This is, perhaps exceptionally, an occasion when a stronger administrative structure may be needed, with shared local budgets. The Scottish model of Community Justice Authorities could not be transposed directly to different organisational arrangements in England and Wales, but similar considerations apply.

The lay magistracy

The lay magistracy has felt under pressure for a number of years. Magistrates have felt that their role and status have been threatened by demands for economy and greater efficiency that have resulted in the closure of court houses and the appointment of legally qualified district judges (previously stipendiary magistrates), while increased demands have been placed on them to undergo training. They have felt that the principle of 'local justice' has been undermined, and they have sometimes suspected that there was a view in the central bureaucracy that lay magistrates were no longer needed at all. They could reasonably hope that the coalition government's commitment to localisation and its support for community justice will provide an opportunity for the role and importance of the lay magistracy to be restated and reinforced.

The trend has been for the lay magistracy to be drawn closer to the higher, legally qualified, judiciary, with sentencing guidelines, more intensive training and more restrictions on out-of-court activities to safeguard their independence. The consequence has been that magistrates have to some extent been separated from local communities and drawn away from some of the recent and prospective developments that are associated with community justice. If some of the restrictions could be lifted and some of the understandings relaxed, magistrates would be enabled to play a larger part in community justice, for example as members of bodies such as probation trusts, neighbourhood justice panels, and police and crime panels; in activities such as restorative justice; or working with any of the numerous voluntary organisations concerned with reducing crime and rehabilitating offenders.

Localisation and citizens' empowerment

Localisation, localism and the involvement and empowerment of local citizens have been on successive governments' agendas for many years. Governments have claimed that their aim is to promote civic values, but they have more often treated citizens as 'consumers', to be appealed to as part of the application of business models to public services, for example in the Citizen's Charter in the early 1990s, or they have seen the involvement of local citizens as a way of achieving their own political objectives, rather than a means of increasing the influence of citizens themselves.

This and other chapters in this book have argued for civil society and local communities to be more actively involved in criminal justice, and for citizens to have a greater sense of ownership of the public services that work for them. Greater involvement is not, however, an entirely straightforward matter. Such achievements depend on gaining the most effective dynamics and the most productive relationship between the citizen and the state, or between civil society and government and public services, in which voluntary organisations can keep their independence and integrity and government can provide the support that is needed in a situation of shortage and austerity.

There is a significant difference between giving greater powers or discretion to authorities, institutions or managers at local level and the genuine empowerment of local citizens so that they can not only choose between the options made available to them, but also decide what the options should be. Unlike previous administrations, the coalition government has promised not only greater powers at local level, but also 'a real transfer of power' to local citizens. Schools, the National Health Service, local government and elected police and crime commissioners were the main instances at the time of writing. Only the election of police and commissioners directly affected criminal justice. The government's emphasis seemed to be more on reducing costs and giving citizens more opportunities to do voluntary work than on their empowerment in the sense of having a significant influence on policy or practice. The full implications of commissioning and payment by results for prisons, probation and services for offenders were still to emerge. See chapter nine for a further discussion.

A wider distribution of power and an increase in authority and discretion at local level are in principle to be welcomed, in criminal justice and elsewhere. So is the increasing involvement and empowerment of local citizens. There are, however, a number of concerns that will have to be resolved. One is the extent to which people will accept local variations in practice and how far they will demand consistency, and how far consistency is a basic principle of justice and what that implies in practice. Another is the resolution of disputes and complaints. Some of the government's language seems to assume that if local people are asked what they want, they will all give the same answer and there will be the means to provide it.[6] Disputes and complaints will continue to arise and have to be resolved, and people will continue to appeal to central government if they are not satisfied. The changes would be much easier to introduce at a time when additional funding could be made available than during a period of economic stringency.

An important report from the House of Commons Community and Local Government Committee (2011) has argued that the government's plans for localisation need greater cohesion and rigour and a stronger sense of priorities, and that there is confusion because different departments appear to have different intentions and expectations. It recommends that mechanisms for local democracy be enhanced and improved, with protection for vulnerable, marginalised and minority groups; and concludes that changes will need to be made to standard procurement procedures if smaller, community-run groups are to compete against big players and that mechanisms for holding providers to account and for intervention in the case of failure need to evolve. The report refers to 'an impression of mixed messages and unanswered questions about the type of localism the government wishes to pursue, and how scrupulous it intends to be in living up to its own ideals' (2011, p 2).

Mechanisms will also be needed to ensure accountability and legitimacy. The interface between local interests and potentially conflicting public or national interests will have to be carefully managed – for example, over the priorities for policing (see chapter six), the location of facilities for offenders and the closure of courts. Local ownership and initiative may be hard to reconcile with consistency and may sometimes lead to 'postcode lotteries'. There will be differences between areas in terms of capacity, employment and housing (for example), and there may be questions about what action should be taken to mitigate their effects.

Two issues stand out from that discussion. One is that the opportunity to generate a stronger sense of social and civic responsibility should not be lost, especially for preventing crime, support for victims and the rehabilitation and reintegration of offenders. The other is that disputes and disappointments should be resolved in ways that are seen as democratic, fair and legitimate, as discussed in chapter one.

---

[6] An example is Oliver Letwin's evidence to the House of Commons Public Administration Committee. Oral Evidence, 12 January 2011. HC 693-i. Questions 1-35.

—

The voluntary and community sector

The Labour government was keen to promote the work of the voluntary and community sector, both generally and in relation to crime and criminal justice and the rehabilitation of offenders. It established the Office for the Third Sector in the Cabinet Office and published the 'Compact', a framework agreement on relations between government and the third sector and how they would work together.[7] The Ministry of Justice published two papers, a *NOMS Third Sector Strategy* for improving policies and securing better public services through effective partnerships (Ministry of Justice, 2008b), and a paper on *Working with the Third Sector to Reduce Re-offending* (Ministry of Justice, 2008c). More detailed advice and guidance to the voluntary and community sector has been published from time to time.

The size of the voluntary and community sector and of its involvement with criminal justice grew dramatically over the period 1980 to 2010, and its work with offenders, in and out of prison, has been transformed. It sometimes operates independently and sometimes in partnership with the public sector. Its work includes advocacy, research, strategic planning through a range of commissions and inquiries, and practical help in the form of funding, advice and support. Its contribution has been incalculable – in the sense both of being very large and also of being difficult to measure. The organisations themselves have been subject to the same pressure as the public sector to demonstrate results and value for money. Yet, as discussed at the end of chapter three, providing reliable evidence that a complex intervention or programme has led to a specific outcome is beyond the capacity of most multi-faceted and dynamic projects, especially when a reduction in reoffending has been the test, and especially for small-scale projects with low budgets providing individualised support.

Debate about how voluntary and community organisations can demonstrate their 'effectiveness' continues, with arguments about whether a reduction in crime or reoffending should be the only or the most important test, and whether other 'softer' measures of social integration or changes in offenders or their families' attitude or outlook could also be used. The question will be of immediate practical importance in any scheme for 'payment by results', as proposed in the green paper *Breaking the Cycle* (Ministry of Justice, 2010a).

---

[7] Now in its 12th year, the latest version is at www.thecompact.org.uk

Strengths of voluntary organisations

Arguments in favour of the voluntary and community sector's involvement, whether in criminal justice or in providing services more generally, are sometimes about the sector's resourcefulness and resilience and its flexibility and ability to innovate. They may also be about the intrinsic desirability of its involvement because of the encouragement it gives to social responsibility and good citizenship. There is evidence from the Economic and Social Research Council's Public Service Programme (see chapter nine) that the sector's ability to innovate is contingent on a policy framework that values such innovation, but between 1994 and 2006 the emphasis moved towards providing a service in accordance with a contractual specification (Osborne et al, 2008). The programme has shown a need to encourage and support a diversity of providers if the sector is to make an effective contribution. There is a danger that the sector might lose some of its distinctive character and effectiveness if contracting has to take place in circumstances of extreme financial stringency, and that some smaller organisations proving specialised services to small groups of people with special needs might be forced to withdraw.

There are some situations, perhaps especially in criminal justice, where government might find it convenient to rely on commissioning large national charities or large private sector organisations to provide services on a large scale. The most innovative and ground-breaking work is, however, likely to be done locally and initially on a small scale, often depending on the initiative and commitment of a few individuals who are able to have some degree of independence. They may set themselves up as separate charities, of which Circles of Support and Accountability (working with sex offenders)[8] and Escaping Victimhood (working with people whose lives have been fragmented by homicide)[9] are examples. They may, however, work as part of a statutory service or a larger charity if the conditions are right, and indeed both victim support and restorative justice had their origins in the probation service. The women's centres set up after the Corston report (Corston, 2007), and consortia of smaller voluntary bodies and grassroots initiatives[10] are

---

[8] www.circles-uk.org.uk

[9] www.escapingvictimhood.com

[10] Such as the consortium being organised by YSS (Youth Support Services) in West Mercia, an established and successful voluntary body that has become the 'preferred partner' of the West Mercia Probation Trust and works with the probation service to commission services from other voluntary services and develop their capacity, and create innovative solutions in working with offenders.

further examples. Another is the Thames Valley Partnership,[11] which brings together the resources of organisations from the statutory, private and voluntary sectors to develop schemes to help people who are vulnerable or in difficulty. The work may focus on groups of people such as prisoners' families, on problems such as domestic violence, or on activities such as the arts. Schemes once tried and tested have sometimes been absorbed into mainstream provision; Circles of Support and Accountability and Escaping Victimhood began in England as part of the Thames Valley Partnership and then became established as separate charities. There are, however, certain functions, especially those involving risk to the public or the sensitive use of discretionary powers, that should be retained within a publicly accountable statutory service – see chapter nine.

Outstanding questions

Serious questions remain about the status of the voluntary and community sector, its relationship with government, its funding, and the balance between its independence and its accountability – questions that the Labour government recognised (Deakin, 2002; Ministry of Justice, 2008d) but that remain unresolved (Etherington, 2007; Benson and Hedge, 2009). Mechanisms and funding will be needed to ensure the survival and development of their partnerships with government and statutory services in the new context of commissioning and payment by results. Government, the Charity Commission and charities themselves are rightly concerned that charities are well run, accountable and make good use of their funds, but that concern should not have the effect of imposing dull uniformity or of creating institutional cultures that are indistinguishable from those of statutory services. Whatever roles the voluntary and community organisations are to undertake, they should perform them as part of civil society and keep their independence from government. If they became in effect agencies of government they would lose their distinctive character, they would become subject to the hazards of political intervention, and the values that inspire their work might be at risk.

The 'Big Society' or good society

Many of the ideas discussed in this chapter helped to inform the vision of a 'Big Society' that became a prominent part of the Conservative

---

[11] www.thamesvalleypartnership.org.uk

Party's election campaign in 2010 and then of the coalition's Programme for Government. There was, however, some uncertainty about what the expression meant and what it involved. In an early speech, the Prime Minister David Cameron[12] said it was 'about a huge culture change' where people do things for themselves rather than rely on government and public services. It was also about 'liberation' and the transfer of power from elites in Whitehall to the man and woman on the street. It meant 'a whole new approach to government and governing' and it was associated with the Conservative Party's political ideal of 'small government'. Other speeches and publications (Herbert, 2010; Home Office, 2010) indicated that the Big Society was to include the involvement of communities and voluntary organisations in policing and the rehabilitation of offenders. The government placed a new emphasis on the 'Big Society' after the riots in August 2011 as providing the means of reasserting moral values and mending Britain's 'broken society'.

What the Big Society means

The Big Society has been interpreted in various ways. It has been interpreted favourably by those who see it as a means of releasing energy and innovation and of creating a new sense of social responsibility; less favourably by those who have seen its main purpose as a means of reducing public expenditure or of 'shrinking the state' for more ideological reasons; and sceptically by those who ask how the vision is to be translated into practices, structures and relationships on the ground, especially at a time of major reductions in government expenditure. Although the government has endeavoured to find new language and give an impression of new thinking, it may be hard to see how projects or programmes carrying the badge of the Big Society will be substantially different from those the Labour government pursued in the past. The government would probably say the difference is that previous initiatives were driven 'top down', with a political and managerial agenda set by Whitehall and Westminster to which those taking part were required to conform, whereas the Big Society will be driven and owned by citizens and communities, or by civil society, without interference from central government. Whether

---

[12] David Cameron gave a speech on the 'Big Society' on 19 July 2010 at Liverpool Hope University. At the time of writing, the transcript can be accessed on the website of the Prime Minister's Office at: www.number10.gov.uk/news/big-society-speech/

that distinction can be realistically sustained, especially at a time of reductions in public expenditure, was unclear at the time of writing.

Nevertheless, whether or not the term Big Society continues to be used, the underlying issues of communities, citizenship, the role of civil society and the position of the voluntary and community sector will remain important, both in relation to crime and for the country's social fabric more generally – not least in preventing any repetition of the riots which took place in August 2011. If a single expression is needed, the 'good society' might be more suitable than the Big Society. It might be better to think of it, not so much as a state of affairs to be created, but as an approach that responds to social and economic problems by mobilising the voluntary and community sector, communities and concerned and conscientious citizens in a spirit of public service and social responsibility. It would be one which fosters consideration for others and a sense of empathy. Barack Obama in his book *The Audacity of Hope* defines empathy as 'a call to stand in somebody else's shoes and see through their eyes' (2006, p 66), the childhood principle which his mother taught him with the question 'How would that make you feel?' and the 'guidepost for [his] politics' (p 67). The good society therefore, while condemning crime and harm to others, would appreciate the resentment felt by people in relative poverty, especially when they are aware of the extreme wealth of others, and understand the frustration of those who feel they do not have a stake in society. But, importantly, the good society would be one which prompts questions rather than dictates answers. Seen in that way, it has much to offer to proposals for preventing and reducing crime and to the reformation and reintegration of offenders, which will be discussed in the following chapters.

Important conditions

Two important conditions have to be satisfied if a government programme of engaging communities is to succeed. One is that the government must be open, realistic and straightforward in what it is trying to do. It is natural that an active and ambitious government should try to enlist the practical support of civil society, but the more it imposes itself the more civil society is itself likely to be weakened, or to turn its energy to activities where government is not involved or to work in opposition to it. A mixture of motives is also likely to lead to uncertainty and scepticism, and a government's good faith may be called into question if, for example, its policies result in the withdrawal of funding from activities it claims to support. The second proviso is that the thinking should be founded on a set of social values that sees those who are vulnerable, disadvantaged or troublesome, or who have committed offences or are at risk of committing offences, as members of society and not as excluded or liable to be excluded from it. That is not to say that they should not have their liberty restricted if necessary by imprisonment or other penalties, but that communities should still regard them as 'their own people'; communities should accept responsibility towards them; and responsibility should be expected from them in return.

FIVE

Courts, punishment and sentencing

The criminal court, symbolised by the blindfolded figure holding the sword and scales, was once seen as the embodiment of all that was best in British justice. By the 1990s, it was coming under criticism as being too expensive, slow, unfairly weighted in favour of the defendant, insensitive to the needs of victims and witnesses, ineffective in finding the truth and punishing those who are guilty, too narrowly focused on the offence rather than the offender, and incomprehensible to many of those who take part and to the public. This chapter considers a set of connected questions relating to the nature of the criminal trial and alternatives to it; the scope of the criminal law; the nature and purpose of punishment as it is administered by the state; the position and treatment of victims and witnesses; and the various forms of restorative justice as part of, or as an adjunct to, the criminal process.

Court proceedings and legislation

Governments have promoted reforms to sentencing and the criminal law at various times over the past 30 years. The Conservative government sought to cut costs and reduce delays as part of the Financial Management Initiative in the 1980s; it set up the Crown Prosecution Service following the report of the Royal Commission on Criminal Procedure (1981); and it established the Criminal Cases Review Commission to review alleged miscarriages of justice, as recommended by the Royal Commission on Criminal Justice (1993). The Labour government sought to improve efficiency, increase rates of conviction and 'rebalance the system' in favour of the public and the victim as part of the reforms associated with the 2003 Criminal Justice Act (Home Office, 2002). Specific measures included the closure of magistrates' courts, restrictions on legal aid, encouraging guilty pleas, 'on the spot' fines, changes to the rules of evidence and procedure, and dispensing with juries in certain cases. Some of them are being extended by the Conservative–Liberal Democratic coalition government that took office in 2010.

Many of the previous Labour government's measures, especially those in the Criminal Justice Act, 2003 relating to evidence and trials without a jury, and indeterminate sentences for public protection, were criticised as threatening the quality of justice. Among the present government's policies, closing magistrates' courts adds to the cost and inconvenience of travel and arguably undermines the principle of local justice. Restrictions on legal aid can put impoverished defendants at risk. Encouraging guilty pleas saves the costs of a full trial, spares witnesses from what may be an unpleasant ordeal and saves victims the stress of what may otherwise be a long drawn out process. On the other hand, it risks oppressive questioning and false admissions. Changing the rules of evidence and dispensing with juries, and imposing 'on-the-spot fines', can all in different ways risk an increase in miscarriages of justice.

Andrew Ashworth and Lucia Zedner (2008, p 44) have argued that:

> [T]he paradigm of the criminal law and the criminal trial is being eroded by the state as it pursues other agendas such as greater regulation, an emphasis on prevention, and an authoritarianism linked closely with penal populism and the demand for public protection.

They further point out the implications of such shifts in policy:

> The challenges to the liberal model of criminal law and the criminal trial … raise questions as to the efficacy, necessity, appropriateness, and effectiveness of the criminal law and its trial processes that cannot easily be put aside.

They identified seven recent trends, which they examined in detail – diversion from the court process, fixed penalties, greater use of summary trials, hybrid civil–criminal processes such as anti-social behaviour orders, creation of offences involving strict criminal liability, incentives to plead guilty and preventive orders.

Attempts to improve or reform the criminal trial itself have in the past been piecemeal alterations to a process that always had conviction and punishment as its objectives. Governments' aims have usually been to make trials more 'effective', or simply less expensive, for example by making it easier to convict suspects (the changes in the rules of evidence in the 2003 Criminal Justice Act), or encouraging defendants to plead guilty and so reduce the cost of a trial (by offering them a shorter sentence). Changes have sometimes been prompted by events, by 'moral panics', or attempts to gain political support. Governments have rarely looked for instances in which criminal sanctions, a criminal trial and criminal convictions might be unnecessary and so could be avoided altogether. Further changes to make courts more effective or cut costs risk compromising the necessary safeguards and creating a process in which emotions, opinions, social pressures and influences from the media would be harder to control. Consistency would be harder to maintain. A better approach may be to look for alternative processes of the kind discussed later in this chapter, and not create shortcuts to a criminal conviction and criminal penalties.

Alternatives to the criminal trial

Imaginative alternatives to the criminal trial have sometimes been proposed. In 1980, JUSTICE[1] made proposals for a 'middle' system of law in which there would be a clear distinction between 'crimes' and 'contraventions', with 'contraventions' generally being enforced by administrative penalties, although with the possibility of a referral to a magistrates' court in the event of a disagreement (JUSTICE, 1980). The idea was followed up in lectures and seminars at the time, but the government's view was that the creation of a new system, with new legislation and a new institutional framework, would be disproportionately expensive and that most of the benefits could be obtained by expanding the use of fixed penalties. Proposals of that kind could probably not be justified on the grounds that they would reduce costs, and the benefits would be found in avoiding the criminalisation of people who would not ordinarily be seen or think of themselves as 'criminals'. No quantified assessment was made of the numbers of people who might thereby be diverted from the criminal process, or of the social or other benefits that might be achieved.

A criminal conviction not only opens the possibility of a coercive sentence; it also carries the stigma of a criminal record that can in some instances have more serious consequences for the person and their family than the penalty itself. Even where the penalty has little or no immediate effect, for example a caution, penalty notice or suspended sentence, the stigma still applies. Governments have for several years promoted the use of penalties where offenders need not go to court if they admit the offence, including cautions, conditional cautions, penalty notices for disorder and cannabis warnings. Out-of-court disposals such as these have obvious advantages in saving everyone – police, courts,

---

[1] JUSTICE is an all-party law reform organisation; see www.justice.org.uk

victims, witnesses, offenders themselves – time and money, and they are especially attractive in times of economic stringency.

With any penalty imposed out of court, however, there is a danger that a defendant might be put under pressure to accept a penalty to 'save trouble', without fully appreciating the consequences. Their use should not be extended lightly, but the danger would be reduced if the penalty did not carry the consequences of a criminal conviction. It could be recorded locally for a limited period, but without being notified to the Criminal Records Bureau to become part of a formal criminal record.

The coalition government has said it would like to simplify the framework of out-of-court disposals, to develop their scope, and explore opportunities for communities to become more involved, for example through community justice panels (Ministry of Justice, 2010a). In some parts of Britain, specialist courts have been experimentally introduced (Berman et al, 2009; McIvor, 2009) following the success of the 'problem-solving courts' and therapeutic jurisprudence in North America, and what has become an international movement (Nolan, 2009). There are different variants, including drug courts, mentally disordered offenders' courts, and courts for low-level offences, but they have in common the closer engagement of sentencers in the rehabilitative outcomes of sentences and in overseeing the defendant's progress (Wexler, 2001). The North Liverpool Community Justice Centre and, to a lesser extent, the Salford Community Justice Initiative, were modelled on the Red Hook Community Justice Center in New York, which provides the court with rapid access to a range of public, voluntary and private sector services to meet the welfare and reintegrative needs of offenders (Thomson, 2010). There is an 'emphasis on solving local public safety problems, changing the behaviour of offenders, and giving local communities a greater voice in "doing justice"' (Berman et al, 2009, pp 7-8).

Ashworth and Zedner (2008) contemplated a new category of 'administrative offences' and 'administrative penalties', resembling in some ways the proposals that JUSTICE put forward 30 years ago but without the creation of a separate administrative structure to apply them. The penalties would be at a low level; if they were to include significant punishment, especially the possible loss of liberty, the procedural protections normally associated with due process and human rights should then apply.[2] More recently, the Law Commission issued a consultation paper on Criminal Liability in Regulatory Contexts

---

[2] The presumption of innocence; proper notice of the charge; adequate time and facilities for preparing a defence; state-funded legal assistance; the right to challenge witnesses; the free assistance of an interpreter; the privilege against self-incrimination.

(Law Commission for England and Wales, 2010). It saw its task as being one of 'introducing rationality and principle into the creation of criminal law'. It argued that the outcome of criminal proceedings may not bring much benefit in terms either of individual retribution or general deterrence, and that reliance on the criminal law as the main means of deterring and punishing unwanted behaviour may prove to be an expensive, uncertain and ineffective strategy. It suggested that the criminal process should be confined to wrongdoing that is 'deliberate, knowing, reckless or dishonest' and that civil penalties should be used for the remainder. The paper made clear that the consultation was not concerned with an improvement in standards of behaviour by the public at large, and it acknowledged that any such scheme would depend on an adequate range of civil measures being available and that effective means would have to be in place to deal with failures to comply. Even so, its analysis and arguments and its task of introducing rationality and principle into the creation of criminal law is one that could usefully be applied more generally.

Criminal offences

Closely related to the criminal trial are questions about the nature and number of criminal offences. Previous chapters have argued that the policies that governments have pursued since the mid-1990s, the legislation they have introduced, the assumptions they have made, the attitudes they have adopted and the language they have used in presenting them to the public have all led to confusion about the place of criminal justice in a modern democratic society. The confusion also extends to the kinds of behaviour that should properly be regarded as 'criminal', and to the place of punishment and the role it should play when it is administered by the state.

Governments have continuously expanded both the number and types of activity or behaviour that it tries to control, and the mechanisms by which it does so. New criminal offences have been created at the astonishing rate of about 150 a year for almost 20 years. They include regulatory offences in matters such as public order, road traffic and health and safety; failure to comply with conditions or instructions; and the offences created under the Terrorism Acts which were discussed later in this chapter. Much of the behaviour so criminalised is or might be innocent and harmless in itself, and it is only the situation or a person's (non-criminal) intentions that make it criminal – something that comes perilously close to 'thought crime', with shades of George Orwell's novel *Nineteen Eighty-Four* (1951). Many were offences of absolute liability for which the prosecution need only show that the person committed the prohibited act, regardless of whether they intended it. There was no defence, and enforcement was at the discretion of the police and the Crown Prosecution Service.

The process of creating new offences did not follow any consistent principles, for example to establish criteria for when a new offence or a longer sentence was needed, what alternatives ought first to be considered, what tests should be applied, how an offence should be enforced, or what purposes it could be expected to achieve. Powers enacted for one purpose, for example to prevent terrorism, were used for other purposes, such as to control nuisances, for which they were never intended – an abuse against which the coalition government has said it would introduce safeguards (Cabinet Office, 2010). Sometimes the government admitted that a new offence might not have any direct effect and that its purpose was declaratory – to 'send a message', for example by changing the classification of cannabis, or to demonstrate action in response to events or expressions of public concern.

Until the 1980s, governments and Parliament adopted a more rigorous approach to the creation of new criminal offences. The criteria were that the behaviour was serious enough to justify a criminal penalty; that the problem could not be dealt with adequately by other means; that the offence was clearly defined and capable of being effectively enforced; that it was not covered by existing legislation; and that there were appropriate provisions for appeal and safeguards against oppressive enforcement. They avoided declaratory offences wherever possible. Even in 1999, the Attorney General Lord Williams said in reply to a parliamentary question about the creation of new criminal offences:

> The Government are mindful that the criminal justice system is a scarce resource and take the view that new offences should be created only when absolutely necessary.
>
> In considering whether new offences should be created, factors taken into account include whether:
> * The behaviour in question is sufficiently serious to warrant intervention by the criminal law;
> * The mischief could be dealt with under existing legislation or using other remedies;
> * the proposed offence is enforceable in practice;
> * the proposed offence is tightly drawn and legally sound; and

- the proposed penalty is commensurate with the seriousness of the offence. (*Hansard*, House of Lords, 18 June 1999, vol. 602, cc57–8WA)

The first of those factors may appear the simplest but is probably the most difficult to determine in practice. There are no objective criteria to establish what is 'sufficiently serious': that is not the same as 'morally wrong', about which opinions will vary between different individuals and cultures, and not every action which is considered morally wrong is sufficiently serious to justify making it a criminal offence. There are also regulatory offences which an ordinary person might see as 'not really criminal' and would suffer no serious social stigma from committing.[3] If the argument is just that 'there should be a law against it', there may be more effective ways of dealing with the problem than by creating and enforcing a criminal offence. An example would be the application of behavioural economics or 'nudging' people towards more acceptable standards of behaviour, but restorative justice and mentoring may be more straightforward and effective.

The coalition's Programme for Government (Cabinet Office, 2010, p 11) included a commitment to 'introduce a new mechanism to prevent the proliferation of unnecessary new criminal offences', and the Ministry of Justice (2011b, p 19) subsequently stated that it had created 'a new gateway to scrutinise all legislation containing criminal offences'. The green paper *Breaking the Cycle* (Ministry of Justice, 2010a, p 63) also indicated that the government would introduce a simpler framework for out-of-court disposals.

Punishment

Successive governments' reforms of sentencing have created confusion about the place of punishment in a modern society, its nature and purpose, the conditions that make it legitimate, and the responsibilities of those who have to be involved in its administration. It has been compounded by the complexity of the legislation and of the arrangements for release from prison, so that the length of a prison sentence pronounced in court bears little resemblance to the time

---

[3] Some forms of behaviour that are dangerous or unpleasant but not what most people would see as 'criminal', for example smoking in public places or failing to wear a seat belt, have been accepted as now illegal and are generally observed. The same approach has been much less effective when it has been applied to the misuse of drugs or alcohol, and some restrictive legislation, for example in the area of health and safety, is widely resented and sometimes disregarded.

the offender will spend in prison. That is one reason for the public's apparent lack of confidence in the sentencing process.

Most people have been brought up to believe that if the state is to punish a person, it should be for something they have been proved to have done; the punishment should be deserved; it should be proportionate to the seriousness of the offence and the culpability of the offender; and the rules of due process should have been followed in what can be seen as a fair trial. Once those requirements have been satisfied, the sentence or punishment can follow, with some room for mercy or compassion where possible. That could once have been said to be the 'British tradition' going back through Dicey (1885) and Blackstone (1765-69) to the Magna Carta.

Persistent offenders

Within that tradition, the sentencing of persistent offenders has troubled governments and the courts for a long time – since the Gladstone Committee in 1895, or even since the stocks went out of use early in the 19th century. Preventive detention as a sentence was found to be unsatisfactory and was abolished by the 1967 Criminal Justice Act. Judges in the 1970s and 1980s were on the whole reluctant to send persistent offenders to prison for longer terms each time they were reconvicted, and sometimes applied the principle of 'progressive loss of mitigation' – slightly longer sentences for the second or third offence, but no additional penalty for persistence after that. The 1991 Criminal Justice Act sought to consolidate that approach and to remove the inconsistencies and anomalies that resulted from the more or less haphazard practice that was being followed at that time. Empirical studies consistently show high rates of recidivism and reimprisonment by ex-prisoners (SEU, 2002; House of Commons Justice Committee, 2009), while the research on resettlement shows the succession of practical challenges that returning prisoners have to face (for example, Crow, 2006; Hucklesby and Hagley-Dickinson, 2007). Based on such findings, it is reasonable to assume that the public will be better protected by investing in effective resettlement for prisoners than by the 'revolving door' of repeated sentences of imprisonment. That is also one of the implications of the Bradley report on people with mental health problems or learning disabilities in the criminal justice system (Bradley, 2009).

The Labour government took a different view when it came into office in 1997, believing that all crime should be met with punishment and that repeated offending should be punished more severely on each occasion ('progression in sentencing'). A judge who passed a community sentence to give an offender 'another chance' when a prison sentence might be expected was likely to be criticised by the media and the sentence might be overturned on a prosecution appeal. The House of Commons Justice Committee (2009, p 5) later expressed its concern that 'an unthinking acceptance has evolved of punishment – for its own sake – as … the only way of registering the seriousness with which society regards a crime'. The idea that courts might be able to make a probation order as an alternative to a sentence or punishment (as they could until the 1991 Criminal Justice Act) now seems very old-fashioned, although the probation order worked well for most of the 20th century, and new thinking about effectiveness in reducing reoffending confirms the value of that earlier approach (see chapters three and seven).

Punishment as crime control

The Labour government also saw punishment as an instrument of crime control – as a means of protecting the public from bad people who should be punished not for what they had done but for the people they were and for what they might do in future (Zedner, 2007b). The use of pre-emptive punishment or 'pre-punishment' has now become a common feature of criminal justice. Offences of conspiracy or of attempting, assisting or encouraging the commission of an offence, and some offences of possessing or carrying (for example, firearms or knives), have been established for some time. There may in some instances have been concerns about proportionality – the seriousness of the harm that is to be prevented, the degree of culpability that should attach to the offence, the standard of proof that is required and the defences that are available (Child and Hunt, 2011) – but they have not in the past presented a problem of principle. More serious issues arise from the scope and potential misuse of the preparatory offences created by the 2006 Terrorism Act, where a simple statement or action may bring a penalty of up to seven years' or even life imprisonment if it is done with the intention or in the knowledge of the possibility that it might encourage or assist an act of terrorism (Zedner, 2010; Squires and Stephen, 2010).

Especially serious, both as a matter of justice and for its practical consequences for the prison service, is the imposition of punishment when it is not based on any act on the part of the 'offender' but on a judgement of the risk they are thought to present – an assessment not related to any knowledge of the individual, but to statistical probabilities based on a sample of offenders with similar characteristics. Actuarial data should not be used to drive decision making but rather to inform it (Crighton and Towl, 2008). There is also an argument on justice grounds when procedures of such doubtful accuracy can be used to justify a person's indefinite loss of liberty, and an argument on economic grounds when the financial costs can be so great.

An example of injustice is the extended periods of detention being served by prisoners subject to life or indeterminate sentences, especially those serving the indeterminate sentences for public protection introduced by the 2003 Criminal Justice Act (Jacobson and Hough, 2010). Their detention may be extended, sometimes for several years, beyond the 'tariff' set by the judge to reflect the seriousness of their offence, not for anything they have done in prison but because they have not been able to show that they are not a danger to the public. That may be because they have not been given the opportunity to attend an offending behaviour course, or because they continue to protest their innocence. The coalition government has announced its intention to limit the scope of the sentence and accelerate the release of some of those who have passed their 'tariff' date (Ministry of Justice, 2010a, p 55-6).

At the other end of the scale is the range of preventive orders, most conspicuously the anti-social behaviour order, but also dispersal orders, control orders, civil gang injunctions, sexual offence prevention orders and others. Their purpose is to prevent harms or risks that are too uncertain, remote or subjective to be directly subject to the criminal process. Their effect is to restrict liberty in ways that may be disproportionate, arbitrary and sometimes oppressive. A breach of the order that may be trivial in itself becomes an offence that may carry a sentence of up to five years' imprisonment. Counter-terrorism offences could be even more oppressive in their application, such as the power to stop and search under Section 44 of the 2000 Terrorism Act, and the power under the 2005 Serious and Organised Crimes and Police Act to designate areas where special offences apply.

What is punishment for?

That punishment still has a place in modern society cannot be seriously disputed. But its relationship with, and its potential for solving, problems of crime and social disorder and of dysfunctional communities and families is much more uncertain. These problems are part of a wider and usually complex situation of relationships, opportunities, temptation and motivation where the punishment of individuals can have only a limited impact.

It is important, though, to be aware of the different meanings and purposes of punishment and to recognise most of them as understandable reactions to wrongdoing albeit generally incompatible with rehabilitation (Canton, 2007). The penal philosopher Antony Duff argues that criminal punishment should be seen as a mode of moral communication, aimed at inducing repentance, reform and reconciliation (Duff, 2001; see also Rex, 2005). His formulation is not easy to translate into policy or legislation, but it provides a valuable challenge to conventional ideas of retributive or consequentialist punishment and deserves serious thought as other modes of punishment and social control come to be considered. He places his arguments in the context of a 'liberal communitarian' view of political society and the role of the criminal law.

Purposes of sentencing

Most attempts to regulate sentencing by statute have ended in disappointment. Chapters two and three have described the main reforms of sentencing that governments introduced between 1991 and 2003, but most of the changes introduced during the past 50 years have been quickly overtaken by further attempts at reform, have never been brought into effect, or are the subject of continuing difficulty and argument. The main reasons for this are that unrealistic claims have been made for the results they could achieve, or that the resulting legislation has been too complicated or too rigid to allow sentencers to use their judgement, or to 'do justice', according to the facts of the case.

Section 142 of the 2003 Criminal Justice Act required sentencers to have regard to:

- the punishment of offenders;
- the reduction of crime (including its reduction by deterrence);
- the reform and rehabilitation of offenders;
- the protection of the public; and
- the making of reparation by offenders to persons affected by their offences.

The statutory recognition of those purposes was generally welcomed, but it was never made clear how sentencers were to choose or to resolve any conflicts between them, or how it might be possible to show whether the purposes had been achieved. Sentences are in practice decided in accordance with guidelines issued by the Sentencing Guidelines Council, and now by the Sentencing Council. The guidelines cover subjects such as the offender's culpability, the harm done and any aggravating and mitigating factors, but they do not say how the different statutory purposes should be applied or how a court is to choose between them.

The different purposes of sentencing reflect different, attitudes to punishment, and different positions about punishment's place in society, which can often conflict (Walker, 2009). The conflict can be especially difficult to resolve if the difference is between moral beliefs, but some resolution is necessary if sentencing and punishment are to have authority and legitimacy.

Complexity and confusion

Notwithstanding the moral aspects, there is a serious difficulty in interpreting the legislation. Lord Chief Justice Lord Judge wrote in his introduction to the Court of Appeal's online annual report:

> What remains less tolerable is the continuing burden of comprehending and applying impenetrable legislation, primarily but not exclusively in relation to sentencing. The search for the legislative intention in the context of criminal justice legislation makes unreasonable demands on the intellectual efforts of judges and lawyers.... The difficulties ... apply to every Crown Court and Magistrates' Court throughout the jurisdiction. The search for principle takes longer and longer, and in the meantime cases awaiting trial are delayed, to the disadvantage of the defendants awaiting trial, the witnesses to the events which bring the defendants to court, and the victims of those alleged crimes. (Court of Appeal, 2010)

The experience described in previous chapters has shown that legislation on sentencing is more likely to work well when its aim is to make the process of sentencing more fair and or consistent, or to resolve what Douglas Hurd in his capacity as Home Secretary in the 1980s called 'muddles' in sentencing. Difficulties are likely to arise when the aim is to achieve an instrumental effect – for example, to limit the prison population, as it was to some extent for the 1991 Criminal Justice Act, or to achieve any of the instrumental purposes set out in the 2003 Criminal Justice Act. They are also likely to arise if the aim is to 'increase public confidence' in sentencing, for example by increasing the severity of punishment to make sure that offenders are adequately punished, or to 'send a message', for example by increasing a penalty or creating a new criminal offence.

There is no evidence that legislation has been successful in achieving any of these aims, but no rigorous assessment or post-legislative review has ever taken place. Any legislation that aims to reduce crime or protect the public by changes to sentencing is likely to ignore the evidence about the limitations of sentencing as a means of reducing crime that came to be recognised in research over a number of years. In particular, it may be counter-productive to introduce refinements such as minimum, mandatory and indeterminate sentences, all of which have a history of causing frustration and potential injustice going back over many years. A study might usefully consider whether the drafting of criminal justice legislation could be made simpler for the courts, prosecutors and others to apply and easier for the public to understand.

More clarity and a stronger foundation of principle are needed if sentencing is to become more intelligible and coherent, and if confidence is to be restored (Ashworth and Zedner, 2008; Loader and Sparks, 2011; Zedner, 2011). The coalition government has said in its green paper that it will 'simplify the sentencing framework and reduce elements of the law that constrain judicial discretion' (p 11), and that it will 'create a simpler, more transparent sentencing framework that is easier for courts to operate and for victims and the public to understand' (Ministry of Justice, 2010a, p 49). The green paper, if it is translated into policy, provides a promising starting point, but much will depend on the scope and detail of the proposals if and when they are translated into legislation.

Victims and witnesses

The past 30 years have seen a transformation in the treatment of victims of crime and of witnesses appearing in court. Victim support schemes grew out of work being done by probation officers during the 1970s and are now nationally organised and funded as Victim Support. The Victim's Charters of 1990 and 1996 gave guidance and later rules on how victims should be heard and supported during the criminal justice process. The work of the probation service became significantly reoriented towards victims and witnesses, and the police were required to give more consideration to victims, with special provisions relating to cases of sexual assault, domestic violence and racial harassment. The Labour government claimed throughout its term of office that it was determined to improve the situation of victims and witnesses and to 'rebalance' the system' in their favour (Home Office, 2002). A Victims' Code of Practice was published in 2005; provision was made for victims' personal statements to be placed before the court; and the government appointed a statutory Commissioner for Victims and Witnesses. And yet there is still a sense among those who support victims that not enough has been done. Louise Casey, the Commissioner for Victims and Witnesses, has said that 'victims and witnesses are still the poor relation' and 'a "sideshow"', while police, prisons, lawyers and the courts focused on the offender' (cited in Walklate, 2011). Victim Support has said that sentencing policy 'as it stands ... disenfranchises the party that has a major interest in the effectiveness of the criminal justice system – the victim of crime' (Victim Support, 2010).

Trials are sometimes seen as a conflict between the victim (good) and the criminal (bad) in which the 'good' has to prevail if 'justice is to be done', and their adversarial nature reinforces that impression. (See the discussion on procedural justice in chapter one.) A trial is essentially a process for assessing the evidence and then deciding on the most appropriate sentence. The parties are the state or the Crown, and the defendant, and the prosecution acts on behalf of the public as a whole, including the victim. Justice is not so much a 'victory' for one side or the other, but the resolution of a situation in a way that is as fair as possible to everyone involved or affected by it. There can, however, be a real conflict of interest between due process for the defendant (who may be innocent, or innocent of the charge being brought) and the extended suffering of the victim. Some guilty defendants 'play the system' by pleading not guilty until the last minute, and some victims will have been badly hurt by the offence against them and then have the added misery of not knowing whether the offender will be found guilty, and anxieties about appearing and being questioned in court, and not being able to move on from the incident until the case is over.

The government's green paper *Breaking the Cycle* (Ministry of Justic, 2010a) placed great emphasis on the importance of the victim and promises a further full review, but its actual proposals were quite limited – more funding for victims' organisations and greater use of existing provisions such as compensation orders and personal statements.[4] Victim Support's own recommendations were not so much for new rights, structures or procedures as for making sure that the existing structure works properly and that what should be done is done (that is, for 'procedural justice'). They argued for greater clarity

---

[4] For a review of the use and effect of victims' statements, see Roberts (2009).

and better explanations of sentencing; better arrangements for paying compensation; more use of restorative justice; and better arrangements for the offender's rehabilitation to ensure that the crime is not repeated. In all these respects, the interests of victims and witnesses are the same as those of any citizen or any criminal justice practitioner.

More still needs to be done to improve the way in which victims and witnesses are treated in practice. The experience of a crime can range from irritating to totally devastating, and the pain or loss can be all the more severe because of the knowledge that it was caused deliberately or culpably by another person, or if it appears that the guilty person may not face any consequences. That should be recognised and taken into account, and victims are entitled to support and appropriate compensation for what they have experienced. But it will not always be possible to give victims satisfaction in terms of the prosecution and sentence of the person who has committed an offence against them: the criminal justice system exists for other citizens as well as victims, and other considerations besides retribution and punishment are necessary in a just and well-functioning criminal process.

Restorative justice

There is widespread support for restorative justice, a lot of experience of its use in different settings, and some evidence of its success (Shapland et al, 2008; Hoyle, 2009). What might be called 'main line' or the 'original' form of restorative justice typically takes the form of a restorative conference where the offender, victim, and members of their families and other supporters meet with a facilitator to discuss what has happened and if possible agree an outcome that may include an apology and some form of reparation. The main claim for restorative justice in that form is the victims' involvement in the process and, it is hoped, their satisfaction with it, and perhaps a transformation in the offender in ways that may not be readily facilitated through the normal process of a criminal trial.

Restorative justice, like support for victims, was first introduced into England through the probation service. Pilot schemes were established during the 1980s, but they were for the most part laborious and time-consuming and the judiciary viewed them with suspicion as interfering with what they saw as the proper course of justice. The idea was revived with a programme of restorative cautioning by Thames Valley Police under the leadership of the Chief Constable Charles Pollard during the 1990s (Young and Hoyle, 2003). The programme lost some momentum after a change of chief constable, but restorative work continued and still continues in the Thames Valley Probation

Service and Bullingdon Prison. Restorative approaches also came to be used successfully in other prisons (Edgar and Newell, 2006), in other settings such as schools,[5] and in dealing with complaints against public authorities.

Restorative justice has come to be widely used in connection with referral orders for juvenile offenders in England and Wales and children's hearings in Scotland, and it has had, and still has, an important role in Northern Ireland. The Independent Commission on Youth Crime and Antisocial Behaviour (2010, p 5) has recommended that restoration should be adopted as a key principle in youth justice and that youth conferencing should become 'the centrepiece of responses to all but the most serious offences committed by young people'.

Three schemes operating at different stages in the criminal justice process in England have been the subject of sophisticated evaluations using random control trials (Shapland et al, 2008; Ministry of Justice 2010b). There was no doubt that victims generally welcomed the opportunity and appreciated the experience when they were able to take part. Evidence of effectiveness in reducing reoffending was less straightforward, but the Ministry of Justice concluded that the size of the impact was a reduction of about 14 per cent. Two of the schemes have come to an end; the third and most successful was the scheme which still continues in the Thames Valley, where it can be used after sentence as a requirement of a community order.

Opinions differ on the circumstances and the types of offender for whom restorative justice can be most successful. The green paper (Ministry of Justice, 2010a) emphasises the benefits for victims, for example in helping them to achieve closure; this is an important aspect, and victims should never feel that they are being exploited for the sake of the offender. For offenders, it suggests that restorative approaches may be best used for low-level offenders as an alternative to the formal criminal justice process or as part of an out-of-court disposal. Experience in the Thames Valley has suggested that it can also be successful after conviction and for relatively serious offenders, including some who have been convicted of offences of violence. The conference should not, however, be treated as a single event, and it should be integrated into a longer-term programme of rehabilitation and reintegration.

Restorative procedures are also used by the police, in a variety of settings – as part of neighbourhood policing, within schools, to settle long-term neighbourhood disputes, as part of reducing reoffending

---

[5] See the Restorative Justice Council's website, www.restorativejustice.org.uk

programmes, and as a means of tackling those crimes and incidents that have a disproportionate impact on communities. Police officers have seen it as a means of uniting local communities around a collective response to offending (Shewan, 2010). A review of the evidence relating to public confidence in the police has shown that restorative meetings mediated by police officers can also improve the public's perception of criminal justice and of the police themselves (Rix et al, 2009).

Some enthusiasts would like to see an expanded role for restorative justice within the criminal justice process, perhaps as part of an explicitly restorative sentence and with legislation requiring it to be considered wherever it is appropriate. Sceptics may continue to question how far formalised restorative justice and the traditional adversarial system could be combined in a single process. It could, however, have a greater role as an alternative to a criminal trial, for example where mental health issues are involved and where 'justice can be done' without recording a conviction or giving the defendant a criminal record. There is also scope for restorative meetings or restorative work to take place after sentence in prisons and the community, and for them to do so on a national scale. Restorative work could, for example, be made more generally available as a 'specified activity' as part of a community sentence under Section 201 of the 2003 Criminal Justice Act, as it is in the Thames Valley. There is also scope to increase its use in youth justice. In all those ways, restorative justice could make a valuable contribution to the legitimacy of the criminal justice process, as discussed elsewhere.

The coalition government showed more enthusiasm for restorative justice than its predecessor (Ministry of Justice, 2010a, pp 22, 68). It did, however, present the arguments in terms of benefits to the victim, with not much reference to the impact on the offender. That is understandable: victims are rightly sensitive to any suggestion that they might be 'used' for the benefit of the offender. Practical experience in the Thames Valley does, however, indicate that restorative justice can have a sharp impact on an offender's understanding of the effect of what they have done and of the feelings of other people, and on their own outlook and future behaviour. This aspect of restorative justice, and the possible application of restorative approaches in a range of situations outside criminal justice, should not be neglected.

Restorative justice may best be seen not only as a defined process, with prescribed procedures, boxes to be ticked, inputs and outputs to be measured and outcomes to be judged in terms of the effect on rates of reconviction, but also as a way of thinking and an expression of social values and a humane but realistic approach to troubled situations and relationships. In that form, it should have a major part to play in promoting confidence and safety in communities and the sense of shared responsibilities.

Conclusion: improving the process

A criminal conviction carries consequences beyond the sentence itself and the criminal process is a time-consuming and expensive process. In a preventive, restorative and enabling system, criminal proceedings should not be pursued if there is a suitable alternative, but once engaged the rules of due process should be rigorously applied. New offences should only be created if they are absolutely necessary, and in accordance with established criteria; existing offences and especially pre-emptive offences should be reviewed against those criteria and repealed if the criteria are not satisfied.

Legislation on sentencing should be simple and straightforward, allowing maximum discretion for sentencers within Sentencing Council Guidelines and indeterminate and mandatory sentences should be reviewed and where possible abolished. New and existing measures, especially restorative measures, that do not involve criminalisation should be developed and promoted.

SIX

Police, policing and communities

The story of British policing over the past 30 years has been one of constant reform and of repeated demands that more change is needed. Governments have sought to make the police more effective in dealing with crime and at the same time to increase efficiency, reduce bureaucracy and cut costs. The public have similarly wanted the police to be more effective in fighting crime, which they have often equated with having a more visible police presence on the streets. Concerns of a different kind have related to police methods in dealing with demonstrations or incidents of public disorder, the use or misuse of police powers, and the treatment of minorities. Dogmatic assertions about what is needed have been matched by scepticism about the extent to which traditional police methods, especially patrol and 'bobbies on the beat', can by themselves have an impact on the general level of crime.

What police are for

Since the earliest days of the public police service, there has been debate about whether the 'job' of the police is to prevent crime and reduce the harm it causes, or whether it is to fight crime, catch criminals and bring them to justice. Accounts of policing and proposals for reform regularly start with a reference to Rowan and Mayne, the first commissioners of the Metropolitan Police, who stated that it was both, but that prevention came first.[1] But it has never been a straightforward choice. For many people, the best way to prevent crime is simply to catch and lock up criminals, and so it may be for some forms of serious or organised crime. Preventing other forms of crime and anti-social behaviour requires different techniques and relationships, and a different culture and mode of operating from those needed for the procedures of investigation, arrest and prosecution. Crime prevention has historically had a lower status and is not so obviously a police function. The practice and culture of policing need to embrace both.

---

[1] 'The primary object of an efficient police is the prevention of crime; the next is that of detection and punishment of offenders if crime is committed' (Sir Richard Mayne, 1829, in his instructions to new police of the Metropolis. Metropolitan Police archives. Source www.met.police.uk/history/definition.htm.)

It has been argued that the nature of policing has changed dramatically, both in response to the increasing demand for public safety and security (Bayley and Shearing, 1996; Johnston and Shearing, 2003), and under the influence of new public management. Policing is now carried out by a range of different, often commercial, agencies and actors responding to market forces, working alongside police forces but independent of them, and so creating a different dynamic and a different relationship with the public. Another view is that the recent changes are part of a continuous process of evolution and development that can be traced back beyond Robert Peel to the early 19th century (Newburn and Reiner, 2007; Reiner, 2010). Whichever analysis is preferred, the fundamental issues are still accountability, legitimacy, culture and functions. In his recent overview of principles for the police service, Peter Neyroud (2011, p 10) has described the need for policing to be 'democratically accountable', 'legitimate', 'evidence-based', 'nationally (and internationally) coherent' and 'capable, competent and cost-effective'.

There is interesting evidence that people may think of police not primarily as providers of personal security, to protect people and their property and detect and arrest offenders, but more for what they stand for and represent as 'moral guardians' of the community's social stability and order and of community values and informal social controls (Jackson and Bradford, 2009; see also Bottoms, 2001, and the discussion of legitimacy in chapter one). It is important that people should think of themselves, and that police should think of them, as part of the community that police exist to serve, and not as being excluded from it or as being in some way 'on the other side'. There should, in particular, be no sense that religious or minority ethnic groups are not part of the same community, or that there is a separate 'criminal class'. There is a special danger if measures to prevent crime, and especially to prevent terrorism, are seen as being directed at a whole religious or ethnic community, with the implication that all members of that community are regarded with suspicion as being dangerous or 'not belonging'. See also the discussion on terrorism and Muslims in prisons in chapter eight.

Demands on police

Changes in the volume and nature of crime, and in the public's and government's expectations, have significantly increased the demands on the police. The demands presented by serious and organised crime and terrorism on the one hand and by anti-social behaviour on the other have become more urgent, and although police-recorded crime has decreased for most offence groups,[2] the public's anxiety and sometimes anger about the general state of crime seem to be as great as ever. Those feelings are natural and justified in relation to terrorism, violence and sexual offences, and in areas where there are exceptionally high rates of property crime; but they may also extend to a more general fear of crime, so that people will see danger in situations where it does not exist or where the chances of becoming a victim are extremely low.

A connected line of argument relates to the policing role in security, not only against terrorism but also in the wider sense of public safety, where security and safety procedures have not only to be managed but also 'civilised' – that is to say, placed in a context of vigilance in protecting the basic principles of justice and human rights and of democratic accountability (for example, through regular reviews by Parliament). That is a task that cannot be left to market forces and has to be carried out on behalf of the state (Loader and Walker, 2007; Jones, 2008). Policing against terrorism should follow the same principles as the policing of ordinary crime, as it did for the most part in Northern Ireland, and the present government has rightly abandoned the language of a 'war on terror', which implies that different rules can then apply if there is the merest suspicion that someone might be linked to terrorism.

The complexity of policing became increasingly evident during the 1980s, with riots on the streets in London, Liverpool and Birmingham (Scarman, 1981) and the findings of police malpractice by the Royal Commission on Criminal Procedure (1981). Further tensions appeared during the policing of the coalminers' strike in 1984 and from the notorious miscarriages of justice that led to a further Royal Commission (Royal Commission on Criminal Justice, 1993). Those events showed that the situations with which police have to deal are much more complex than catching criminals, and involve issues of legitimacy and of social, racial and procedural justice. Police were at that time facing a problem, not to say crisis, of public confidence, which showed itself in a lack of cooperation by the public and a reluctance by juries to convict on unsubstantiated police evidence. Measures to correct that situation included the reform of police procedures in the 1984 Police and Criminal Evidence Act, the creation of the

---

[2] The crime statistics released in May 2011 show that in the 12 months up to December 2010 recorded crime decreased by six per cent (Ministry of Justice, 2011a, p 12). On the other hand, compared against the year 2000, 'the proportion of sentences given for indictable offences to offenders with 15 or more previous convictions or cautions rose steadily from 17 per cent in 2000 to 29 per cent in 2010' (p 69).

Crown Prosecution Service, the reform of arrangements to deal with complaints against the police, and the beginning of a movement towards community and neighbourhood policing.

Further complications came with new forms of crime (for example, cyber crime) and new technology, and from the changing environment within which police had to operate, including their developing relationships with their partners and contacts – local authorities, other statutory services, voluntary organisations, representative groups and members of the public (Flanagan, 2008). Looking ahead, problems of public order may increase if groups such as the English Defence League and the British National Party become more active. There may be further demonstrations against the government's social and economic policies, with problems for the police in keeping control and in their use of controversial methods such as 'kettling', where large numbers of people may be contained in a small area for considerable periods of time. Difficult situations arise when peaceful demonstrations are infiltrated by small numbers of people who are intent on causing trouble or when there is public disorder on a large scale. The riots which took place in August, 2011 were an extreme example. But in all cases, the police response has to be proportionate and legitimate.

Developments in policing

Three major developments can be seen to have occurred over the past 20 or 30 years (Flanagan, 2008; Jones, 2008). One is the increasing range of policing functions that have come to be performed by private security companies. Some of the functions are performed under contract to central or local government, for example security checks and the protection of public buildings; others are carried out as services to the private sector in places such as shopping malls, department stores, supermarkets and 'gated' estates. Companies working for central or local government are to some extent publicly accountable through their contracts; those working for the private sector are accountable only to their employers or clients. All are primarily accountable to their shareholders and customers, rather than the public at large.

Another development has been increased control by central government, and increased centralisation through the creation of national agencies, and the influence of HM Inspectorate of Constabulary and the Association of Chief Police Officers, with a corresponding loss of authority and influence for police authorities and their elected members. The 'tripartite structure' (Home Secretary, police authority and chief constable) that had its origin in the 1964

Police Act was no longer suited to the situation as it had become 40 years later. The consequence was a 'democratic deficit', felt especially by minority ethnic communities (Bowling et al, 2008), but also by other groups or individuals who felt themselves to be marginalised and neglected, and felt that the police were not 'there for them'.

A third has been the increased involvement of members of the public, for example through neighbourhood watch and in community consultative groups, as lay visitors to police stations, as independent members of police authorities, or as respondents to consultative procedures. All these activities can be seen as examples of 'community involvement' and as part of the 'citizenship' discussed in chapter one, but most of those who take part do so as well-informed and thoughtful individuals and not usually as representatives of a 'community' to which they consider themselves to be accountable, while others may still feel excluded.

A wider role and its limitations

In practice, police do much more than prevent and respond to crime. Controlling road traffic and attending accidents and civil emergencies are obvious examples, but, as Greater Manchester Police demonstrated by its 'Twitter experiment', how much the police do and how many calls they may receive have very little to do with 'policing' as it would usually be understood.[3] It might be suggested that the police should stop responding to calls which are not about 'real' policing, as it is narrowly understood, in order to concentrate on higher priorities, especially at a time of austerity. The police could not, however, arbitrarily refuse to respond to such calls without some loss of public confidence and goodwill, as well as loss of the public's cooperation in preventing and investigating crime when the need arises.

Sometimes, as discussed in previous chapters and provided the offence is not too serious, harm can be more successfully reduced by means that do not involve the criminal justice process. Examples include the harm caused by the abuse of drugs or the misuse of alcohol, many offences committed by children, some forms of anti-social behaviour, and some

---

[3] Greater Manchester Police reported that: 'The calls have ranged from those that are not police matters, including someone who called to say there was a rat in the house, and that the cat may be responsible, and a woman reporting a man shouting "you're gorgeous" at her, to serious offences including injuries to a child' (www.gmp.police. uk/mainsite/pages/68ff568654153da6802577bd001fd68a.htm).

of the regulatory offences discussed in chapter four.[4] Moreover, citizens might themselves be more ready to demand and enforce considerate behaviour, not necessarily by intervening in a confrontation when there is a risk of violence, but by intervening to check the 'incivilities' from which more serious problems can develop. HM Inspectorate of Constabulary (2010a, p 11) has argued that:

> Most importantly, individuals and communities must mobilise their defences by re-establishing acceptable rules of behaviour for those in public spaces or impacting on their neighbours, for example, youths who congregate in town centre streets on Friday evening; drunks who habitually urinate in shop doorways; aggressive driving in residential streets. To some degree, the police and other agencies and partners can help with this, but the approach must involve doing it with the people on the receiving end of this behaviour.

See also the report of the Eighth Oxford Policing Policy Forum (Longstaff, 2010).

Given that harm can sometimes be reduced more successfully by non-criminal measures, it may also be asked whether or how far the police should lead or coordinate the preventive action that needs to be taken. The situation may for practical purposes be one where if the police do not act, no one else will, or where, in a 'can-do' spirit of service to the public, the police make an offer to take the lead in a particular enterprise that others round the table are only too pleased to accept. The leadership or involvement of the police could, however, create an impression that the issue to be resolved is one of crime and criminality, where little distinction is made between crime and matters that are not or need not be treated as criminal, and the solution is simply to find an offender who can be identified, punished and given a criminal record. There is also a temptation to think that once the police or other criminal justice agencies are involved, they will take over responsibility and other agencies will be absolved from any responsibilities of their own.

---

[4] Other possibilities are some instances of tax evasion and some types of fraud, but there the argument is more often that the offences are too serious for the offender to escape a criminal penalty and the relatively affluent people who commit them should not receive more favourable treatment than those who are convicted for example of benefit fraud.

Advancing police accountability

Most discussions of police accountability have concentrated on political, managerial or financial accountability or on subjects such as the handling of complaints. Various measures have been introduced or proposed for strengthening police authorities, for the election of their chair or members, and for elected commissioners, as the coalition government now intends and as is discussed later in this chapter.

Successive governments have promoted the publication of information, and much more information is now available to citizens about crime in their area and the performance of their police force. That development, and the openness and transparency that should follow from it, are of course to be welcomed. It is not, however, clear how far the public will have the time or the inclination to make sense of the material without some independent person who can interpret the information and explain its significance. Without that – or perhaps in any event – many people will rely on the often selective and sometimes misleading reports that appear in the media. Nor is it clear how the publication of information would enable the public to make choices, or to bring about changes in police practice, without representatives who can assemble the arguments and put their case.

Just as important as the mechanisms and structures of accountability at force level is local accountability to the citizens and communities the police serve. Sir Ronnie Flanagan[5] (2008, p 96) concluded his review of policing by saying:

> However, some things are clear if we wish to … increase trust, confidence and satisfaction with policing.… [T]he greatest gain to be made is from improving the quality of interactions between individuals involved in delivering policing services (including officers, staff and volunteers) and members of the public. And the second is … [the need to] … better support the capacity of accountability bodies to fulfil the functions expected of them.

There is also an important tradition of accountability to the law, going back to the founders of the Metropolitan Police and famously expressed in the ruling in *Blackburn* ([1968] All E.R.763), that, in all matters of law enforcement, the Metropolitan Police Commissioner is responsible 'to the law and to the law alone'. Police may sometimes have appealed

---

[5] In his former role as HM Chief Inspector of Constabulary.

to that tradition as a way of resisting what they saw as unwelcome interference from ministers, but the importance of the tradition is not to protect chief officers but to assert a separate (and some people might say higher) duty to the courts and the law of the land (Chakrabarti, 2008; Jones, 2008). No one would want that duty to result in frequent litigation, but nor should it be overtaken or displaced by administrative reform (see also chapters one and nine).

A special issue of accountability relates to the Association of Chief Police Officers (ACPO). The association is a representative body working on behalf of the chief officers who are its members; a professional forum that shares ideas and best practice; and an operational body that coordinates resources and helps to deliver effective policing as well as coordinating the strategic policing response in times of national need. Its status is as a private company limited by guarantee and as such it has no effective accountability to ministers, Parliament or the public (Chakrabarti, 2008). The Home Office and ACPO have acknowledged that the situation is unsatisfactory, and in the consultation paper *Policing in the Twenty-first Century* (Home Office, 2010) the Home Office indicated that it was working with ACPO to agree a more appropriate structure. Peter Neyroud (2011) has made proposals that were under consideration at the time of writing – see below.

Bureaucracy and culture

Accountability and bureaucracy are closely related. Excessive bureaucracy has been a matter of complaint for several years, and several reports (Flanagan, 2008; Berry, 2009; HM Inspectorate of Constabulary, 2010b) have shown that attempts to reduce it have so far had a limited effect. The main complaint has been that it keeps police officers in police stations when they ought to be on the streets, and that the main culprit is central government with its previous emphasis on performance indicators and micro-management.[6] The demand to reduce bureaucracy is not, however, straightforward. What one person may see as bureaucracy, another may see as accountability. For a public service to know and to be able to explain what it is doing, what it costs and what it expects to achieve is a necessary part of democratic accountability. For the police, it is essential for their authority and their actual perceived legitimacy. The demands

---

[6] The same applies, of course, to the work of probation officers, youth justice workers and other criminal justice practitioners, who are similarly constrained to excessive hours in front of computers and paperwork.

for more effective police accountability have come from a different direction, but they are not to be ignored.

Police culture has received a great deal of attention over the past 30 years, both from the Inspectorate of Constabulary and from researchers (Smith, 1983; Westmarland, 2008; Loftus 2010). Much of the attention has focused on attitudes and behaviour in matters of race, gender and sexuality. Those are still important issues; Neyroud (2011, p 41) found that although discrimination has been for the most part successfully eliminated in the recruitment process, there are still problems in relation to appointments to the higher ranks of the service and in the culture of the service as a whole. Other important aspects relate to the service's attitudes to risk, innovation and change; its readiness to share power in partnerships and joint working; its views of other services and of the communities it serves; the dynamics of its internal and external relationships; what it regards as 'real' police work; and what sort of work is valued and rewarded. As Louise Westmarland (2008) has pointed out, there is not a single 'police culture', and the ways in which the different cultures react with one another or are expressed in action – on the streets, in meetings, in offices – will vary between different places and situations and between different officers.

Police reforms, 1994-2010

Chapter three briefly described the reforms successive governments introduced in the period from 1994 to 2008. Legislation gave the Home Secretary increased powers to direct and regulate local forces, and other reforms included the formation of the Home Office Police and Standards Unit, the Serious and Organised Crime Agency and the National Police Improvement Agency. At local level, they included changes in the composition and functions of police authorities, improvements in cooperation between forces, the introduction of community and then neighbourhood policing, and the appointment of police community support officers. Police gained greater powers to deal with terrorism, for example the controversial power to 'stop and search' under Section 44 of the 2000 Terrorism Act. Expenditure on the police increased by almost 50 per cent between 1999 and 2009 (Mills et al, 2010) and allowed police to 'throw money' at problems rather than look for other solutions or show evidence of value for money (Lambert, 2009).[7] The Sheehy (1993) and Posen (Home Office, 1994) reviews of police responsibilities and rewards and of core and ancillary tasks showed that government regarded the job of the police as being more to fight crime than to prevent it. That view was later confirmed by the language used in speeches by the Prime Minister Tony Blair (2004, 2006) and in the white paper *Justice for All* (Home Office, 2002).

The performance of the police has improved in many ways over the years, especially the integrity of their procedures and their relationships with other agencies and probably also with communities and victims. Even so, there has continued to be a strong demand for more improvements to be made and for further changes in the service's structure and accountability and in the arrangements for democratic control. The Labour government's green paper *From the Neighbourhood to the National: Policing our Communities Together* (Home Office, 2008) proposed that police authorities should be directly elected, but the subsequent white paper *Protecting the Public: Supporting the Police to Succeed* (Home Office, 2009) was more cautious and limited in its vision and concentrated on plans for 'smarter working'. The white paper also announced that the elaborate array of targets and performance indicators would be replaced by a single target of improving public confidence.[8] The proposals to amalgamate police forces to create a much smaller number of strategic regional forces, favoured by Charles Clarke during his time as Home Secretary (2006-08), have so far not been revived (except in Scotland).

The coalition's reforms

The headline proposal in the coalition government's discussion paper *Policing in the Twenty-first Century* (Home Office, 2010) and in the Police Reform and Social Responsibility Bill is for directly elected police and crime commissioners, who, together with chief constables, will 'lead

---

[7] The House of Commons Home Affairs Committee (2007, p 45) noted that the increase in expenditure came after the main fall in crime and that the 'reduction in overall crime levels does not seem to have been directly related to additional resources'. It is significant that comparative research across 16 European countries has shown that the greater the proportional expenditure on public order and safety, the lower the level of public trust in the police (Kaariainen, 2007).

[8] The performance measures to which the Labour government attached so much importance produced inconclusive and confusing results, and it is arguable that performance may actually have suffered from them (House of Commons Home Affairs Committee, 2007; Jones, 2008).

the fight against crime and anti-social behaviour' (p 3). Police and Crime Panels drawn from locally elected councillors will hold them to account and police authorities will be abolished. Frontline staff will be 'crime fighters: freed up ... to get on with their jobs' (p 3). The paper refers to the importance of reconnecting the police with the communities they serve, and to the need for enabling them to meet the new challenges of crime and anti-social behaviour.

The playing field on which the government put forward its other proposals for police reform is for the most part well-trodden ground. Apart from the direct election of police and crime commissioners and changes in police conditions of service, the issues it has identified and the proposals it has made are not particularly contentious. They include a transfer of power away from government to police professionals, and a change in the focus of government away from micro-management at local level and towards serious crime. Some existing structures are to be combined in a new National Crime Agency. The government will 'empower the Big Society ... making sure that everyone plays their full part – wider criminal justice and community safety partners, the voluntary and community sector and individuals themselves' (Home Office, 2011, p 9). There are separate proposals for modernising the workforce, covering such matters as police recruitment, pay and conditions of service – a familiar issue but one where successive governments have so far made little progress. By implication, the obsession with police numbers as a measure of a government's success or failure – an obsession that had affected the politics of policing for over 40 years – would at last be abandoned.

More radical proposals have come from Peter Neyroud's (2011) report on police leadership and training. His main recommendation was for a chartered police professional body that would be responsible for key national standards; the main functions of ACPO would be merged into the new body and it would be supported by a new council of chief constables. There would be a radical overhaul of the qualifications for entry into the service to widen the range of potential applicants; a transformation of the culture and provision of police training; and a new approach to the development of careers for the future strategic leaders of the service. Those recommendations are timely and arguably overdue. They focus mainly on structure and process, and the intention is clearly that changes in culture and dynamics will follow when the new arrangements are in place. The report has less to say about what those changes would be, except in relation to women and members of minority groups, or about the wider social and political context (apart from a reference to the 'Big Society'). Nor does it say much about the relationships between the police and other criminal justice services or other agencies in the public, private or voluntary sectors. Whatever changes are made there will be a close connection between confidence in police and the fear of crime; and confidence in police will depend ultimately on the quality of their day-to-day encounters with the public (Skogan, 1994). Generally good relations can be seriously damaged by a single bad experience.

Police and crime commissioners

This chapter was written at a time when the Police Reform and Social Responsibility Bill was still before Parliament, and on the assumption that its radical and controversial proposals for elected police and crime commissioners will become law in some form, despite their rejection by the House of Lords in May 2011.

The consultation paper argued that the public:

> [...] do not know how to influence the way policing is delivered in their community, let alone get involved.... Police and Crime Commissioners ... will be powerful representatives of the public leading the fight against crime and ASB [antisocial behaviour]. They will ensure that:
> * the public can better hold police and senior officers to account;
> * there is greater engagement in policing both in terms of priority setting and active citizenship;
> * there is greater public – rather than Whitehall – ownership of force performance; and
> * the public have someone 'on their side' in the fight against crime and ASB. (Home Office, 2010, p 10)

The government claims that police will become more accountable and more responsive to the public and their local communities and there will no longer be a 'democratic deficit'. The public will in turn come to feel a greater sense of 'ownership' for their local police force and become more ready not only to cooperate with the police but also to develop a stronger sense of responsibility for taking their own action to prevent crime and deal with some instances of anti-social behaviour when it is possible and appropriate to do so. Members of the public would therefore take part in the 'co-production' of policing, perhaps doing things that the police would otherwise have to do at greater cost, through schemes such as neighbourhood watch; or, more questionably because open to misuse, by being more active in reporting suspicious persons and situations or providing intelligence. In a more positive form of co-production, although in the language of a business model, both offenders and victims could be seen as 'service users' and the knowledge and experience of both could be drawn on to improve the quality of the service the police provide and also to encourage the wider involvement of other citizens (Longstaff, 2011).

On some subjects the consultation paper contained very little detail, or said that the government would consider them later. Commissioners and criminal justice agencies will be statutorily required to work with one another so as to provide an efficient and effective criminal justice system in the police area. At the time of writing, it was not yet clear what responsibilities or authority commissioners are to have for functions not directly performed by the police; what powers or duties they might have in relation to private security companies; how commissioners can ensure that they can effectively represent, and be seen as representing, minority, disadvantaged and marginalised groups and individuals; and which police functions might come to be performed by the private or voluntary sector or by communities or individuals themselves.

Much will depend on the environment in which the changes take effect, and on the interests and motivation of those who put themselves forward for election as commissioners. They may see it as one step in a political career, perhaps leading eventually to government office; as an opportunity for service to their communities, perhaps after a career in the police service itself; or as a means of gaining some local reputation and status. The most obvious danger is of a form of politicisation in which policing would become subject to populist competition between parties or to the 'tyranny of the majority', or where the media had inappropriate influence or relationships, so that professional decision making and police independence become undermined (Jones, 2008; Blair, 2009, p 288). That would be the opposite of what the government intends, but there are no actual checks to prevent it.

Difficulties could arise if a commissioner represented a party different from the national government, especially if the commissioner used his position as a platform from which to attack the government or where a commissioner intervened to demand the use of water cannon or plastic bullets (for example) as a political response to a situation where the police judged that they were not operationally justified. Or the situation might become one where political accountability to a ruling party displaced the important principle of legal accountability to the courts and the rule of law, discussed earlier in this chapter. It is not clear how much influence police and crime panels will have on commissioners or chief constables, or more generally; how their influence will be used; or how panels will in practice be composed. Their role and legitimacy may prove to be as significant as those of elected commissioners.

Other concerns were less widely discussed. As the consultation paper recognises, the commissioner would have to take account of national demands and priorities, and of policing interests that extend beyond the force area. That might be difficult for a commissioner elected on what might be a narrow platform of promoting the electors' local interests. There is potential for conflict between an elected commissioner, with a local democratic mandate, and the new National Crime Agency with its authority to 'undertake tasking and coordination of the police and other law enforcement agencies to ensure networks of organised criminals are disrupted and prevented from operating' (Home Office, 2011, p 5). A commissioner could certainly be a prominent public figure in the force area, but it is not obvious that a single person, whether or not elected, would necessarily be seen as accessible and responsive to local concerns or as ensuring 'greater public ownership of force performance', especially if he or she were a representative of a political party that many people might not support. Candidates in an election might exaggerate the local problem of crime, so increasing the public's fear of crime and reducing their sense of security. A commissioner elected on a low turnout, with the votes of only a small proportion of the electorate, might lack credibility or even legitimacy.

Issues of 'engagement' and 'ownership' arise in practice at a very local level and it is hard to see how a commissioner could make much difference to communities' sense of 'empowerment' at that level. A review of the evidence on public confidence in the police has shown the importance of engaging with communities at local level, of interventions that are adapted to local areas, and sometimes of changes in the organisational culture of the police if they are to take local engagement seriously (Rix at al, 2009).

Perhaps more than any other public service, the police must be seen as equally available and accessible to all sections of the population, to minority or marginalised groups as well as to the articulate middle class. With or without elected commissioners, police must be able to engage with communities in the widest sense if they are to have authority or legitimacy (see chapter one), and serious attention should be given to the skills, relationships and mechanisms that enable them to do so. Democracy is about more than elections, and success in an election will not provide that authority or legitimacy on its own.

Policing in the future

The future direction of policing will depend on the interaction between the government's reforms; the financial and economic pressures both on the police and on others with whom they work – local authorities, other statutory services, voluntary organisations; and on the leadership and culture of the police themselves. It could be affected by the threat of terrorism or events such as deaths that could be attributed to failures in police practice or organisation; or to social unrest, from whatever cause, resulting in public lack of confidence in the police service. Arguments for structural change above force level – amalgamations or new formations at national level, perhaps with more specialised operational capacity – may again be heard.

Issues such as terrorism, serious and organised crime and anti-social behaviour are well recognised and receive constant attention. Police and government have given less attention to preventive work among young people or to the relationship between young people and the police (Longstaff, 2011). Increasing tension has arisen from the policing of protests and demonstrations, involving young people and sometimes their parents who do not normally have much contact with the police and who do not fit the stereotype of 'trouble makers' and 'criminals' – labels the police may apply to those they think of as their 'opponents'. In a different part of the social spectrum, gangs of young people can present a serious threat to other people and to their own members, and it can be hard for police or their own communities to judge how best to deal with them. From one perspective, the issue may be one of intelligence, that is, information shared freely between the police and other services and agencies including schools and hospitals, or information obtained by the use of undercover agents.[9] From another perspective, it may be one of police culture and leadership and of the need for better mutual understanding. Crucially, it is about the accessibility and legitimacy of the police and of respect for the law, as Neyroud (2011) recognised in his report.

Pressure to achieve economies will almost inevitably lead to changes in police practice – to reductions in some types of activity and withdrawal from others. Whether, where or how the police might be replaced are still open questions. Some activities may be transferred to the private sector or to voluntary and community organisations; others might be left to citizens and communities themselves. The pattern,

---

[9] Use of undercover agents is a practice that came under severe criticism early in 2011 because of abuse and failures of accountability.

and certainly the capacity, of voluntary organisations and communities will be different in different places – see the discussion of outsourcing in chapter nine.

Whatever the intentions of government, commissioners and the police themselves, police will have to respond to the public's expectations if they are to keep the public's confidence and their own authority and credibility. That should not mean agreeing to whatever the public want, even if it were possible to do so, but establishing good communications and a relationship of mutual trust. Police have been working on those for several years, but they will be more important than ever in the period to come. There may need to be a clearer understanding of what police should and should not be expected to do and how they should do it. Like the idea of justice itself, policing needs 'public reasoning and government by discussion'– see chapter one – and places where that discussion can take place – see chapter nine.

There may be a temptation for police to withdraw to their core tasks and concentrate on their crime-fighting role, and to be impatient of demands from 'undeserving' groups or the distractions caused by complaints and law suits. Events such as the riots in August 2011 may increase that temptation, and some of the language of the consultation paper may seem to encourage a movement of that kind. That would, however, be the opposite of what the government has previously said it intends, and of what it proposed in the consultation paper's discussion of communities.

Neither the government nor the police service as a whole seems at present to have a coherent vision of policing that goes beyond responses to changing circumstances and immediate situations. The most positive influences are likely to come not from government or academics or think-tanks but from the leadership, culture and professional standards of the police themselves. These may come to be transformed as a result of structural changes such as those that Neyroud has recommended. Much will depend on whether the new institutions, and the service itself, is inward looking and wholly preoccupied with immediate responses to pressures and events, or whether they can engage positively with civil society, other public services and government. This, in turn, will depend on the service's readiness and skills to work in partnership with others, observing but when necessary overcoming professional and organisational boundaries, and respecting differences of culture and outlook; and on its integrity in resisting inappropriate pressures from the media or self-interested politicians at national or local level. Future relations between the public and the police also require the ability of the country as a whole to achieve a public understanding of situations where the criminal justice process should and should not be engaged, and of the nature and use of out-of-court disposals. Police will need to be fully prepared to anticipate, prevent and control any further riots of the kind which took place in August, 2011. For that they will need adequate numbers of officers and suitable equipment, but intelligence, the trust of local communities, and proportionate, sensitive and effective methods will be no less important.

SEVEN

Community sentences and desistance from crime

Community-based interventions and sentences provide opportunities for applying the constructive, encouraging and enabling principles advocated in this book. Supervision of offenders in the community has traditionally fallen to probation services and the youth offending services of local authorities. This chapter therefore looks at shared aspects of these two public sector services. Although probation and youth justice have separate histories, infrastructures and bodies of professional and academic expertise, they both have their roots in social work and what has been called 'penal welfarism' (Garland, 2001), and they have each relied on a similar practice model for working with those under their supervision. The evidence base on their effectiveness is also linked. During the past 30 years, seismic changes have altered their governance, their statutory purpose and, therefore, their professional priorities and working culture.

A detailed account would need to have regard to differences in the legislative and organisational structures and the distinct histories of probation (Raynor and Vanstone, 2007) and youth justice (Morgan and Newburn, 2007), but, in the context of community responses to crime, it is worth bringing both services together in order to consider valuable common ground, particularly as they relate to shared concerns for promoting welfare, social inclusion and rehabilitation. Even though in recent decades these public sector community services have been politicised and driven by 'the neo-liberal legalistic ethos of responsibility and punishment' (Muncie and Hughes, 2002, p 1), there is research evidence to suggest that most practitioners in these services are still motivated by an ethic of care, and they continue to attract people who want to help people (Burnett and Appleton, 2004; Annison et al, 2008).

The way they were

In their former capacity as branches of social work, probation and youth offending services applied a welfare model of service delivery. Although engaged in tackling 'social problems' for the benefit of the broader society, they were primarily focused on looking after the interests and wellbeing of those they saw as their caseload – and termed 'clients'.[1] The traditional model of working with offenders in the community was through a one-to-one relationship that combined mentoring with monitoring, and practical help to them and their families with casework, to support the psychosocial development of the person (Burnett, 2004a). This relational model, and the subsequent 'work with offenders', relied on respectful, friendly or warm interaction, and the willing cooperation of the service user (Burnett and McNeill, 2005). Although supervision of those who had offended was imposed through a court order, in the case of probation orders and juvenile supervision orders, the client was offered support that they could decline.[2] For a period, 'after-care' for those leaving prison and not subject to licence was offered, as a matter of course, on a voluntary basis.

Care and control

The tension between the 'care and control' (or mentoring and monitoring) elements of supervision was an accepted characteristic of probation work. Practitioners were 'officers of the court', as were social workers with court duties. This dual role was well summarised by the influential Morison report, which specified that 'the probation officer's prime concern is with the well-being of an individual, but he is also the agent of a system concerned with the protection of society' (Home Office, 1962, p 23). The same report defined casework as 'the creation and utilisation for the benefit of an individual who needs help with personal problems, of a relationship between himself [sic] and a trained social worker' (Home Office, 1962, p 24). Such casework addressed the problems that the individual and their families themselves presented, in discussion with the practitioner, as reasons for their offending and barriers to more settled, fulfilling lives.

Obvious advantages of this service model are that it *works with* the person towards their goals; it is swimming with the tide of their intentions, and so is far more likely to gain their compliance than an arrangement that has punishment or public protection as its central purpose. At its best, probation and youth work was a combination of

---

[1] This terminology was influenced by the language of psychotherapy and solicitors, rather than by commerce where the concept of 'client' conforms to a business or customer model, but it does suggest that the practitioner was representing the interests of the individual as opposed to the interests of the community, or both.

[2] In practice, they were unlikely to do so because the alternative may have been a custodial sentence or, in the case of a juvenile, being taken into care, but this entry into an agreed arrangement set the tone for the relationship that followed.

personalised life counselling and connecting people to the services, treatment and resources that they needed to sort out their problems and to move on from anti-social behaviour to more socially acceptable, happier lives. People referred to probation and social services were themselves seen as victims of social inequalities or psychological problems – statistically, they were, and still are, likely to be from impoverished backgrounds and to have been brought up in less favourable and perhaps abusive conditions – and for all but the most uncooperative the emphasis was on providing some of the support or opportunities they had previously lacked. For those sentenced to supervision in the community, the concept of punishment was very understated, if mentioned at all.

Effectiveness and accountability

A common failing was that casework was carried out in a one-to-one vacuum, without formal partnership arrangements for calling on other resources or services to address the structural disadvantages, and largely without reference to a shared body of reliable professional knowledge on what is effective in rehabilitation. Without such access, more attention was given to changing the person, getting them to change their circumstances and hoping for good fortune to arise. Practitioners drew on an eclectic mix of techniques, theories, religious beliefs and homespun philosophies (Raynor, 1985; Raynor et al, 1994). The plan of work, or what much later came to be called the 'sentence plan', was largely a matter for the discretion of the officer, under the supervision of senior officers who encouraged a 'you know what's best for your client' approach. There was little accountability, and minimal central inspection from the Home Office.[3] Even in the 1990s, when partnerships with other services and group programmes were becoming increasingly available, there were wide variations, from one practitioner to another and from one area to another, in the content of casework that the individual service users received, such as whether it was focused on office interviews, home visits to the family, or referral to services and opportunities in the community (Burnett, 1996).

It is a moot point whether traditional practice was effective in reducing offending. Practitioners believed that they did help to rehabilitate those they supervised, but there was an absence of evidence

---

[3] Inspection reports up to the early 1980s read more like 'social enquiry reports' (later called 'pre-sentence reports') on the chief probation officer and sometimes other senior staff than a report on the service's performance.

to demonstrate this (Raynor et al, 1994). Belief that law-breaking tendencies could be changed by criminal justice interventions peaked in the 1960s but declined in the 1970s and 1980s, when 'nothing works' became the prevailing orthodoxy. Another factor in a backlash against the rehabilitative enterprise was a sense of injustice that different sentences could be imposed for the same crime, and justified on welfare grounds. The 'justice model' (dubbed 'just deserts'), based on sentences that are proportional to the wrong done rather than subject to arbitrary variation, became the primary rationale for sentencing in the 1991 Criminal Justice Act, but with an emphasis on alternatives to custody.

One of the criticisms made against youth justice and probation practitioners was that they focused on improving welfare while neglecting to address the offending behaviour, and sometimes seeming to excuse it (Audit Commission, 1989, 1996; Home Office, 1997). Whether or not probation was an effective means of reducing recidivism has not always been central to the work of the probation service; at various times in its history, more emphasis has been placed on providing help. The specified mission of probation officers for a sustained period of the service's history was to 'advise, assist and befriend' offenders. Later on, concerns that the treatment model was ineffective and led to injustices through disproportionate periods of supervision gave rise to the 'non-treatment paradigm' (Bottoms and McWilliams, 1979), which reframed probation work as a collaboration between the worker and the offender aimed at providing help with problems defined by the offender. In youth justice, the main responsibility prior to the reforms following the 1998 Crime and Disorder Act was to look after the welfare of children and young people who had come into conflict with the law.

When, for the first time, the probation service was given an official statement of national operations and purpose (SNOP)[4] (Home Office, 1984), it marked the beginning of a sustained period of review and readjustment in which the service was required to be more accountable and to provide evidence of its effectiveness. Questions about the value and achievements of the service came from both outside and within. A report by the Audit Commission (1989) called into question the efficiency and cost-effectiveness of the probation service, and similar criticisms were raised in respect of youth justice services in the report *Misspent Youth* (Audit Commission, 1996). There was little by way of evidence to suggest that community sentences led to lower reconviction

---

[4] The introduction of SNOP came to be seen as the beginning of central Home Office direction for probation services. Until then, the movement had actually been in the other direction, to give services more autonomy over things like senior appointments.

rates than custodial penalties, and the few studies that had been conducted showed disappointing outcomes.

Faith in rehabilitation was gradually revived from the late 1980s, following new evidence that some interventions may be effective if appropriately implemented. By the last decade of the 20th century, rehabilitation had renewed credibility and legitimacy. The Home Office in 1998 launched its own 'What Works?' agenda, otherwise known as the Effective Practice Initiative. Funding was allocated from the Crime Reduction Programme to develop a range of 'pathfinder' programmes, including cognitive behavioural programmes, for general offending behaviour, domestic violence, sexual offending and substance abuse. These were followed by resettlement pathfinders for short-term prisoners, and pathfinders concerned with basic skills provision, unemployment, the needs of women who offend and enhanced community punishment orders. Probation services were invited to develop pilot versions of group work programmes that were reviewed by a panel of experts and, if up to standard, given accreditation.

The re-formed probation and youth justice services

Around the turn of the millennium both services were overhauled via separate, but conceptually and chronologically close, acts of legislation. With regard to youth justice, the 1998 Crime and Disorder Act required all local authorities with social services and education responsibilities to replace their social services youth justice teams with multi-agency youth offending teams, subsequently known as YOTs, bringing together social workers, probation, police, health and education staff. The Act specified that all those working in the youth justice system would work to the overriding aim of preventing offending by children and young people. The Youth Justice Board was also introduced to monitor the performance of the 155 YOTs set up in England and Wales. In 2001, the 54 independent probation services in England and Wales were reorganised to form one service, under a central directorate. The resulting National Probation Service was firmly identified in policy documents as a 'law enforcement agency delivering community punishments' (Wallis, 2001). Both services were thus uprooted from their social work, welfare-oriented backgrounds and replanted into a law and order framework. That might have been a suitable time to consolidate and develop the changes that had been made.

Other major changes followed. Just two years after the establishment of the National Probation Service in England and Wales, the report of the Correctional Services review, *Managing Offenders, Reducing Crime* (Carter, 2003) proposed that the probation service and the prison service should be restructured into a new National Offender Management Service (NOMS). This was launched in 2004. The creation of NOMS reified an idea to merge the services that had been mooted for some time, with the prospect of the probation service ceasing to exist (Nellis, 2004). Instead, it was retained as a distinct public sector service, alongside the prison service, with both as part of NOMS. Service delivery models were introduced with a view to integrating custodial and community elements of sentences (so-called 'seamless sentences') and integrating the work of both services (termed 'end-to-end management') – see Hough et al (2006) for critical analysis of these developments. This was followed by the 2007 Offender Management Act, which gave the Secretary of State the power to make arrangements for the provision of probation services, selecting from competitive bids across a range of providers in the public, private and voluntary sectors (and referred to, inelegantly, as the 'contestability' of services – see chapter nine).

Changes too far

All of these developments were further incremental changes in what has been a sustained and gradual paradigm shift *towards* punishing and managing people who have offended and *away from* caring and helping. There is a general consensus among academic commentators that these so-called reforms have been damaging, misguided and a waste of public money, and that successive governments have been over-responsive to simplistic and sometimes erroneous interpretations of public opinion.

With regard to youth justice, several authoritative critiques of contemporary shifts in penal policy have pointed to detrimental aspects of these developments. Youth justice policy especially is seen as deeply flawed. For critics of the 'new youth justice' in England and Wales, its 'defining hallmark ... is a new punitiveness' (Goldson and Muncie, 2006, p 92) that has insufficient regard to children's human rights and the 'material realities of poverty and inequality' (p 102). The new measures introduced by the 1998 Crime and Disorder Act and subsequent legislation were seen as evidence of 'American-inspired "institutionalised intolerance" towards those under age 18' (Muncie, 2008, p 109), particularly the abolition of the presumption of *doli incapax*[5] for those aged 10 to 14, the targeting of pre-criminal disorder and incivility, and the introduction of parenting programmes. The huge increase in the number of children being detained in the juvenile secure estate, and the move away from cautioning to final warnings and prosecution, reflect a devaluing of what is in the best interests of the child and other principles that formerly shaped decisions.

With regard to probation, numerous critics have pointed out that the National Probation Directorate was over-ambitious and over-zealous in its adoption of the accredited cognitive behavioural programmes, and its pursuit of high targets and strict enforcement standards (Merrington and Stanley, 2000; Hedderman and Hough, 2004; Mair, 2004). The then Chief Inspector of Probation, Professor Rod Morgan (2003), went as far as to describe some aspects of the process as indicating 'programme fetishism' or a policy of putting too many 'eggs in one basket'. The early evaluations of the community-based programmes had less-than-encouraging findings (Hollin et al, 2004; Roberts, 2004). High numbers of people referred to the programmes either did not commence or did not complete them; this leaves open the possibility that those who completed them and whose offending was reduced were different in some way from those who did not and therefore might have made the same progress with or without the programme.

Raynor and Robinson (2005, p 132) note that critical criminology has tended to dismiss the What Works? movement in Britain as coercive and reductionist, but without having regard to the more nuanced debates and evidence surrounding effective rehabilitation. The real story, they argue, is more complicated:

> The last ten years have seen a mixture of successes and failures and an even larger volume of inconclusive outcomes: the process of judging what is working, what is promising and what would be better abandoned will continue for years, and conclusions drawn at this point are necessarily provisional. However, our own provisional conclusion at this stage would be that the 'What Works' movement in Britain tried to move too fast too soon: the correctional services, under considerable political pressure, tried to do

---

[5] There had been a rebuttable presumption that a child under 14 was not capable of committing a criminal offence (*doli incapax*). For a prosecution to succeed, there had to be evidence to show that the child 'knew what he/she was doing'. It was not usually difficult to produce such evidence and the presumption no longer served any useful purpose or made any practical difference. Its abolition did, however, have great symbolic significance.

many of the right things but were often not able to do them in the right way.

They add that the probation service seems likely to have to pay the price.

The repeated restructuring of the probation service has led to change-fatigue and demoralisation (Robinson and Burnett, 2007). Initially, the probation service had welcomed evidence-based policy. As noted by Judy McKnight (2009, p 328), a leading figure in Napo:[6] 'the Probation Service stood to gain from such an approach. All the evidence showed that the Service was successful; that it had itself learnt the lessons of "what works."' But, looking back, that movement and the associated injection of funding to set up accredited programmes is viewed, more cynically, as an appeal to punitive populism:

> It transpired that New Labour did not literally mean 'what works', for example in reducing reoffending. They meant 'what works' in appeasing the views that emerged from a simplistic interpretation of focus groups, even if those views meant increasing prison numbers further and meant playing down the success and effectiveness of probation, toughening up its image and its language. (McKnight, 2009, p 328)

The story is one of an over-politicisation of crime and justice policy and misuses of research by government, counterproductive aspects of managerialism, and the excessive and unwarranted use of custodial sentences. Law and order politics, in which successive governments have been over-responsive to simplistic and sometimes erroneous interpretations of public opinion, has driven a febrile agenda, which itself needs to be brought under control (Loader and Sparks, 2010). It might be argued, however, that the punitive intentions of the policy shifts have been overstated (Matthews, 2005) and that positive aspects of the reforms should be acknowledged too.

For better or worse?

The legislation for services to work in partnership, to make crime and justice the responsibility of all public sector services, and to involve other sectors could be regarded as a positive development. Although multi-agency collaborations had featured in a series of crime prevention

---

[6] Napo is the professional union for the probation service.

initiatives since at least the mid-1980s (for example, Crawford, 1994; Liddle and Gelsthorpe, 1994), the Labour government continued the trend of previous government to promote a mixed-economy service provision, and with a strong emphasis on harnessing the potential of the third sector (Pycroft and Gough, 2010). This promised better prospects for shared responsibility within communities for tackling neighbourhood problems associated with offending and for supporting reparation by, and the social inclusion of, former offenders.

One of the hopes for the joined-up approach in youth justice was that it would provide better and quicker access to the educational and employment opportunities that they had lacked and to the mental health or substance abuse services that they needed (Burnett and Appleton, 2004). Similarly, there was some optimistic anticipation that these comprehensive partnership arrangements in youth justice would provide a positive example for adult community penalties (Bottoms et al, 2001; Faulkner, 2006). Adam Crawford (1999, p 511) suggested that the emergence of Crime and Disorder Regional Partnerships might provide 'fertile soil in which a more progressive criminal justice policy, one which turns away from the punitive populism of recent years, could begin to establish itself and flourish'. Such partnerships were an example of a trend towards involving the 'local state' and civil society in a significant role in the regulation of crime and anti-social behaviour (Matthews, 2009, p 351).

The introduction of the pathfinder programmes as part of a national action plan for reducing reoffending (SEU, 2002; Home Office, 2004) meant that there would be a broader range of high-quality interventions to be drawn on in a holistic approach to rehabilitation that fully recognises the multiple social as well as individual factors in crime. Also, whatever it did wrongly, the investment in rehabilitation helped focus the minds of probation officers and prison staff on 'the concepts and methods of evidence-based effective practice, a situation which would have been unthinkable only ten years ago' (Raynor and Robinson, 2005). While evidence-based practice has been sullied by its association with managerialism and false hype about effectiveness, it did provide a needed challenge for those less skilled and less industrious practitioners who hid neglectful or inappropriate practice behind the respected screen of officer autonomy.

These potentially positive developments unfortunately have not been used primarily for rehabilitation in the sense of efforts to lead better lives, but essentially for risk management and public protection. The major reforms of the probation and youth justice services were driven by political and economic factors, and the ends of saving money and gaining public confidence ran contrary to the goals of helping individuals lead more fulfilled and law-abiding lives. In particular, the popular appeal of punishing offenders and erring on the side of public protection created some tensions between the steps to achieve those ends and factors that best serve rehabilitative ends, such as giving the offender the benefit of any doubt and opportunities to remain in the community. The very tools that were intended to enhance professionalism and inform the quality of transformative work with offenders (see, for example, Roberts et al, 1996), instead have, in a climate of risk management and increased workloads, served to undermine skilled casework and have resulted in over-defensive assessments by practitioners who are too busy to get to know those they supervise (Fitzgibbon, 2007). The effect is an inflation of risk estimates leading to more 'revolving-door' prison sentences and social exclusion.

Taken to extremes, the techniques of managerialism are not compatible with the time, flexibility and interpersonal skills needed to assist desistance. They have the effect of automating practices that previously involved discretion and professional reflexivity. Some commentators have characterised the results as 'korrectional karaoke' (Pitts, 2001) and the 'McDonaldisation' of practice (Oldfield, 1994), with tasks broken down into mechanised processes that can be performed without thought. Such an approach is the antithesis of the sensitivity and ingenuity required to respond to the complex realities of the people they supervise. As Rob Canton has observed (2007, p 236), work with offenders 'is a morally significant activity and not reducible to techniques of effectiveness'.

It is some consolation, therefore, that a strong practice culture may result in practitioners finding ways of working around new policies that militate against their values and the purposes that drew them to the profession they joined. As found in numerous studies that focus on practitioners and how policies are activated 'on the ground', directives from the centre can be mediated or resisted (McAra, 2004) and the 'translation of policy into practice depends on how it is visioned and reworked (or made to work) by those empowered to put it into practice' (Muncie, 2005, p 54). Such a dynamic was observed in a study of the implementation of policies to move youth justice away from social work culture (Burnett and Appleton, 2004). Youth justice workers were keenly aware of the revised goal to focus on reducing offending, but in their day-to-day practice continued to prioritise the welfare of supervisees, thus conforming to the observation of John Muncie (2005, p 55) that: 'A social work ethic of "supporting young people" may well subvert any partnership or national attempt simply to responsibilise the young offender.' Recent research shows that a wish to help people deal with their problems and lead better lives still motivates recruits into the public sector criminal justice services (see, for example, Annison et al, 2008).

Alternative models for achieving rehabilitation

In the light of disappointing results from evidence-based programmes and the limitations of experimental criminology – see section on 'The revival of rehabilitation' in chapter three – increasing attention is being paid to 'theoretically engaged descriptive criminology' (Hough, 2010, p 14). This means that, beyond the accredited programmes that were adopted for mainstream rehabilitative practice and beyond the risks-needs-responsivity paradigm, several alternative bodies of research are now informing contemporary rehabilitative practice. These include psychotherapy and counselling, desistance from crime, therapeutic jurisprudence and procedural justice. They are separate bodies of research, each with their own leaders and following, but there is increasingly a convergence between them, experts within each area having identified insights and applications that cross over and have relevance with their own (for example, Wexler, 2001; Birgden, 2004; McGuire, 2003; McNeill et al, 2005; Ward and Maruna, 2007).

In common, they point to the importance of the subjectivity of offenders and what the interventions mean to them; of relationships and *how* people are treated as distinct from what sentences they get; of strengths-based perspectives that focus on the positives in what people can and could do; and of natural change processes attributable to factors outside the 'treatment', 'intervention' or 'court sentence' and that might occur as part of psychological development or by engaging the support of family and community networks, and through collaborations and restorative processes.

Psychotherapy and the common factors model

Research in psychotherapy has led to a long-term debate on whether any specific method of intervention or technical approach is more effective than another in bringing about change, or whether positive outcomes can be attributed to some common factors; this is known as the 'specificity versus commonality' debate (Hubble et al, 1999; Wampold, 2001). A recurring finding in comparative studies is that no method is any more effective than the rest, and, instead, it is the common processes that apply to all and the so-called extra-therapeutic factors that are primarily responsible for bringing about change.

The common processes in question include therapist style – with accurate empathy, respect, warmth and genuineness being shown to be critically important – and the resulting 'working alliance' (in psychotherapy, the 'therapeutic alliance') through which a bond is formed and agreement reached on the goals and tasks. An aspect of this is that it is person-centred: it looks at the relevant issues from the person's own perspective and it is concerned with them holistically rather than being restricted to the problem that brought them into therapy or under supervision. The skill of the practitioner and something radiating from them, as well as the approach taken, is crucial in engaging someone in the change process and gaining their confidence. As observed by Andrew Bridges (2011, p 1), the recently retired Chief Inspector of Probation, there are people in probation and youth offending work who stand out as having 'what it takes to *influence other people for the better* through the way that they talk with them and listen to them' (emphasis in original).

That 'therapist factor' elicits and interacts with the equally crucial 'client factors' in his or her response to the proposed programme of work: motivation, abilities, sense of purpose and expectation of a positive outcome. Also, the milieu and ethos in which contact takes place has long been identified as critical to outcome, whether coldly businesslike or one that is conducive to 'healing' (Frank, 1961). The same conversation and instructions will be received differently in a bureaucratic risk-management context than would be the case in a more friendly context in which the personal improvement and wellbeing of the individual is valued, even if not the object of the meeting. According to Lambert and Barley (2002), who carried out an extensive overview of studies that distinguished these 'common factors' variables, 30 per cent of client improvement is attributable to such variables in contrast to 15 per cent attributed to the specific procedures and techniques used.

Such common processes can be readily identified as applicable in the helping professions more broadly, including medicine, skills training and education, and also in work with offenders. An extra challenge for the latter, though, is that they are involuntary clients. A good working alliance can override this, but in the context of enforcement is harder to achieve and sustain. Offenders, as noted by Marshall and Serran (2004, p 315), are typically a 'difficult population to work with at least partly because they are often defensive and oppositional'. Compared with many psychotherapy patients, they are also likely to have suffered from social inequalities that require wider solutions. Beyond the common processes within treatment, *extra*-therapeutic factors have been identified as having an even greater effect – 40 per cent in Lambert and Barley's survey. These include everything that applies outside the framework and delivery of the treatment, not least service users' economic and material circumstances, their skills and individual differences, their cultural and developmental needs, and the opportunities and misfortunes that arise for them.

Desistance from crime

What happens beyond or 'outside' of the criminal justice system is one of the starting points for desistance research. Its core assumptions are that offending behaviour is typically linked to a stage during youth from which individuals move on, with or without intervention from the criminal justice system, but that 'growing out of it' is usually a gradual process rather than a decisive moment, and getting to that point may involve relapses because of difficulties faced and related ambivalence (Burnett, 2004b).

Desistance research has advanced understanding of how repeat offenders eventually stop, and the processes involved in the interplay between subjective variables and structural variables (Maruna, 2001; Farrall, 2002; Giordano et al, 2002; Laub and Sampson, 2003). Giving up crime is the combined outcome of developing maturity, transitions in life to employment, lasting relationships and other attachments to society, and changes in how a person makes sense of who they are and what is important to them. A useful distinction is made between 'primary' and 'secondary' desistance to differentiate those who have paused their offending from those whose non-offending is accompanied by 'the role or identity of a "changed person"' (Maruna et al, 2004, p 274).

Because desistance theory sees the process of giving up offending as belonging to the offender, it shifts the emphasis away from 'what works to what helps' (Ward and Maruna, 2007, p 12). This significantly changes the nature of supervision – from imposing programmes on people as objects, to working alongside them as subjects of their own activities and intentions. Thus, 'desistance is the process that offender management exists to promote and support' and 'approaches to intervention should be embedded in understandings of desistance' (McNeill, 2006, p 55).

A desistance-focused approach will place less emphasis on needs and deficits, or at least will balance attention on these with a focus on abilities and potential to lead a more rewarding life. Such strengths-based approaches are also restorative, concerned with what the ex-offender can contribute to his or her family and community, and how their life can become useful and purposeful. The most systematically developed strengths-based approach is probably the Good Lives Model developed by Tony Ward and his colleagues (Ward and Stewart, 2003; Ward and Maruna, 2007). This emphasises working with offenders in ways that support their own efforts to attain, by legitimate means, the 'primary human goods' that all people crave: 'experiences, activities, or states of affairs that are strongly associated with well-being and higher levels of personal satisfaction and social functioning' (Ward and Maruna, 2007, p 21).

As well as Shadd Maruna (Maruna, 2001; Ward and Maruna, 2007), desistance researcher Fergus McNeill has been particularly helpful in developing an understanding of how this body of work can be applied in reducing reoffending, in developing appropriate practitioner skills (McNeill et al, 2005) and in a strengths-based, restorative framework (McNeill, 2006, pp 56-7):

> Practice under the desistance paradigm would certainly accommodate intervention to meet needs, reduce risks and (especially) to develop and exploit strengths, but whatever these forms might be they would be subordinated to a more broadly conceived role in working out, on an individual basis, how the desistance process might best be prompted and supported. This would require the worker to act as an advocate providing a conduit to social capital as well as a 'treatment' provider building human capital. Moreover, rather than being about the technical management of programmes and the disciplinary management of orders, as the current term 'offender manager' unhelpfully implies, the forms of engagement required by the paradigm would re-instate and place a high premium on collaboration and involvement in the process of co-designing interventions. Critically, such interventions would not be concerned solely with the prevention of further offending; they would be equally concerned with constructively addressing the harms caused by crime by encouraging offenders to make good through restorative processes and community service (in the broadest sense).

In setting out this restorative framework, McNeill also argues that enabling ex-offenders to participate and be included in society is not only a means by which they can make amends and perhaps begin to perceive themselves in different prosocial ways, but is also a way in which some amends can be made to them. In the context of the social inequalities and exclusion that contribute reasons for offending, there is a moral requirement for a 'rights-based approach to rehabilitation which entails both that the offender makes good to society and that, where injustice has been suffered by the offender, society makes good to the offender' (2006, p 56).

Therapeutic jurisprudence, procedural justice and legitimacy

The strengths-based, positive psychological principles that characterise desistance theory are shared by a cluster of approaches within what Susan Daicoff (2006) has termed the 'comprehensive law movement'. These include 'therapeutic jurisprudence' and 'procedural justice', and 'problem solving courts' and 'restorative justice'. Therapeutic jurisprudence was developed by David Wexler and Bruce Winick (1996) and is best exemplified by the problem-solving courts movement (referred to in chapter five). Tom Tyler's research on procedural justice has focused on people's perceptions of fairness and legitimacy (Tyler, 2006a, 2009; see also chapter one).

Therapeutic jurisprudence is the 'study of the role of the law as a therapeutic agent' focusing on the 'law's impact on emotional life and psychological well-being' (Wexler and Winick, 1996, p xvii). Initially concerned with the effects of legal practices in the mental health field, it is now more broadly concerned with the rehabilitative outcomes of legal decisions, rules and roles. Implicit is the idea that judges and magistrates and other legal actors can be part of the solution, or indeed part of the problem (Wexler, 2001), and that an 'ethic of care' and procedures with an eye to the defendant's reintegration needs can contribute to therapeutic outcomes, while still maintaining the integrity of other legal values such as due process and justice.

Procedural justice theory is similarly concerned with people's experiences in legal settings, particularly their perceptions of fairness and their trust in authorities, which in turn rests on how they are treated – whether with respect and whether they are given a voice, for example. A central concept of 'procedural justice' theory is 'legitimacy', which, as Tyler (2006b, p 375) explains, is

> a psychological property of an authority, institution, or social
> arrangement that leads those connected to it to believe that
> it is appropriate, proper, and just. Because of legitimacy,
> people feel that they ought to defer to decisions and rules,
> following them voluntarily out of obligation rather than
> out of fear of punishment or anticipation of reward.

In short, it is 'the belief that authorities, institutions, and social arrangements are appropriate, proper, and just' (Tyler, 2006b, p 376; see also chapter one, this volume).

Thus, people abide by decisions if they feel they are morally appropriate and if they accord with their sense of what is fair. This applies in all professional and personal relationships they have, when others make requirements of them that may be onerous or that are not of obvious benefit to them. They are more likely to go along with a directive or request if they trust the person imposing it and if they feel obligated to them in return for decent or kind treatment. Research into experiences of probation has shown how probationers make more effort to comply with the requirements of their order and the suggestions of their probation officer when a relationship of trust and helpfulness has been established (Rex, 1999; Burnett, 2004a).

Where next for community-based practice?

Probation and youth justice services are once again at a crossroads. It would be heartening to see them secure a more prominent and appreciated place in criminal justice, with renewed professional status now that their training requirements have been further revised. After years of being criticised by politicians, Nick Clegg, as Liberal Democrat home affairs spokesman, called for the probation service to be 'cherished, not undermined' (Foreword in Napo, 2007). With regard to youth justice services Frances Done, present Chair of the Youth Justice Board (YJB), claims there has been 'real progress, over the last few years, in significantly reducing the numbers of first-time entrants to the youth justice system, reducing the frequency of reoffending and dramatically reducing the numbers of young people in custody – and at the same time making custody safer and more effective'.[7] However, the deep budget cuts determined in the October 2010 Spending Review, the intended absorption of the YJB into the Ministry of Justice and the replacement

---

[7] Statement on the future of the YJB made by Frances Done on 4 October 2010. Source: www.yjb.gov.uk/en-gb/News/futureoftheYJB.htm

of the director of the probation service by a director of NOMS are all indications of further diminishment of these services. It seems likely that they will become increasingly invisible within the multi-agency, multi-sector mix for responding to anti-social and criminal behaviour.

At its best, traditional one-to-one support was task-focused and problem-solving, and it was strengths-based and steered by a working alliance and action plan for steps towards the person's prosocial goals. Also at best, there were local partnership arrangements and teams of volunteers who provided support, and, although it was too much a matter of chance and individual persuasive powers, probation officers could call on the goodwill of local services and employers to provide opportunities for cooperative clients. Some recent trends therefore have a striking resemblance to that older model – although, in the context of contemporary criminal justice, the engagement of the third sector is set to be more prominent and organised, funds permitting. Professional bodies naturally object to the new commissioning arrangements on the grounds that members' jobs are at stake and a reasonable fear is that services will be commissioned from substandard providers on the basis of cost considerations. An optimistic view is that this opens up the prospect of creative, re-energised provision that will, through competition, push up standards.

Promising projects during a time of austerity

The clearest and most obvious insights from research as well as the experience of practitioners are as follows:

- Moving from a criminal past to a law-abiding future can be best assisted by a combination of personal support and assistance to access services.
- The most effective change agents are the offenders (and ex-offenders) themselves. That is, personal change comes from within and interventions can only work if the recipients perceive them positively and want to take advantage of them.
- Therefore it is necessary to engage the volition and motivation of offenders;[8] and to build up their confidence in their own ability to achieve and sustain a law-abiding lifestyle.

---

[8] At various points in this book we have avoided using the label 'offender', in an effort to practise what we preach about the self-fulfilling effects of continuing to identify a person by their status as an offender. We appreciate though that where practitioners and others are also being discussed, its omission may result in a lack of clarity. This section seems to be a case in point.

- This in turn will depend on whether offenders' basic needs, at least, can be met, and a network of support services or pathways to access them will be important.
- Change also takes effort and perseverance and a willingness to learn necessary skills and make necessary adjustments to behaviour.
- Some of this may be difficult or against offenders' immediate wishes, and their willingness to be directed and sometimes challenged by a key worker will depend on their perceptions of the legitimacy of the sentence and the service, and whether a collaborative working alliance has been established, which in turn will depend on whether they have been treated with respect as persons with needs and potential.
- A service that is available on an optional basis may be best placed to secure initial engagement, although it could complement a court order or post prison licence. More importantly, the integration or reintegration of ex-offenders into the community is more likely to succeed with a service that is problem-solving and empowering as opposed to one that is essentially surveilling and controlling.

Two recent projects that seem to capture the mix of elements highlighted here are the Transition to Adulthood (T2A) programme funded by the Barrow Cadbury Trust (T2A Alliance, 2009; Burnett and Hanley Santos, 2011) and the London Youth Reducing Reoffending Programme – also known as the Daedalus project (Ipsos Mori, 2010).

The T2A programme includes three pilots projects and an alliance of organisations with the purpose of developing and promoting better provision for 'young adults' in the criminal justice system, recognising that this is a stage in life when the adjustments and passages in the life-course are at their most challenging and when those already involved in offending are at risk of becoming the most prolific. The pilots were set up in three areas, with a dual function: to demonstrate effective work with young adults at risk, and to explore and promote strategies for bridging the gaps between services and ensure joined-up provision for young adults. Early results have been positive.

The T2A workers (called transitional workers, or community engagement workers) act as mentors and 'brokers'. The contact is optional on the part of the service user, and the meetings are focused on an 'action plan', determined mainly by the service user but with the agreement of their worker, to help them improve their situation and behaviour. The emphasis is on linking the service user to resources and opportunities in the community and on 'being there' for them to provide advice and support during times of crisis. One of the pilots employs mainly ex-offenders to work with service users. All of the teams engage volunteers to act as mentors.

The T2A pilots have also demonstrated some different ways in which voluntary sector services can be engaged in mainstream services. One of the pilots is based in a probation service and employs its own staff as transitional workers, but staff work closely with a local consortium of voluntary sector organisations as well as other partners in order to refer the young adults to the openings they need. Two of the pilots are led, very successfully, by voluntary sector services, but it is expensive to sustain dedicated T2A teams and, like all voluntary sector organisations, they face a precarious future in the present funding environment. In an interesting development, the YSS, which developed one of the pilots, has been selected by West Mercia Probation Trust to be its 'preferred partner'. In this arrangement, its role will be to work with the probation service to commission services from other local third sector providers, and to develop the 'capability and capacity of local voluntary organisations to create innovative solutions to working with offenders'.[9]

The London Youth Reducing Reoffending Programme (Daedalus)[10] has some similarities to the T2A programme. It is a multi-agency project, led by the youth charity Rathbone[11] to support the resettlement of young people during and following custodial sentences. The young people are allocated a 'resettlement broker' while they are still in Feltham Young Offender Institution, to support them before and after release in their efforts to turn their lives around. It is funded by the London Development Agency and European Social Fund (in contracts to a total of £9 million until May 2012) and other agencies involved are Nacro, St Giles Trust, Catch 22, Serco and London Probation Trust. It is the first 'payment by results' programme to address resettlement and reducing reoffending. Not surprisingly, therefore, it is described in terms of 'outputs' (starting the project; initial entry into education, training and employment) and 'outcomes' (remaining in sustainable education, training and employment for a minimum of six months). The initial findings focus on the service users' perspectives of the project and are reported to be positive (Ipsos Mori, 2010).

Both these projects are concerned with supporting young people through difficult 'transitions', a concept that features increasingly in

---

[9] www.westmerciaprobation.org.uk

[10] Also referred to as LYRRP and with sub-projects called Heron and Inspire, reflecting its multiple facets and partners.

[11] www.rathboneuk.org

policy and academic discourse. There are various points where people need to make a transition from one life stage to another, or from one institutional context to another, and may struggle to make that transition because of the obstacles they face and thus become more vulnerable to involvement in offending. In criminal justice, transition points suggest a way of focusing scarce resources.

Questions might reasonably be raised about the extent to which it is right to provide help for offenders in circumstances where they might be at a disadvantage, such as help in finding a job or housing, when non-offenders in similar circumstances would equally benefit from such support. Different conceptions of justice, as discussed in chapter one, raise different priorities for consideration here. Following the egalitarian principles of Rawls (1971), it would be appropriate to provide additional opportunities and resources for people who have greater need, irrespective of their past. Applying virtue-based arguments, on the other hand (MacIntyre, [1981] 2007; Sandel, 2009), it might be argued that impoverished *non*-offenders are the more 'deserving poor' and ought therefore to be privileged over people who have offended if resources are scarce. On a case-by-case basis (for example, one job, two applicants), it would be understandable for desert or reliability (the likelihood of a further offence) to be a decisive factor, as well as other factors to be taken into account in assessing merit and need. As a basis for policy, the same principles of humanity, and the same ethic of care, should extend to all; from a consequentialist perspective, the benefits for all are greater if policies have the effect of enabling desistance and so reducing the number of future victims.[12]

Conclusion: rehabilitation with a difference

David Garland (2001, p 8), writing at the beginning of the century, observed that 'rehabilitation programmes no longer claim to express the overarching ideology of the system, nor even to be the leading purpose of any penal measure'. Instead, the 'rehabilitative possibilities of criminal justice measures are routinely subordinated to other penal goals, particularly retribution, incapacitation and the management of risk' (p 8). The encouraging messages from recent research and collaborative projects indicate that it would be appropriate to have

---

[12] Many would argue that the tension in each of these perspectives could be overridden in the long term by policies that decrease the gap between the rich and the poor, thus reducing the need and stress arising from both absolute and relative poverty (Wilkinson and Pickett, 2009).

a renewed focus on rehabilitation (as the so-called 'rehabilitation revolution' seemed to promise), but under a new name and with some critical differences.

The overview of theoretical frameworks and practice discussed in this chapter brings into prominence the importance of interpersonal relationships, of people's own understandings and their personal agency in the process of change, and of criminal justice professionals and others as agents of change. The implications of these for supervision in the community are as follows:

- The professional relationship that staff have with 'offenders' is paramount. That was enshrined in the long-standing mission statement of the probation service, 'to advise, assist and befriend', and is consistently reiterated by practitioners to be of utmost value (Burnett and McNeill, 2005), but it has had to be rediscovered by policy makers, in so far as it was sidelined by a focus on group programmes. Desistance research, therapeutic jurisprudence and legitimacy concepts have contributed to raising the profile of this relational aspect of the work.
- There needs to be the right balance between interventions to change people and mobilising resources to change their social circumstances. Although sentences must follow the principle of proportionality, the appropriate elements of community supervision should be determined and adjusted on a case-by-case basis. Again, this can only be done if practitioners have the time and interest to get to know the individual and their circumstances.
- The willing engagement of service users in interventions should not be underestimated. Listening to the user's perspective, and inviting their own agenda for action, are also prerequisites for engaging them in the process of change.
- People are responsive to someone who cares about their interests and believes in their potential, whereas they may feel discouraged and demoralised by someone preoccupied by management targets and the risk they pose. The phenomenon of improved behaviour in response to the high expectations of others – or the converse – referred to variously as the Pygmalion effect, the looking-glass self, labelling effects and self-fulfilling prophesy effects, is empirically supported by experimental psychology and psychotherapy research, and equally has relevance to the reintegration of former offenders (Maruna et al, 2004).

Criminal justice workers therefore matter. In turn, their own confidence and morale is affected by the way they are perceived and valued in society. Their ability to deal appropriately with the multiple problems and chaotic lives that often correlate with offending requires discretion and good judgement and in-depth understanding informed by high level professional training.

Most important of all is the personal agency and self-determination of the individual. Where social behaviour is concerned, it is at the level of the individual's response that interventions work. The person agrees to engage and, importantly, applies their efforts because what is offered is in their interests, and is helping them deal with their situation and move towards their – legitimate – goals. The most effective interventions will engage and sustain individuals' own efforts through inclusion and encouragement, and enabling the choice to lead more socially acceptable lives. Community supervision of offenders by statutory criminal justice services perhaps took a wrong turn (even if for the right reasons) when the notion of punishment in the community took precedence over rehabilitation, and control replaced the concept of care. As the Aesop fable The Wind and Sun (cited at the beginning of the book) so vividly symbolises, getting someone to change an aspect of themselves is more readily achieved by engaging their volition.

EIGHT

Prisons: security, rehabilitation and humanity

Discussion about prisons sometimes reveals, but often conceals, a deep-seated difference in attitude towards people who break the law and receive sentences of imprisonment. The difference is between those who are sympathetic to their plight and those who are not; that is, between those who see prisoners as fellow citizens who have erred but are capable of change and who are still entitled to decent, humane treatment and help when they need it,[1] and those who see them as a distinct class of people – 'criminals' – who have forfeited all such claims and have no place in 'our' society.[2] In practice, the differences in perspective can usually be resolved or ignored when there is a job to be done, but they sometimes emerge in a form where reconciliation seems difficult or impossible. In this chapter, we review the present situation in English and Welsh prisons and recent and current proposals for reform. We then argue for a parallel agenda that we hope will help to resolve some of the differences, by focusing on relationships and on the themes of citizenship, community and legitimacy discussed in previous chapters.

---

[1] As Catherine Appleton (2010, p 208) found in her study of discretionary lifers, 'even those who have committed some of the gravest crimes are capable of, and do, change'. See also the discussion in the Introduction, present volume, on different perceptions of human nature.

[2] An example is the dispute over whether prisoners should have the right to vote in parliamentary elections. For some people, the answer is obvious – prisoners are still people and human beings, they are still citizens of this country and if it is practicable for them to vote, they should be permitted to do so. To allow that is an affirmation of their status and an indication that they are expected to take a responsible place in society after their release. To others it seems outrageous – prisoners have by their offence forfeited any right to a place in society or to any influence on its decisions or institutions. It is a pity that the debate on prisoners voting in the House of Commons on 10 February 2011 had very little to do with the merits of the case and was more about the jurisdiction of the European Court of Human Rights and the rule of law as it applies to government.

English and Welsh prisons today

Prisons in England and Wales have been on the verge of crisis for as long as anyone can remember. Overcrowding was already a problem in the late 1950s, when the white paper *Penal Practice in the Changing Society* (Home Office, 1959) announced the first programme of new prison building since the end of the 19th century. It reached a point of crisis at various times, for example in 1987 (see chapter two), again in 2007 and most recently after the riots in August, 2011, but the prison service has so far always managed to pull through without drastic measures such as the wholesale release of prisoners. No one now expects overcrowding and the demands it makes on staff and inmates to be anything but a normal part of prison life, with other priorities being subordinated to it.[3]

Safety and security

Prisons have to be safe and secure. Crises of safety and security have occurred at various times – for example, disturbances by prisoners and escapes by notorious prisoners. Both can do great damage to the confidence and reputation of the prison service. Disturbances include those at Gartree in 1978, Wormwood Scrubs in 1979 and, most seriously, those at Manchester and other prisons in 1990, which led to the Woolf report (1991). Escapes include most dramatically that of George Blake from Wormwood Scrubs in 1966, which led to the Mountbatten report (Home Office, 1966, discussed later), and further escapes in the early 1990s that led to a series of reviews culminating in the Learmont report (1995) and the dismissal of the director-general of the prison service Derek Lewis. All those events had a profound effect on prison staff, and on prisoners themselves, which continued for years afterwards. Disturbances still occur from time to time, for example at Ford in January 2011, but not on the scale of some of those in the past, and there has been no escape from inside a secure prison for some time. That is an important achievement.

In day-to-day life, keeping prisons safe and secure and accommodating prisoners in establishments that are appropriate to their security classification must inevitably be key priorities for prison staff. Once those priorities have been met, whatever capacity is left can be used to keep prisoners usefully occupied – with work, education and

---

[3] The old standard of Certified Normal Accommodation with one prisoner to a cell has given way to 'operating capacity', in which two prisoners sharing a cell is the norm.

courses designed to help towards their resettlement and reduce their likelihood of reoffending. Activity is not, however, an optional extra: safety, security and control depend on a sufficient level of activity to provide a safe environment. The achievement is to reach the end of the day with everything done that has to be done and the prisoners safely in their cells. A good inspection report or a good performance rating will be a welcome bonus and reward for hard work; it will also protect the prison from market testing (discussed later). Even so, that is a limited ambition for anyone who hopes that prisons might do more than minimise future harm, to society or to prisoners themselves, as well as punishing or trying to repair the harm that has already been caused to victims and offenders themselves.

Achievements and continuing concerns

For the most part, the prison service docs the basic things very well indeed. Anne Owers (2010, p 8) said in her valedictory lecture as HM Inspector of Prisons:

> Over the last nine years there is no doubt that prisons have become better places – better able to keep prisoners safe, provide a decent environment, offer some purposeful activity and provide some resettlement opportunities.

Even so, she acknowledged that progress has been patchy and precarious and gains can too easily be lost through changes of staff or circumstances (prisons are especially dependent on the personality of the governor). She found that the best prisons, usually open or resettlement prisons, are outward-focused, using release on temporary licence to allow suitable prisoners to do voluntary or paid work and making links with employers and voluntary agencies. Concerns remain over subjects such as suicides and self-injury; provision for those suffering from mental health problems; the position of women and young offenders, especially children; treatment for the misuse of drugs and alcohol; and the situation in high security prisons where prisoners with very long sentences are detained, including terrorists and leaders of criminal gangs.

Special problems arise from the large number of prisoners now serving indeterminate sentences (see chapter five), with the consequence that they will not be released until they are deemed 'safe' and it is certain that they will not commit further offences. No such guarantee can ever be given, but prison staff and the Parole Board are made to feel as if it will be seen as 'their fault' if such a prisoner does reoffend;

they are reluctant to take risks accordingly, and the prisoner may be detained indefinitely. That situation is indefensible in terms of humanity, fairness and legitimacy. This is partly a result of the development and promotion of risk assessment tools whereby policymakers, practitioners and politicians may be seduced by the purported accuracy of such methods, but it also reflects the political and managerial culture in which the prison service now operates. Putting aside the well-documented problems with such approaches to risk assessment, there seems to have been far less consideration of the fairness or justice involved in decision making based on such forms of risk assessment (Towl, 2004).

Pressures and their consequences

Overcrowding and the pressure of numbers are a constant drag on the system's capacity and capabilities. The prison population almost doubled between 1993 and 2010, and was over 87,000 at the time of going to press. Expenditure on prisons increased by nearly 40 per cent in real terms between 2003-04 and 2008-09, or from £2.52 billion to £3.98 billion a year. Even so, the lack of activity for prisoners is still a chronic problem, with too many of them spending too much time without any constructive occupation, whether it be work, education or attendance at courses. There are often no activities for prisoners at weekends. The usual problems are poor management exacerbated by a lack of funding to pay for instructors, teachers and equipment and lack of staff to provide supervision. Those problems are likely to continue and become more intense with reductions in prisons' budgets.

Prisons are rightly averse to taking risks with safety or security, but the institutionalised instinct of staff when placed under pressure or challenged is to look first to the interests of the institution as they see them. This can be a problem if staff find that institutional compliance conflicts with appropriate professional standards. The 'best prisoners' are deemed to be, not those most likely to rebuild their lives after release and benefit from support in doing so, but those who conform to the prison's customs and expectations and do not bring themselves to notice. Rehabilitation[4] and resettlement are seen as a matter of prisoners attending and completing courses, giving the right answers to questions, and enabling staff to

---

[4] The word 'rehabilitation' implies the, generally, dubious assumption that a prisoner can reclaim or re-establish a stability and lifestyle which many have never in fact experienced.

tick the right boxes.[5] The measurement of such courses tends to be characterised by an overreliance on psychometric data. With a few exceptions, such as the therapeutic community at Grendon (Genders and Player, 1995; Stevens, forthcoming) and open and resettlement prisons – and despite the spread of behaviour change programmes – prison regimes are not, for the most part, about helping prisoners genuinely to change their attitudes, outlook or motivation, and still less about helping to create an environment in which prisoners can be enabled to make progress when they are back in the community. This is not to say that individual prison officers, psychologists, programme leaders and so forth are not intent on genuine change: such efforts obviously vary with the individual. But the predominant culture in prisons is driven by considerations other than rehabilitation.

Life in prison

The day-to-day interactions between staff and prisoners, and among prisoners themselves, are among the most important constituents of prison life (Liebling et al, 2011). They can be occasions for reassurance and encouragement, but also for humiliation in many ways.[6] The effect is often unintended or unexpected, although the action itself may be deliberate. The arrangements for reception into prison and for visits, the handling of requests and applications, and the nature and fairness of disciplinary proceedings are obvious examples. So are the ways in which prisoners are able to be 'themselves' – the possessions they are allowed to have with them, the clothes they wear, the food they eat, the kinds of conversation they can have with staff and with each other. The relationships between prisoners and staff and their potentially abusive nature are reflected in everyday language in prison – for example, prisoners *refuse* and governors *decline*. Such terminology reflects power relationships rather than real behavioural differences (Towl, 2010).

Prisons are often isolated institutions, geographically and socially. They are functionally connected with other services and those who supply goods to the prison, but have few connections with the communities in which they are located. Names of new prisons have even been chosen so that they will not be associated with neighbouring towns or villages. Staff may socialise more with their

---

[5] Based on personal communication with Graham Towl, former Head of Psychology for prisons and probation services.

[6] See, for example, Dexter and Towl (1995), who found that routine rituals of humiliation were meted out to suicidal prisoners.

own colleagues than with others who have different backgrounds and occupations. Prison staff are used to holding themselves a bit apart from others and in their working lives they do not always take easily to partnerships with other agencies unless they are on their own terms. The institutional reluctance to join in partnerships and make contacts with communities may be reduced as the composition of prison staff becomes more diverse: about 70 per cent of the direct entrants to the Accelerated Promotion Scheme for prison governors over the past 10 years have been women. Even so, women – and, still more, members of minority ethnic groups – are underrepresented at the highest levels of the organisation.

Prison service culture

It is as difficult to generalise about the culture of the Prison Service, as it is about that of the police (see chapter six). Values and attitudes will vary depending on background, professional role, experiences and ideology. They are different for governors, prison officers and other prison staff (Liebling, 2004). Contrasting 'stories' are told from different perspectives – those of government, prison governors, prison officers and academic observers. They have been the subject of a revealing and significant study by Crewe and Liebling (2011), which shows how governors' values have evolved over a number of years in response to the changing demands on prison staff. The most obvious demands are those presented by the need for greater security, with more prisoners with a history of violence serving very long sentences; the changing character and the increasing size and diversity of the prison population; a demanding and restless workforce; and more insistent political demands of ministers.

Optimism and disillusion

Until the 1950s and early 1960s, the leaders of the prison service believed that the service could change people's lives through a 'welfarist' process of assessment and treatment (Garland, 2001; see also chapter seven), especially in borstals[7] but also in training and open prisons.

---

[7] Borstal institutions and the sentence of borstal training were formally established by the 1907 Prevention of Crime Act for young offenders aged 15-21 (for a time 15-23) for whom the courts thought there was some prospect of reform. They were modelled on the English public school system, with houses, house masters and matrons, and for many years they were considered a great success, due partly to their selective intake. Staff wore plain clothes. Following the 1982 Criminal Justice Act, borstals,

They presented that belief to the service and to the world in a spirit of confident liberal humanism. Charismatic leaders among prison commissioners and prison governors were admired, and inspired young men and some young women to join the service with the promise of a career in which they could help people and 'make a difference'. The reality, as it was experienced by most prisoners and staff, was very different. Crewe and Liebling found that some of those who joined the service at that time were appalled by the collusion, self-deception and sometimes abuse of power that they found. Even as late as the 1980s, women's prisons and female staff were treated as a less important service.

Disillusion set in, as it did for other aspects of criminal justice as described in chapter two. The escape of George Blake from Wormwood Scrubs in 1966, and the Mountbatten review (Home Office, 1966) that followed, were a traumatic experience for the prison staff and their leaders at the time. The demoralisation of senior managers and greater assertiveness on the part of prison officers and the Prison Officers' Association led to a period of anxiety and instability that continued until the 1990s. In that situation, liberal humanitarians came to be seen as, and perhaps often were, bad managers, and they lost credibility and respect. The earlier belief in prisoners' welfare and rehabilitation gave way to an insistence on security, order and control, and the service became increasingly aware of its need for a confident and watchful style of management, and a 'credo of management' (Rutherford 1993), with efficiency as an end rather than a means, came to dominate. In the changed ethos, the service came increasingly to value 'operational experience'[8] above qualities such as imagination or originality, and because of the special demands, pressures and risks associated with prisons it tended to regard itself as different from other public services. It was not inclined to look for ideas from outside the organisation. Responsibility for welfare and preparations for release was assigned to probation officers seconded from the probation service, to the resentment of many prison officers, with important and arguably damaging consequences for the way in which prison officers saw their work.[9]

---

youth custody centres and then young offenders' institutions lost any special character and identity. The special priority that was once given to young adults has gone and the age group that once enjoyed the privilege of borstal training (as it was sometimes seen) is now arguably the most neglected in the prison system.

[8] The distinction between 'operational' and 'non-operational' staff in prisons seems in effect to be between governors and prison officers on the one hand and other members of staff on the other.

[9] David Faulkner's personal recollection from the time.

Attitudes and beliefs

From the 1970s onwards, people were selected for governor grades more for their ability as managers than for their interest in changing prisoners' lives. They had liberal views on equal opportunities, sexuality and race relations, but they attached more importance to performance and efficiency, and to fairness, due process and objectivity, than to care or compassion. As in politics and other areas of criminal justice, 'liberal' was not a description they wanted to accept. They were not inclined to be sympathetic towards prisoners, and they were sceptical about how far people were capable of changing. They were more comfortable than their predecessors would have been with the view that prisons should be places of punishment. As Crewe and Liebling (2011) put it, they had been 'socialised in a period where the most fundamental questions about what prisons are for have become subordinate to questions about how best to manage them' (p 192).

Since the late 1960s, there has been a deep sense of scepticism, within and outside the prison service, about the extent to which prison sentences can have more than a marginal effect in changing a person's future life and behaviour for the better. There is evidence to support this scepticism in consistently high rates of reoffending among former prisoners. Some penal reformers have been reluctant to acknowledge the possibility that prison might ever be rehabilitative for fear that it would encourage even higher rates of imprisonment, while a few have dismissed aspirations towards a 'benign prison' as a persistent myth (Carlen, 2002, p 78). From the opposite perspective, some people think that prisoners are simply not worth the attention that a serious attempt at rehabilitation would involve.

The May Committee (Home Office, 1979) thought that the organisational aspiration should be 'positive custody', while King and Morgan (1980) thought it should be 'humane containment'; both took a sceptical view of the scope for rehabilitation. In spite of encouragement from Sir Stephen Tumim as HM Chief Inspector of Prisons, the prison service was too preoccupied with immediate concerns over security to pay much attention to rehabilitation until the mid-1990s.

Attempts at prison reform

Until the 1990s, governments' attempts to reform prisons were mostly in response to operational crises – escapes, disturbances, industrial action by prison staff. They were variously focused on security (the

Mountbatten report [Home Office, 1966] and a series of related reports); and the structure and management of the organisation (the May committee [Home Office, 1979]). The Woolf report (Woolf, 1991), occasioned by the disturbances at Manchester and other prisons in 1990, was unusual in arguing not only for improvements in prison conditions and the treatment of prisoners, but also that prison reform should be considered in the wider context of criminal justice as a whole including sentencing. Those reports, and especially the Woolf report, brought some necessary and welcome changes. Equally significant reforms during that period were, from the present authors' perspective, the creation of the positions of 'HM Chief Inspector of Prisons' and 'Prisons Ombudsman';[10] the reform of adjudications to provide for more procedural justice in dealing with offences against prison discipline; the relaxation of restrictions on prisoners' correspondence; allowing prisoners access to telephones; and the growth in the number and range of charities working with prisoners and their families inside and outside prisons. An important influence was the emphasis on 'decency', promoted by successive directors–general and the Prisons Inspectorate, which resonated with academic work on legitimacy and humanity in prisons (Sparks et al, 1996; see also chapter one).

Management and market testing

The prison service was subjected to the same managerial pressure as other public services – the Financial Management Initiative and the demands for economy, efficiency, effectiveness in the 1980s; the service's establishment as an executive agency, nominally at 'arm's length' from ministers, in 1991; and New Public Management, with its array of performance measures and indicators in the 1990s (see chapters three and nine). The formation of the National Offender Management Service followed in 2004, bringing further changes in the organisation at headquarters and in the intermediate structure between headquarters and establishments (Hough et al, 2006; see also chapter seven). The prison service was less affected than the probation service, perhaps because it was more successful in resisting the changes, but they still led to a period of uncertainty and instability.

Market testing and the contracting out of prisons to the private sector were politically controversial when they were first proposed in the 1980s, and they were understandably opposed by members of the

---

[10] The title changed to 'Prisons and Probation Ombudsman', and the role expanded, soon after the establishment of the National Probation Service in 2001.

prison staff. Contracting out of prisons and prison services is now more or less accepted in this country and not much is heard of the earlier objections, for example that prisons should not as a matter of principle be run for private profit and that a 'market' in prisons would provide a commercial incentive and therefore political pressure for an increase in the use of imprisonment.[11] A comparison between public and private prisons by the National Audit Office (2003) concluded, however, that no general verdict was possible on whether one could be regarded as better than the other. Effects on public prisons have included a slightly greater readiness on the part of the Prisoner Officers' Association to accept lower levels of staffing, and a constant search for economies by governors and others, while private prisons have been more innovative in matters such as recruitment and the use of technology and in developing constructive relationships between staff and prisoners.

A more recent study (Crewe et al, 2011; Liebling et al, 2011) found significant differences in the way in which staff in public and private sector prisons used their power and authority. Broadly speaking, those in private sector prisons maintained good relationships but showed weaknesses in control, organisation and consistency; those in public sector prisons were confident and knowledgeable, delivering regimes that were safer and more reliable, but uniformed staff were more jaded and cynical than those in the private sector and this limited the levels of care and humanity that prisoners received. There were, however, differences between prisons in each sector. The study concluded that it is difficult to say whether private sector prisons are 'better' or 'worse' than those in the public sector, but the issue raises profound questions about the role of the state in punishment, the difference between privatisation's effects on quality and quantity, and the role, identity and status of the prison officer.

Prison programmes to reduce offending

The Labour government gave a new impetus to rehabilitation and the reduction of reoffending when it came into office in 1997 and made substantial new funds available both for research and for new programmes, as described in chapter three. The practical, operational and sceptical culture of the modern prison service, the procedures

---

[11] The Supreme Court of Israel has decided to prohibit private operation and management on the grounds that it is constitutionally unlawful and permits a potential violation of human rights (Liebling et al, 2011).

and disciplines of New Public Management (see chapters three and nine), and the political aims of the new government fitted well together. The key to success in reducing reoffending was thought to be found in courses or interventions based on psychological approaches, bolstered by international evidence of their effectiveness, and typically cognitive-behavioural in their methods. The belief in scientific (or more accurately technological) approaches resembled in some respects the situation 40 years before, as described in chapter two.

Between 2000 and 2005, the number of the service's psychological staff was increased from 400 to 1,000 to design and deliver the new courses that aimed to reduce reoffending. The government's intention, across government as a whole, was that policy should be based on 'what works' and should emphasise not only inputs and outputs, but also outcomes or results where measurement was more difficult. In the event, efficiency prevailed at the expense of effectiveness. Consistently with the techniques of New Public Management, efficiency could be judged by measuring inputs (such as the number of courses provided or the number of prisoners taking part in them) against key performance indicators. The programmes themselves were 'manualised', that is to say, staff followed standard sets of instructions and ticked boxes as requirements were satisfied or procedures completed. Outcomes – the effects particular courses might have had on the progress of particular individuals – were more difficult to measure and less attention was given to them.

The enthusiasm for such programmes and the zeal with which they were 'delivered' contributed to the 'dumbing down' of much psychological practice (Towl, 2004; Crighton and Towl, 2008). That was not just a matter of technical skills, but was also about the core of psychologists' professional and ethical conduct as independent practitioners. One significant problem was that the programmes were too prescriptive and did not allow the use of sufficient professional judgement. There was something Orwellian about the language associated with them, for example, 'treatment integrity', dosage' and 'criminogenic factors'. Such language can imply a level of understanding of criminal behaviour and a degree of scientific accuracy that goes beyond the evidence.

Prison staff can claim some success in reducing reoffending, but it is hard to attribute that success to any particular course or intervention by the prison service, or to distinguish between the effect of interventions while the prisoner is in custody, of those made by the probation service after release, and of other events in a person's life that may have had no connection with their treatment by either service. Structured interventions, to be effective, need to be tightly targeted in terms of time and place and appropriateness in terms of offenders' characteristics. These factors may in turn feed into any impact studies on efficacy, so that it is unclear whether it is the approach itself that is or is not effective or the policy and operational arrangements for the implementation of the work.

There was perhaps too much reliance on international evidence and some small-scale studies in the United Kingdom to justify so large an investment in programmes that were expensive and ultimately proved ineffective. There was, however, a close fit both with managerialism and with the political needs of the time. Inputs could be clearly measured. Something could be 'seen to be being done'. Professional and political interests may have prevailed over the lack of evidence.

Preparing prisoners for their return to the community

The top-down reforms of prison service organisation and internal practice were easier to implement than the less structured but equally important arrangements to promote greater collaboration between services and more responsive provision that government and practitioners realised were essential to support the resettlement of prisoners and if significant improvements in reoffending rates were to be achieved. The Bradley report (2009) on people with mental health problems or learning disabilities has already been mentioned in chapter four. The report of the Social Exclusion Unit (SEU, 2002) on reoffending by ex-prisoners identified the lack of a unified rehabilitation strategy in addressing factors associated with reoffending, particularly those relevant to the rehabilitation of certain groups – women, young adults, black and minority ethnic groups and remand prisoners. It recommended that there should be a long-term, wide-ranging National Rehabilitation Strategy involving a cross-government approach to meeting resettlement needs including improved access to housing, healthcare, benefits, employment, education and training.

A House of Commons Home Affairs Committee (2005) inquiry into prisoners' rehabilitation endorsed the SEU findings and focused particularly on provision to help released prisoners access accommodation and employment as the best way of ensuring their rehabilitation. Criticisms included too much time in cells and non-purposeful activity, inconsistency of provision across the prison estate and inadequate provision for those with mental illness, unconvicted prisoners and 18- to 21-year-olds. For resettlement, it recommended greater use of day-release schemes for gaining work experience, and identification of labour shortages and skills gaps in the external labour market to be matched with vocational training and work programmes in prisons. For prison regimes, it recommended greater use of therapeutic communities (following the Grendon model) and a community approach (developing close ties between prisons and local services) to complement 'normalisation' of the prison experience (following a model operated in Sweden) whereby, instead of setting up specialist provision otherwise unavailable to inmates, the task of the prison and probation service should be to facilitate offenders' access to existing services.

The response to those reports has been well intentioned but patchy in its application and effect, and its impetus has been affected by the change of government and cuts in public expenditure. Some recent resettlement projects – for example, the London Youth Reducing Reoffending Programme (Daedalus) and the RESET[12] projects, and the resettlement aspects of the Transition to Adulthood programme (see chapter seven) – do, however, lend hope that a multi-agency approach that combines supportive relationships and that 'brokers' access to accommodation, health services and employment can help to break the revolving-door cycle of offending and prison sentences.

Prisoners trying to make a law-abiding fresh start after release will be liable to fail if they lack the basic materials for settling down, supportive prosocial relationships and viable routes to employment and some of the rewards of 'a good life'. While opportunities are essential, the Home Office Resettlement Pathfinder, which included a social skills programme and cognitive behaviour courses, also revealed the importance of ex-prisoners' own thinking, self-concept and efforts in becoming integrated back into the community (Raynor, 2004; Clancy et al, 2006). A more constructive resettlement policy would draw on the rich body of research on desistance and the termination of 'criminal careers' (e.g. Maruna and Immarigeon, 2004; Farrall et al, 2010) and would include public recognition of the challenges involved, even including rituals of reintegration to acknowledge the change of identity and status (Maruna, 2011).

Terrorism and Muslim prisoners

Prisons must clearly play their part in resisting terrorism. There are two issues – the treatment of the 100 or so prisoners serving sentences for terrorist offences, and the danger that other prisoners might be

---

[12] RESET stands for resettlement, education, support, employment and training.

'radicalised' by influences during their time in prison. Maximum security is obviously needed for prisoners known to be likely to prepare or commit acts of terrorism. For the remainder, a distinction has to be made between manipulative people preying on vulnerable prisoners and getting them to do things they would not otherwise do, and prisoners who find a religious faith – Muslim, Christian or any other – during their time in prison. As in policing – see chapter six – staff should think of Muslim prisoners as part of their prison's community, and not as separate or potentially dangerous. As Nick Hardwick, HM Chief Inspector of Prisons, recently said:[13]

> 'I think it is important not to see Muslim prisoners as some homogeneous group who are all in danger of becoming extremists. What works in terms of preventing radicalisation is what works with the prison population as a whole: running good prisons, expecting people to behave themselves, keep them safe, give them purposeful activity and give them the sort of help they need to resettle and build their lives successfully. There isn't a special, magic solution for Muslim prisoners.'

Prisoners' work in prisons

The green paper *Breaking the Cycle* (Ministry of Justice, 2010a) promises that prisons will become 'places of hard work and industry', along with a renewed emphasis on existing types of intervention such as offending behaviour, drug treatment and violence reduction programmes. Rehabilitative work done in prisons will be followed up through integrated offender management after the prisoner is released. Prisoners will work a full working week of up to 40 hours, and, with the cooperation expected from the private sector, the work done in prisons will generate an income that will be used to pay for prison programmes, support prisoners' families and help compensate victims.

Those promises are ambitious, but they are not essentially different from the aspirations the prison service has held for many years. The problem in the past has been that a working week for prisoners, and the disciplines needed for productive and profitable industry, demand a significant change in a prison's priorities and character. Attempts during the 1970s to establish an 'industrial prison' and to increase the involvement of the private sector had short lives. To succeed, risks will

---

[13] Interviewed on World at One, BBC Radio 4, 7 June 2011.

have to be taken and the obligation to meet the contract has to be placed ahead of the prison's institutional convenience. Officers' shift patterns would have to be altered. Provision would still have to be made for requirements such as exercise and visits, as well as the courses and other activities needed to support the prisoner's resettlement. Pressures on prison capacity are likely to make it difficult to maintain a stable workforce or to provide training for the skilled jobs that might be needed for a profitable industry.

Disappointments with similar interventions in the past should not, however, stand in the way of a programme that should receive general support. The current government's plans have enthusiastic support from the Howard League, although the League's own proposals only envisage that in the long term 'there should be at least two prisons where large numbers of prisoners are engaged in real work with a range of businesses', with further prisons being identified where 'real work can take place' (Howard League for Penal Reform, 2011, p 3). The report recognises that major changes would be needed in organisation, in providing the necessary infrastructure of commercial contracts, and in training or recruiting governors and managers with the necessary skills and commercial and operational independence. Neither the Howard League report nor the government have shown how the profits would be collected and then distributed among the various purposes for which they are intended.

From the present authors' perspective, prison life should certainly include work which approximates, as nearly as possible, to work and working conditions as they are outside. The government's plans in this regard should certainly be supported. That should not, however, be at the expense of the other activities necessary for a well-functioning institution. It is especially important that the work done should be of a quality and the working conditions should be of a standard that enables prisoners to take some pride in what they are doing and obtain some satisfaction from it, but prisoners will also need as many as possible of the other ingredients of a responsible and stable life.

Prisoners as people

Increasing emphasis is rightly being placed, in prisons and in criminal justice more generally, on the need for prisoners and others who have committed offences to take responsibility for what they have done – to admit it, not to put the blame on others, not to make spurious excuses, to understand and acknowledge the pain and damage they have caused, and to make amends to society or the victim in so far as it may be possible to do so. That is important; it seems to be what the public increasingly and appropriately expect; and it is an essential part of restorative justice, as discussed in chapter five.

Responsibility and active citizenship

Taking responsibility should be more than an expression of remorse, however sincere it might be, and it should look forward as well as backwards (Pryor, 2001). Prisoners are effectively deprived of all responsibility once they arrive in prison. They should be encouraged to think and do something about their responsibilities for their own future, for their families, and for taking their place in society after they are released. Equally, there should be opportunities to – and the expectation that prisoners should – take responsibility both for as much as possible of their daily lives in prison, and then for their lives as citizens, with their families, in their communities and at work.

Speaking to the All Party Penal Affairs Group in the House of Commons in 2011, the Archbishop of Canterbury, Dr Rowan Williams,[14] said:

> 'If we lose sight of the notion of the prisoner as a citizen, any number of things follow from that, and are indeed following from that.... The prisoner as citizen is somebody who can on the one hand expect their dignity as a citizen to be factored into what happens to them, and can reasonably expect that penal custody will be something that contributes to, rather than takes away from, their capacity to act to as a citizen in other circumstances. Thus issues around restoration, around responsibility, around developing concepts of empathy and mutuality are all part of what seems me to be a reasonable working out of what it is to regard a prisoner as a citizen.'

Erwin James (2011, p 3), the insightful and articulate former long-term prisoner and now successful writer, has written:

> It is a fallacy that people in prison are content to wallow in a state of irresponsibility just waiting for the day when the gates are opened.... My experience in prison was that, amongst the mixture of chaos and control and the corrosive prison culture, there were indeed pockets of opportunity

---

[14] Available at www.prisonreformtrust.org.uk/PressPolicy/News/vw/1/ItemID/114

from which to gain a sense of positive engagement with others, inside and outside.

Stephen Pryor, a former prison governor, has written (in personal correspondence):

> One of the biggest hurdles is the prisoner perspective which the present system allows and determines. The sentencing and 'prisoning' processes all presume a prisoner who is not competent, not responsible, antisocial and a criminal to the core. The adversarial outcome is of a wholly guilty (or totally innocent) person. The state of imprisonment carries with it the status of prisoner, whether convicted, sentenced, appellant, otherwise competent or not. A prisoner ... comes quickly to accept the role of prisoner so defined. On that basis, and only on that basis, will he or she be able to find safety and meaning in prison.

Time well spent

The Prison Reform Trust has promoted the theme of prisoners as citizens for a number of years, most recently in its important publication *Time Well Spent* (Edgar et al, 2011). The report defines active citizenship as being when prisoners 'exercise responsibility by making a positive contribution to prison life and the wider society' (p 10); to be allowed responsibility is a necessary condition for making a contribution (Burnett and Maruna, 2006). It lists five types of active citizenship roles that are performed at present. Peer support schemes are those where prisoners help and support one another within the prison setting. Community support schemes involve work with or on behalf of other people outside the prison. Examples include those on day release to help in charity shops, and ex-prisoners who provide advice and support other prisoners following their release (Farrant and Levenson, 2002; Boyce et al, 2009). Another example is the partnership schemes between some open prisons and their local Citizens Advice Bureau, whereby prisoners on temporary release can work as volunteer advisers answering requests for information from members of the public (Burnett and Maruna, 2004). In other projects, prisoners take part in restorative justice programmes, where they are encouraged to acknowledge the harm they have caused and to make amends; they can take an active part in prison life, for example through membership of prison councils or other forums; or they can join arts and media projects such as prison-based radio stations or newspapers, or performing arts programmes.

Time Well Spent gives a number of examples and explores the steps that prisons can take to expand the opportunities they provide. It makes four recommendations:

- Government should acknowledge the contribution that volunteering and active citizenship can play in rehabilitation, developing work in prison and the wider concept of the 'Big Society'.
- The prison service should produce and implement quality standards for active citizenship, encouraging prisons to expand on the opportunities available.
- Prisons should do more to involve officers in the development of volunteering and active citizenship.
- Prisons should identify policies that inhibit the exercise of responsibility by prisoners, and revise such policies as required.

Government and the prison service should make these proposals the basis of a serious programme of action as part of their plans for prisons and the rehabilitation revolution.

Women prisoners

The special situation and special needs of women prisoners, and women offenders generally, have long been recognised, but they have been especially difficult for government and the prison service to handle. Well-intentioned efforts to promote equality of treatment and opportunity in the 1970s and 1980s, and for women's prisons to be integrated into the male-dominated regional structure of the rest of the service, may in some respects have added to the difficulty they found. Baroness Corston's review (Corston, 2007) contained some important insights when it argued for (as on the cover of the report): 'The need for a distinct, radically different, visibly-led, strategic, holistic, woman-centred, integrated approach.' Its radical proposals included the creation of small, geographically dispersed, multi-functional custodial centres and a network of community centres offering support in such matters as accommodation, health and life skills. Consistent with the arguments in this volume, it emphasised the themes of decency, community and legitimacy.

The government cautiously agreed with the majority of the report's recommendations (Ministry of Justice, 2008d). Considerable efforts were made and some success was achieved in establishing the community centres, although their future is precarious in view of the current cuts in public expenditure, and custodial centres remain a distant prospect. Some improvements were made, for example to make the searching of women prisoners less humiliating, and new machinery was established for consultation across government departments. Evans and Walklate (2011) point out, however, that while Corston wrote in the language of women, vulnerabilities, harm and troubled lives, the government's response reverted to the language of offenders, diversion from crime and risk to the public. It was written against a presumption of penal populism and its horizon was limited to the criminal justice system.

Prisoners' families

The families, especially the children, of people who are sent to prison are often themselves the 'innocent victims' of the offence. Emotional stress, material deprivation, greater likelihood of poor performance and exclusion from school, and a greater risk of committing offences both at the time and in later life are recognised dangers. Forty-five per cent of prisoners lose contact with their families while they are in prison, and the reoffending rate after one year for those who do is 70% compared with 52% for those who stay in touch.[15] One hundred and sixty thousand children have a parent who is in prison; the boys are three times more likely than other children to become involved in anti-social or delinquent behaviour and are twice as likely to develop behavioural problems. The government promotes and coordinates initiatives to support the families of offenders, and enthusiastic work is done at local level, involving statutory services and voluntary organisations such as the Revolving Doors Agency, St Mungo's and Barnardo's. Action for Prisoners' Families[16] lists 64 national and local charities that work with families, and provides links to their websites. One example is POPS – Partners of Prisoners and Families Support Group – based in Manchester, formed in 1988 and now supporting over 250,000 families a year and employing almost 100 staff and 30 volunteers.[17] Another example is the Thames Valley Partnership whose Family Matters programme[18] coordinates support at local level and offers training and support.

---

[15] www.justice.gov.uk/publications/docs/research-factors-reoffending.pdf

[16] www.actionpf.org.uk/links

[17] www.partnersofprisoners.org.uk

[18] www.thames-valley-partnership.org.uk

Conclusion: reducing the need for prisons?

Opinion is sharply divided between those who think more should be done to help prisoners towards their rehabilitation and resettlement and those who think conditions should remain as they are or be made more punitive. It is, however, clear that the government's plans for prisons and for a 'rehabilitation revolution' depend on two contingencies. One is the willingness and motivation of prisoners to do what is expected of them, both in prison and in the community after their release. The other is the country's acceptance of those who have committed offences as people who should have a place in society where they can become responsible citizens and should be allowed some help in achieving and sustaining it.

The first contingency is a matter for the criminal justice services and the courts and their authority, legitimacy and ability to motivate; the second is a matter for political leadership and civil society. The danger is that a combination of restraints on public expenditure and hostile public and political attitudes will bring about increasingly impoverished conditions and distant relationships between prisoners and staff. The emphasis would be on industrial output rather than the ability to hold down a job after release; on statistical rates of known reoffending rather than genuine rehabilitation; on formal and sometimes unthinking compliance with what are seen as political or managerial expectations; and on appearances to satisfy political and public opinion. All those would be to the detriment of opportunities and motivation for prisoners to rebuild their own lives and help to rebuild the lives of their families. Distant and formalised relationships between prisoners carry the risk that prisoners will increasingly see their identity as prisoners and offenders (or criminals) and react accordingly, forming relationships based on separation from the rest of the world and hostility towards it and sometimes based on ethnicity or religion with the danger of radicalisation. Some practical reconciliation between the opposing points of view is needed if progress is to be made.

NINE

The role of government in criminal justice

The situation in criminal justice is part of a wider context of reforms of the way in which public services and government operate, in Great Britain as a whole but particularly in England. Especially in criminal justice, but also across the whole range of government activity, ministers have for the past 30 years been more active than at any time since the post-war Labour government, both in promoting new policies and legislation and in the day-to-day running of their departments. They have also become more ambitious in what they try to achieve. Chapters two and three described the weight and volume of the reforms that Conservative and Labour governments introduced between 1979 and 2010, the results they achieved and the lessons to be learned from them. Chapter four considered the means of preventing and reducing crime, and chapters five to eight examined some of the current issues for the administration of justice and the management of the criminal justice sector. How these lessons are applied and how these issues are addressed cannot be separated from the government and governance of the country as a whole – the processes by which legislation and policy are formed and put into effect and how services are provided and managed. That is the subject of this chapter.

The current Prime Minister David Cameron has stated that he 'wants one of the great legacies of the government to be the complete modernisation of our public services'.[1] Localisation, new arrangements for commissioning, the position of the House of Lords, and changes in parliamentary procedure are all under discussion. At the time of writing, these changes mainly affect public services such as health, education and those provided by local government, and the proposed reforms consist mainly of cuts in public expenditure, contracting out services to create competition, and allowing the 'Big Society' to take over functions previously performed by publicly funded statutory services. The same approach is being applied to criminal justice, but here the pace of change is slower and the details are less fully developed.

---

[1] www.number10.gov.uk/news/latest-news/2011/01/public-service-reform-2-58857

From 'old' to 'new' public administration

What has been described as the 'old' public administration prevailed in British government and public services from the end of the First World War more or less until the change of government in 1979. Its characteristics included centrally determined rules and guidelines, administered by a strong central bureaucracy; stability in structures and processes; continuity and lifetime careers; and a dominant position for professional specialists and practitioners (Hood, 1991). Across large areas of criminal justice, and of government and public services generally, civil servants and practitioners were aware of ministers in the background; they knew they should not expose them to embarrassment, but they were often able to do their jobs with little contact with ministers or interference from them. Prison governors (though not usually prison officers) and probation officers had quite a lot of scope to go their own way.

Public servants thought of themselves more as performing a function, and as doing so according to the rules and their own professional standards, than as achieving outcomes or results. At least from the end of the Second World War onwards, it could always be expected that new tasks would bring new money and more staff. There was not much encouragement and quite a lot of resistance to doing new things with existing resources. Ministers were usually ready to defer to the judgement of their advisers – their own officials, the professional leaders of the services and professions, and the 'great and the good' whom they appointed to the various committees and advisory bodies.

Traditionally, those with advisory and decision-making roles within the criminal justice system had benefited from the experience, professional wisdom and judgement of individuals both within Whitehall and in what would now be called interest groups and stakeholders; they also had opportunities to consult and agree policies within these forums. This approach included a readiness to make use of Royal Commissions and departmental committees as a means of assembling the best advice and counsel, and of giving credibility and authority to the policies that were based on their reports. It respected and took account of academic research and academic thought. Government departments and public services had a sense of their own history and values, which they thought ministers should value and respect (as they usually did). All public servants were committed to serving the national interest, rather than any party political interest, at least as they saw it.

That approach was, however, slow; its results might be well informed and reflect the best of conventional thinking, but it could be seen as elitist and out of touch with the experience of 'ordinary' people and of women and minorities. Advisers came to be thought of as typically white, middle-class men, remote from the practical world of business and economics and 'everyday life'. That approach was more comfortable with principles and qualities than with numbers and quantities. It did not suit the changing social and economic circumstances of the 1980s and 1990s, or governments in a hurry or bent on radical transformation. It was already coming under criticism from the Labour and Conservative governments of the 1960s and 1970s (Fulton, 1968), and especially from the Conservative government during the 1980s (Ryan, 1999; Loader 2006).

The drive for reform: ministers, politics and the media

The drive to reform public services received a new impetus when the Conservative government came into office in 1979. It had two main features, both of which were later accentuated after the change to the Labour government in 1997. One was much greater activity on the part of ministers, who came under greater pressure to prove themselves to their colleagues (especially the Prime Minister) and to the public and the media. The other was what came to be called 'New Public Management'.

Ministers had lost confidence in their traditional sources of advice and in the professionals who were thought to have been responsible for the decline in the country's economic performance during the 1970s. They were regarded as 'self-seeking service providers' whose interests had to be subordinated to those of the 'customer'. Ministers thought 'they knew best'. They effectively deprived themselves of their traditional sources of wisdom and advice, political judgement was substituted for professional advice; and a new 'elite' emerged composed of political advisers, consultants, commentators and politically aligned think-tanks (Ryan, 1999; Walden, 2000; Oborne, 2007).

Ministers' greater involvement in judgements about how public services should be delivered led to a loss of professional leadership, and the politicisation of large areas of public business. Almost any problem became political, and the need to score or refute political points became more important than the need to resolve the problem itself. Governments claimed that the focus of their policies was on practical outcomes and effective means of achieving them, but their greater concern often seemed to be with appearances and presentation.

The external pressures were also changing. The 'establishment' and the old elites in the professions, the old universities and their networks were no longer so powerful. New demands were coming from new directions – from women's organisations, from a range of minority interest and pressure groups, and from campaigning organisations that often focused on single issues such as animal welfare, the environment or victims' or prisoners' rights. Some of them provoked hostile reactions that ministers also had to take into account. The media, especially newspapers, were under financial pressure and in the competition for readers and advertising their reporting and editorial comment became more critical and sometimes more sensational (Ryan, 2003). The pressures are likely to continue, with new forms of communication and new ways of forming associations and gathering support through the internet that also provide opportunities for government and the services themselves.[2] The combination of localisation, the mass of information that the government is making available, and the government's financial stringency will also create new pressures, the full extent of which is still to appear.

The New Public Management

The term 'New Public Management' (NPM) was coined by Christopher Hood (1991) to refer to the new models of management based on neoliberal economics that were being promoted during the 1980s, especially in Great Britain and the United States. Key elements included (Osborne, 2010, p 3):

- the use of management models taken from the private sector;
- competition, contracts and the construction of 'markets';
- hands-on management, by generalist managers rather than professionals or specialists in the service concerned;
- separating 'operations' from 'policy', and purchasing or commissioning from providing;
- an emphasis on the measurement and control of inputs and outputs, and on performance management and evaluation;
- assessment and management of risk.

The intention was to reduce the influence and discretion of purportedly self-interested service providers and career civil servants; to separate 'purchasing' from 'providing' or 'delivery'; to focus on outcomes rather than process; and to create a 'performance culture' based on rewards

---

[2] For example 'crime mapping' (www.police.uk) or the 'twitter experiment' of Greater Manchester Police mentioned in chapter six.

for success and penalties for failure. The art of government was treated as a branch of management, and management consultants and business people were more valued as sources of advice than career civil servants, practitioners or academics. The process of reform began in earnest under the Thatcher government's Financial Management Initiative and through a series of initiatives such as the creation of 'Next Steps' agencies, privatisation and contracting out. It gathered pace after the Labour government was elected in 1997.

Some aspects of NPM – those to do with setting objectives, quantifying and measuring inputs and outputs, and judging how far the intended outcomes had been achieved and whether they represented value for money – were a necessary part of responsible management, public accountability and good government. Many public servants welcomed them at the time. The achievement of NPM was to change the focus from the services' internal performance, as measured by its own and governmental rules, assumptions and expectations, to their external performance in terms of outcomes, results, effectiveness, efficiency and value for money. The country was arguably more democratic, in the sense that government and public services were more sensitive to public opinion, and perhaps more in touch with 'real life'; and public services were in many respects more efficient and better managed.

NPM later came to be widely criticised for the bureaucratic burden that targets and indicators placed on services and for their sometimes perverse effects. Targets for the police (Berry, 2009; Home Office, 2010) are one of the best known examples of targets originally expected to reduce crime by 'bringing more offenders to justice' but which had the effect of needlessly criminalising more children and young people; but there are other examples in prisons and probation and throughout the public services. The extent to which the 'target culture' has damaged the probation service is well illustrated in a recent report of the Probation Association (2011), aptly entitled *Hitting the Target, Missing the Point* and in the House of Commons Justice Committee's (2011) criticism that three quarters of probation officers' time is spent on work which does not involve direct engagement with offenders. HM Chief Inspector of Prisons found that the prison service, perceived from Whitehall and Westminster through its performance data, became a virtual world with little resemblance to reality (Owers, 2010). In particular, she criticised the sacrifice of quality in the pursuit of quantified results; the disincentive for collaborative working; the culture of blame and competitive individualism that was sometimes a consequence of 'driving up performance' and failure to meet rigid targets; and the unsuitability of commercial models of marketing and competition when applied to public services that serve the population as a whole, including its most disadvantaged members.

Moving on: a new public governance?

New models and new patterns of working began to appear in the late 2000s. Theories of 'public value' (Benington and Moore, 2010) reasserted a focus on citizenship and the claims of citizens to the services that are authorised and funded through the democratic process.[3] These theories argue that public services are complex systems with characteristics that are qualitatively different from markets or private sector business principles. They need systems of networked governance through which public agencies work with citizens so that together they can both improve services and generate democratic legitimacy and trust. 'Public value' should take the place of 'shareholder value' in the private sector. The new theories are distinguished from NPM by their emphasis not on the performance of individual services but on the outcomes of partnerships and other forms of collaboration between different government departments, local authorities, services and bodies such as voluntary organisations and users' groups. Public administration scholars have described them as a 'New Public Governance' (Osborne, 2010) and they are to some extent reflected in the coalition government's white paper *Open Public Services* (Cabinet Office, 2011).

There are now various situations in criminal justice where partnerships are formed between departments, services or voluntary organisations to deliver services. Recent examples in prisons or for resettlement of ex-prisoners include the resettlement project, known as RESET (see footnote 13, chapter eight) (Hazel et al, 2008); the Daedalus project (Ipsos Mori, 2010); and multi-agency arrangements for supervising offenders in the community (Burnett and Appleton, 2004; see also Pycroft and Gough, 2010). Some partnership arrangements focus on community safety, such as Multi-Agency Public Protection Arrangements (MAPPA) (Baker and Sutherland, 2009), Multi-Agency Risk Assessment Conferences (MARAC), and Circles of Support and Accountability (Nellis, 2009). People becoming involved with the criminal justice process who have mental health problems or learning

---

[3] The government would argue for a much broader definition of 'public services' to embrace services that are provided for the benefit of the public, for example 'social enterprises', but which are run and funded by the voluntary or private sector.

difficulties are another area where all those considerations come into play (Bradley, 2009). Such projects are easier to plan than to deliver and can be fraught with obstacles and result in disappointing outcomes.

Further criticisms and proposals for reform

Numerous reports made proposals for improvement in public services and government during the last years of the Labour administration. They covered subjects such as localisation, professionalism and strategic leadership (Cabinet Office, 2008); collaboration between local authorities, partners and frontline professionals (HM Treasury, 2009); improving the relationships between policymaking and frontline professionals (Omand et al, 2009; Sunningdale Institute, 2009); improving leadership across public services (Benington and Hartley, 2009); improving the contribution the humanities and social sciences can make to policymaking (Wilson, 2008); and strengthening departments' expertise in commissioning and using relevant research (Bichard, 2009).

The Economic and Social Research Council promoted a Public Services Programme involving 100 researchers from 14 disciplines working in universities across the United Kingdom[4] and beyond. The programme included several studies and findings that were especially relevant in a period of austerity, for example on the relationship between public expectations and public confidence, and the possible need to lower expectations if confidence is to be maintained; on the comparative effectiveness of different types of incentive (such as targets, competition or professional pride) in different situations; on the scope for choice and different kinds of choice in a situation of scarcity; on the implications of those choices for accepting and managing risk; on the consequences for local empowerment and control and the delegation of decision making; and on the implications for the voluntary and community sector.

One of the more comprehensive reviews was the report *Good Government: Reforming Parliament and the Executive* from the Better Government Initiative (BGI, 2009). It reviewed the way in which successive governments had functioned over the previous 20 years, and made a range of recommendations that covered policymaking and the processes of government; the role of the centre of government (Prime Minister's Office, Cabinet Office and Treasury) and its relationship with other governments; the implementation of policy and the delivery of

---

[4] www.publicservices.ac.uk

services; relations between the executive and Parliament; and the civil service (BGI, 2009). Some of the discussion that follows reflects the arguments of this report.

All the reports made useful proposals and all had implications for criminal justice as well as for other areas of public service and government. They were supported by an extensive academic literature (for example, Bochel and Duncan, 2007). They were, however, contributions to debate, including evidence to parliamentary committees, rather than reports that the government formally considered and accepted or rejected.

Policy and legislation

There was broad agreement in all these reports that the processes of policy formation, legislation, management and implementation needed to be improved, and that there should be better connections between the processes to ensure more effective delivery of services on the ground. Too often a policy's impact on the ground was different from that which the policymaker intended. As observed by Muncie (2005, p 55), 'The translation of policy into practice depends on how it is visioned and reworked (or made to work) by those empowered to put it into practice.' There was also agreement that change cannot be successfully achieved by imposing standard models or processes without engaging the people who will have to carry it out. It needed the active engagement of the workforce, and the consent and if possible the support of those who would be affected by it. Communities should feel that courts, prisons, the police and probation services, as well as schools and hospitals, are 'their' institutions, in which they can take some pride and towards which they have some responsibility.

Policy and legislation should be the outcome of open and responsive consultation that draws on experience and expertise from a range of relevant sources. Those who will be directly affected by the policy, especially those on whom the department will rely for delivery, should feel that they have been part of the process by which the policy has been formed, even if they do not agree with the outcome. Consultation should take place at the stage when policy is being formed – the traditional purpose of a green paper, although the process should also include conferences, seminar and debates – and not left until the main decisions have been taken and the government is only interested in detail and the means of putting its intentions into effect. No one should be excluded from the process on the grounds that their views may be critical, that their general position is thought to be unfavourable to the government, or that their views are less valuable or legitimate than anyone else's.

Inclusive processes of consultation and policy formation will be especially important for the increasing and changing forms of collaboration that can now be expected from the policies of the coalition government. The principles of procedural justice apply as much to the process of forming policy and putting it into effect as they do to public services' engagement with the public. Differences in power, status, and capacity, and in culture and expectations, will have to be resolved in ways that carry authority and legitimacy, as they must within the coalition itself. Instructions from central government or even legislation may no longer be effective or even have much relevance. Skills and competences will have to be reviewed. There will need to be a stronger relationship of trust between ministers, public servants and the citizens they serve. Improvements in relationships and dynamics should be reflected in more orderly and less febrile processes of policy formation, consultation and implementation. As the House of Commons Justice Committee has said, 'means must be found for encouraging and informing sensible, thoughtful and rational public debate and policy development' (House of Commons Justice Committee, 2009, p 7).

Ministers and public servants

Hood and Lodge (2006) describe the relationship between ministers and public servants in terms of a 'bargain'. They have civil servants particularly in mind. The relationship may be one of broadly two kinds, although neither excludes the other. Public servants may be treated as trustees, constituting a self-managed or autonomous estate, or as agents who are servants of their political masters. The former view might now be seen as elitist, old-fashioned and a relic of the 'old' public administration; the latter might now seem more modern and democratic. The effect of NPM and of successive governments' policies of reform has been to move public services in the latter direction. The shift might at first sight seem to be entirely right and proper, but the situation is not straightforward.

Civil servants

Civil servants can be seen as servants of the Crown, accountable to their departmental ministers but politically independent and with a wider duty to promote good government and to serve the public interest on behalf of the nation as a whole (Chipperfield, 1994). That view was on the whole accepted until the 1980s, when the Armstrong Memorandum (1985, amended 1996) stated that while civil servants are the servants of the Crown, 'for all practical purposes the Crown in this context is represented by the government of the day' (p 1), but the distinction between the public interest and party political advantage still remains.

Leaving those constitutional issues aside, it is becoming generally acknowledged that civil servants working in Whitehall need to understand the subject matter of an individual government department and its broad policy area, as well as possessing generic skills in subjects such as policymaking, analysis of evidence and resource management. Rapid movement of civil servants between jobs and subject areas led to a serious weakening of corporate memory with the risk of failure in strategy, policy and delivery. Developments in leadership and management training for public service professionals has been too concentrated in individual departments, with too few connections between departments, services, and different professional disciplines and backgrounds. More attention to career development and succession is needed to make sure that there are staff in departments who have the necessary skills, experience and corporate memory. Increasingly, 'the civil service will need to work across boundaries, collaboratively and flexibly, enabling others to be part of the creation of the answers and not doing so in isolation with ministers in their own departments'.[5]

Cross-cutting issues

Governments have tried for many years to deal with what have become known as 'wicked issues' (intractable problems involving several departments or services), 'silos' (lack of communication or understanding between departments or services), 'joined-up government' and 'managing the criminal justice system as a whole'. The system of cross-cutting public service agreements seemed to work well, but changes in the machinery of government to split or combine departments often proved costly, disruptive and ineffective. The mechanisms of NPM have often worked to frustrate cooperation, as managers have concentrated on meeting their own targets and have had no incentive to help others, and chapter three argued that top-down attempts to 'manage' criminal justice 'as a system' have the effect of

---

[5] As explained by the Government Connect programme director, Philip Littleavon, on the Civil Service Live network (http://network.civilservicelive.com/pg/pages/view/263961).

shifting the focus and diverting energy away from problems and issues on the ground and towards the system for its own sake.

Practitioners and professionals

Public servants such as police, prison and probation officers and professionals in health, education and social care have duties and responsibilities to the public and to the law, and to those in their care or charge, that are independent of their duties to ministers. Their accountability should not only be to a political authority (see chapter six and Chakrabarti, 2008, for the situation as regards the police). Those who are members of recognised professions have their own forms of statutory regulation, for example by the Health Professions Council, and their own professional associations, such as the British Psychological Society. Both issue ethical guidance and provide some accountability to the public for the professional standards to which services are provided. Ethical codes require professionals to preserve their independence in their relations with management and if necessary with ministers.

Recent governments have been generally suspicious of professional or services cultures, regarding them as working to promote the services' own interests and resist change. There has been some force in that argument but cultures can also work to promote professional pride and standards that are more deeply rooted than the performance measures of NPM. The situation is complicated, as chapter five has shown, in relation to the police; there are some occasions when cultures have to be challenged, and others where they need to be supported. Ben Crewe and Alison Liebling have made an important study (Crewe and Liebling, 2011) of the extent to which 'humanity' has been and still is a part of the culture of the prison service; a similar study might usefully be made in the probation service (are the service's traditional functions to 'advise, assist and befriend' things that probation staff think they still do or ought to do? – though see Vanstone (2004), Napo (2007) and Whitehead and Stratham (2007); see also chapter seven, present volume). A study of the culture of the 'old' Home Office and now of the Home Office and the Ministry of Justice would be revealing and probably instructive.

Activities that are important for reducing crime, helping victims or preventing reoffending may involve several departments, local authorities or voluntary organisations, but they may not be a high priority for any of them or contribute directly to their formal objectives. Differences of power, influence, professional culture and capacity have to be reconciled to create a sense of shared ownership of the task in hand and of shared satisfaction in its successful completion. Command models based on authority and top-down communication do not work in settings of that kind and new ways of working based on consultation and mutual confidence and respect have to be found. Representatives at meetings may have to speak for colleagues – it will not do to say 'that is not my responsibility'. A determination to get something done may have to overcome a cautious instinct to protect positions and avoid risks. Continuity in post, depth of experience, and the wisdom and respect that flow from them may need to be more highly valued. Success depends on the skills, capacity, motivation and relationships of those on the ground, but there are important issues of policy, management and leadership to be taken into account and new answers may need to be found to the familiar questions about accountability, organisation and structure, and skills and competences.

Training

Reports are rarely written that do not include a recommendation for more training. That is usually well justified, but the training should be of a kind that encourages public servants to work across cultures in a spirit of mutual trust and respect and without sacrificing values that are important. The Bradley report (Bradley, 2009), for example, made a point of recommending joint training wherever possible, but public servants should also have time and space for reading and reflection, and for reflective discussion among themselves and with others who have relevant experience and insights. They should be able to do so in informal settings where they can share impressions and ideas without feeling politically constrained, in the spirit of the Chatham House Rule.[6]

The way forward seems increasingly to be through multi-disciplinary teams such as youth offending teams and those for mental health that Bradley recommended (Bradley, 2009). At government level, it may be through 'programme boards', again as Bradley recommended, but arrangements for funding would have to be adjusted to match – Whitehall has never had much appetite for 'programme budgets'. The problem has been recognised for many years in the context of custodial and non-custodial sentencing; it might be more productive to address that problem than to search for new ways of making sentencing more

---

[6] 'Participants are free to use the information received, but neither the identity nor the affiliation of the speaker(s), nor that of any other participant, may be revealed.' See www.chathamhouse.org.uk/about/chathamhouserule.

'effective' in preventing crime, or for even more intricate guidance to sentencers in the hope that it will bring a closer alignment between sentencing practice and prison capacity.

Risk, innovation, research

Some issues have continued to have relevance throughout all attempts at reform. In particular, debate has continued over the nature and consequences of risk management procedures, the place of new initiatives and innovative practice, and the usefulness of commissioned research from academic and consultancies.

Managing risk

Assessments of risk are a necessary part of many of the functions governments have to perform, in criminal justice as elsewhere. They can identify significant correlations, but have limited accuracy in predicting future behaviour (Armstrong, 2004; Towl, 2004). Whether in protecting children from possible abuse or in making decisions to release a prisoner on parole, the statistical methods should still be combined with qualitative judgements. The application of a formula, or 'ticking the boxes', should not be a substitute for the informed exercise of responsible discretion. On the other hand, more precautionary clinical judgements may result in more false positives than actuarial techniques, as found by Roger Hood and colleagues (2002) in a study of Parole Board judgements of the risk of sex offenders. What is needed, they suggest, is assessment procedures that take account of both static and dynamic risk factors. Risk assessments need to take account of a person's circumstances and prospects in their lives as a whole (McAra and McVie, 2007; McNeill and Weaver, 2007; Crighton and Towl, 2008), which are to a large extent outside the system's knowledge and certainly its control – as Phil Wheatley, then the Director-General of the National Offender Management Service, himself acknowledged (Wheatley, 2010). Rod Morgan has described the effect that the mechanisms of risk assessment have had on pre-sentence reports, case management and decisions about parole, arguing that they have added disproportionately to the work of the prison and probation services while damaging offenders' prospects of rehabilitation and increasing rather than reducing their risk of reoffending (Morgan, 2008). A similar concern is implicit in the Bradley report's recommendations on offenders with problems of mental disorder.

Government's task is not only to assess and reduce risk but also to manage uncertainty. It should do so in ways that are outward-looking, confident and properly informed. For understandable political reasons, governments are more reluctant to accept risk than the private sector, but absolute certainty is an illusory goal and protection may be bought at disproportionate cost – financially (Lambert, 2009) or in its interference in people's lives. It is a basic function of government to maintain law and order and preserve the Queen's peace, but no government can guarantee its citizens absolute protection against crime, still less against bad behaviour. The attempt to do so can turn protection into oppression, or it can excuse people from their proper responsibilities as citizens. For a government to acknowledge the limitations of what the criminal justice process can or should do to prevent or reduce crime is not defeatist but realistic. What is defeatist is to fail to explore the more promising alternatives.

One of the consequences of a period of austerity may be a need to accept lower standards and a higher degree of risk than government or the public have demanded in the past. That may in turn imply a need to lower public expectations if public confidence is to be maintained (James, 2009). It may be especially difficult to do this in areas such as policing, prisons and probation where government and opposition parties have for several years insisted on and promised greater safety and protection for the public, even though the degree of protection they have led the public to expect may sometimes have been unrealistic.

Promoting innovation

A culture that gives priority to risk management – which in practice often means risk avoidance – will not be favourable to innovation, but the need for new ideas and new ways of doing things is likely to be even greater during a period of austerity. The Labour government regularly emphasised the importance of innovation in public services and in government, for example in its white paper *Innovation Nation* (DIUS, 2008), and there is an extensive academic literature. The National Audit Office (2009) has carried out a survey of innovation across central government and reviewed some specific initiatives; its report identified some success factors and made some useful but not especially penetrating recommendations. Other contributions to the debate have been more critical (Osborne et al, 2008; Bichard, 2009; Osborne and Brown, 2011).

Innovation has to be supported by a favourable culture and climate in the organisation as a whole, and it needs to be recognised, valued and rewarded, although not necessarily financially. If it is imposed from the top down, it will only be sustainable if it is fully accepted on the ground. It will be vulnerable if a key 'champion' moves to another position. Innovation from the bottom up may be more easily sustained, but it may still be suppressed by lack of interest from senior managers, by pressure from competing priorities, or by the volume of existing work. 'Pilots' are superficially attractive – they show that 'something is being done' and they are cheap to fund as an 'extra' without disturbing existing programmes. They are common in the private sector where new process will be trialled and new products market tested. They went well with the culture of NPM. But for public services it may be unsafe to assume that an innovation that has been carefully nurtured in one place will be equally successful in other places or different circumstances. What is done as part of a self-conscious pilot may not work in the same way if it becomes part of a normal routine.

Innovation may not always be what an organisation needs – persistence, patience and a continuous search for improvement and excellence within existing practices may sometimes be more important. Staff may for a time be excited by the sense that they are doing something new and different, but 'initiativitis' – too many initiatives promoted for their political effect – can be demoralising, especially when the interest of ministers and senior managers moves on to another new scheme and another new priority. Osborne and Brown (2001, p 1) argue that:

> [T]he dialogue about innovation in public services currently found within public policy ... is a flawed one, often both at odds with the existing evidence and lacking a holistic understanding of the nature of innovation and its distinctive policy and managerial challenges.

The new situation of financial austerity will compel government and services to revise their attitudes towards innovation. Instead of relying on new money to fund a new initiative, they will have to find ways of doing new things within the capacity that is already available. Or sometimes it may be more sensible to concentrate on doing the existing job better than to try to do something different (especially if part of the reason for doing something different is to impress and 'look good'). Innovation that involves stretching existing capacity, challenging existing ways of working and finding and motivating new collaborators may be more painful, but the effort and the results may be more sustainable.

Research and expert advice

The nature and relevance of the evidence that is available or might be obtained to support a government policy varies according to the subject and the discipline involved. It is significantly stronger, more widely accepted and more likely to be conclusive in medicine (for example) than in criminal justice. Government will sometimes be able to commission research that will settle an issue; sometimes the issues are too complex, or the study would be too expensive or take too long. Government may sometimes be able to rely on an expert committee to assemble evidence and give advice that it will normally accept; sometimes, and especially where the evidence is likely to be inconclusive or disbelieved, ministers will have to make a political judgement taking the relevant evidence into account but not necessarily regarding it as the determining factor.

Ministers have to consider evidence and advice in their wider social, economic and political context; they are entitled not to act on the evidence or the advice if they choose, but they should then be ready to justify their decision to Parliament and ultimately to the electorate. Good practice would also expect them to give a reasoned explanation to those who have provided the advice. There is general agreement, not always observed in practice, that statistics and evidence from research should always be published and made publicly accessible, together with any expert advice that may be based on them.

The relationship between evidence, policy and politics, and the role of scientific or other expert advice, became major issues in the BSE crisis[7] in 1996 (Phillips, 2000; Fisher 2007), and again in the disagreement between the government and the Advisory Council on the Misuse of Drugs over the classification of cannabis that led to the dismissal of Professor David Nutt as chair of the council in October 2009. The relationship can be especially difficult in criminal justice. The evidence is sometimes counter-intuitive and often inconclusive, especially if it is based on small samples or pilot schemes. Ministers ask 'What causes crime?' or 'Will this work?' and the answer is often 'We don't know,' or 'It depends.' It may be 'We can find out,' but sometimes – although

---

[7] The numerous issues raised by the BSE crisis, in which a number of people died, thousands of cattle were infected and millions were slaughtered, included the relationship between the government and its expert Spongiform Encephalopathy Advisory Committee, the confusion between their respective functions and responsibilities, and the government's initial failure to recognise the seriousness of the problem.

neither ministers nor criminologists would willingly admit it – the honest answer is 'There is no way of knowing for certain.'

The situation is frustrating for ministers and criminologists, and also for those policy advisers, practitioners and voluntary organisations that devise and want to promote what they believe to be promising ways to reduce crime or to support offenders or their families or victims. The results may 'feel' good but it is difficult and sometimes impossible to prove a direct causal link between the work they want to promote and a reduction in crime or reoffending. The usual and often correct answer is 'Try harder', but there comes a point where action has to be guided not by evidence of measurable results but by social values and a social conscience. The House of Commons Justice Committee (2009, p 134) has recommended that the government 'gives consideration to the most appropriate means of drawing together existing research with a view to devising a transparent and coherent model for directing resources more effectively to prevent further expansion of the criminal justice system and increases in costs'. The evidence report (Ministry of Justice, 2010b) associated with the green paper *Breaking the Cycle* is an excellent example of what can be done.

The complaint has been that in spite of its declared commitment to evidence-based policy, the Labour government had variously ignored or misused scientific evidence or research in order to maintain public confidence, limit public expenditure or, the critics would claim, to appease public opinion (see Hope, 2008; and Walters, 2008 for an especially critical view; see also Stevens, 2011). Some arguments are more convincing than others but it is another area of what Amartya Sen called 'pervasive plurality'. There is a long-running argument among criminologists about the nature of their discipline, what it is for, what it does and how to do it. Part of the debate is concerned with the relationship between the craft or science of criminology, and policymaking and politics. Loader and Sparks (2010, p 117) say that 'criminology's public role is most coherently and convincingly described as that of contributing to a better politics of crime and its regulation'. Garland (2011) and Loader and Sparks (2011) have discussed the different views of where criminology should position itself in relation to government and policymaking, and hope that a more productive relationship may be possible in future, without prejudicing criminology's integrity and academic independence. A more realistic and perhaps more respectful understanding of the interactions between academic knowledge, government policymaking and professional practice may be needed on all sides.[8] Academics might then become better equipped to assemble and present their knowledge and their research, and government and practitioners to make better use of the knowledge that can be made available.

Commissioning and contracting out

The coalition's green paper (Ministry of Justice, 2010a) said that criminal justice services would be commissioned competitively from a variety of providers in the public, private and voluntary sectors and increasingly on a basis of payment by results. The management of prisons would continue to be put out to tender and further prisons might be (and subsequently were) transferred from the public to the private sector. The only functions reserved for the public sector seemed to be professional advice to courts and the custody and supervision of those offenders who present the greatest danger to the public. Further details were to be published during the summer of 2011.

The division between the public and private sectors in relation to prisons was hotly debated during the 1980s when it was argued, for example, that the custody of convicted offenders should always be reserved for the public sector as a matter of principle, although the same principle did not apply to prisoners on remand or prison escorts (Windlesham, 1993, pp 275-89). Arguments of that kind are now rarely heard in England (but see Crewe et al, 2011 and Liebling et al, 2011, and the section on management and market testing in prisons in chapter eight of the present volume), and the coalition government has given the impression that almost any function now performed by the public sector should be open to competition. It may be time to consider whether any parameters or 'red lines' should now be recognised.

Differences between the sectors

It is facile to argue that either the private sector or the public sector is somehow always superior to the other, and to claim that the discipline

---

[8] Bhikhu Parekh's analysis (in Jahanbegloo and Parekh, 2011) of the role of political philosophy and its difference from political science is illuminating in this respect, and bears comparison with criminology. Political philosophy, he suggests, 'has a normative dimension and among other things, provides principles to judge existing institutions ...' and is 'reflective, concerned with meaning and significance' (p 41) whereas political science 'is empirical, aims to arrive at generalizations based whenever possible on causal connections, and has a predictive orientation' (p 41). Each is interdependent but asks different kinds of questions.

of the 'market' enables the private sector always to do a better job than the public or voluntary sector, or alternatively to claim that the public or voluntary sector has an ethos that makes it in some way superior to that of the private sector. None has a capacity or an ethos that is unique to itself, that is never found elsewhere; and there are as many differences within the sectors as there are between them. Organisations in any of the three sectors can learn from one another, share particular objectives and contribute their own capacity or expertise to a common purpose. In partnership with others they may be able to do things that none of them could do individually.

Even so, some essential differences remain. The public sector acts on behalf of the state, of the citizen or the public, and in pursuit of a public interest that is democratically determined. It is paid for from taxation. The private sector acts on behalf of its shareholders and exists primarily to make a profit; it is paid for by the charges it makes to its customers. The voluntary sector operates independently of both. Many voluntary organisations are charities set up to carry out the purposes set out in the charity's trust deed as interpreted by its trustees; most of those in the criminal justice sector have been set up to meet a particular need or serve a particular purpose or 'client group'. They are funded by a combination of donations, subscriptions, endowments and grants from government. There is still a fundamental difference between serving the public (or government), serving the shareholders and serving a charitable purpose, and there often remains an underlying difference in outlook. Those differences have important implications for the function that each can most appropriately perform and the situations in which it can do so.

Functions and decisions

Within the criminal justice sector, important distinctions can be made between the kinds of functions that have to be performed and the types of decisions that have to be made. It seems to be accepted that certain functions should as a matter of principle be the responsibility of the state, acting through democratically accountable statutory services and in some instances the courts. They clearly include the power to use lethal force, in the rare circumstances when that is needed, and also the power to arrest or prosecute a person to deprive them of their liberty, or to inflict other forms of punishment, especially if the punishment carries with it a criminal record with all the handicaps that implies. The arguments are broadly constitutional and democratic, and relate to principles such as public accountability, legitimacy and human rights.

Once a person has become subject to the criminal justice process, decisions have to be made about how individuals are to be treated. As well as the courts' judgements about guilt and sentence, they include professional decisions about the degree of security that is needed to protect the public; the kind of programme, treatment or other intervention they may need to stabilise their lives and reduce their risk of reoffending; how that need can best be met from the provision that is available; their suitability for release from prison on licence; and the action to be taken to enforce the conditions of a licence or to respond to a significant change in a person's circumstances. All of these involve crucial judgements about a person's character or possible behaviour that may affect the public's safety, the person's liberty and position in society, and the situation of their family. They should accordingly be made within a statutory framework, in accordance with due process, and with accountability to Parliament and by public servants who are free from considerations of their organisation's profitability or commercial advantage. Not only advice to courts and to the Parole Board but also offender management, with the authority to take action on breach or to apply to vary conditions, are functions that should be reserved for the statutory services.

Practical implications

If these principles are accepted, some functions could then either be provided by the public sector or commissioned from suitable providers in the private or voluntary sector according to suitability, availability and cost. Several considerations should, however, be taken into account.

Large companies such as G4S and Serco, and some large voluntary organisations, will naturally seek large, profitable national contracts, and government itself is likely to find a small number of large national contracts easier to manage than a large number of smaller local contracts. Large national contracts can provide some degree of accountability to ministers and Parliament through the contract itself, although with serious limitations because of commercial confidentiality, but they do not provide for accountability at local level. Strong arguments have been put forward, by government and others, for diversity of provision, greater localisation, more involvement of local citizens, and local discretion to respond to local circumstances and take advantage of local opportunities. There are important functions, for example work with vulnerable, disadvantaged and minority groups, that may not be commercially attractive but that voluntary organisations and community organisations are willing and well able to undertake, often on a very local basis – see for example the House of Commons Communities and Local Government Committee's report on localism.[9] There is also scope for useful forms of co-creation in which stakeholders are involved in service design, and of co-production in which people – who could include ex-offenders – are routinely involved in service delivery (Bason, 2010). Large national contracts may be suitable for some purposes, but there are many instances where they would not.

Neither administrative advantages nor the political influence that large private sector companies can command should distort the decision-making process so that its focus moves away from the public interest, or the interests of justice, and towards convenience of the companies' own commercial advantage. The providing organisation's individual ethos and the way it treats its staff will affect the staff members' relationships with offenders and others with whom they work, and ultimately the quality and legitimacy of the service it provides. The line between protecting the public interest and offering a contract that contractors will find acceptable may not be an easy one to draw, but the distinction is crucial.

Payment by results

The intended shift from payment for services delivered to payment by results will involve difficult judgements about the kind of results that are expected and how their achievement is to be measured (Collins, 2011). Reductions in reoffending will be relevant but will depend on so many variables in individual personalities and circumstances that they will be simplistic and inadequate as a test on their own. Payment by results may not be suitable for smaller contracts with charities that may not be able to raise funds to put 'up front', or see reducing reoffending as their only or main priority, but may have an invaluable contribution to make.

Responsibility and accountability

There are voices in the government suggesting that the proposed police and crime commissioners should become responsible for the functions that probation trusts currently perform, while Ian Loader and colleagues (Lanning et al, 2011) have argued for local authorities to be given this function as part of a programme of 'justice reinvestment'

---

[9] www.publications.parliament.uk/pa/cm201012/cmselect/cmcomloc/547/54702. htm

(see chapter ten). Local authorities have responsibility for most of the services on which an offender's rehabilitation is likely to depend and are therefore well placed to furnish multi-agency provision for offenders and ex-offenders as citizens – as they would for any other citizen. At present, however, probation trusts have become well established and seem to be the natural choice. Building on the established contacts and experience of the probation boards, they have good relationships with their important partners and stakeholders, they are locally accountable, and they are already well connected with their local communities. They could become better connected, for example by improved communication and consultation, the development of neighbourhood justice panels, closer connections with courts (especially if magistrates and judges become more involved with offenders after sentence, as *Breaking the Cycle* suggests they might), and the appointment to trusts of elected members of local authorities. Acting on this basis, they can be expected to work effectively with police and crime commissioners when they take up their positions in due course. They would directly provide the core services indicated above; other services could be provided directly or outsourced to the private or voluntary sector according to circumstances. There may be scope for some large national contracts for some 'standard' services, of which approved accommodation and some unpaid work might be examples, but large providers should not have a monopoly. It will enrich resources and reduce transaction costs if there is room for smaller local contracts and for less formal partnerships or service level agreements, for which probation trusts will be the natural commissioning authorities.

TEN

Policy, politics and the way forward

The title of a recent book – *The Eternal Recurrence of Crime and Control*[1] – has strong resonance for us. Every new government, and every new Home Secretary or Justice Secretary, promises new initiatives to deal with crime, and sometimes a new appointment or a new report brings the promise of a different emphasis and a new approach. All too often, what emerges proves to be more of the same – more legislation, more reorganisation, more punishment. The recurring problem is the assumption that reducing everyday crime and the harm it causes is a matter for more intensive governance or tougher measures against the people who commit it. We began this book thinking that the formation of the coalition government and its promise of a 'rehabilitation revolution' and a reduction in the use of imprisonment could augur a genuine turning point. More recent events began to follow the familiar pattern, no doubt spurred on by the riots which took place in August 2011 and the public and political reactions to them, but we hope that such a change may still be possible.

This chapter brings together the main conclusions we have drawn from the previous chapters, and relates them to current issues for policy and practice. It reviews the coalition government's policies and proposals as they were becoming established after the change of government in 2010, and offers a longer-term framework for the future development of policy, legislation and practice.

We set out in the Introduction some of the principles and themes we believe should be followed. Integrity, decency, transparency and trust are essential if the governance and administration of criminal justice are to command the respect and compliance of those who work with them in the criminal justice sector, and of those who work with them and those who are affected by what they do, including victims of crime, offenders and the wider public. That applies to the formation of policy and the preparation of legislation as well as to the operation of the courts and the professional practice of the criminal justice services. We have argued for an approach to criminal justice that is focused first on

---

[1] Downes et al (2010)

people and their capacities, situations and relationships, and on treating them with humanity, respect and dignity, and only then on reforming institutions, structures and systems. We support the arguments for civil society and local communities to be more actively involved in criminal justice, and for citizens to have both a greater sense of ownership of the public services that work for them and of responsibility for the social fabric of the communities in which they live their lives.

Our arguments have been based on experience and evidence gathered over the past 20 or 30 years, including our own experience and research, and on an attempt to show how what is right may be distinguished from what works or what is politically helpful, while acknowledging that all three may in some extreme instances be overtaken – we hope temporarily – by what is politically imperative. We recognise that feelings and opinions about crime and how to deal with it may sometimes be deeply divided. Some means of reconciliation has to be sought in those circumstances, and we have made suggestions for ways in which reconciliation might more often be achieved.

Lessons from experience

We have argued in previous chapters for less detailed and less politically driven direction from central government and greater trust in and discretion for professionals and practitioners, as well as for a more realistic appreciation from government – and it is to be hoped from the media – of what the criminal justice process cannot and should not be expected to achieve. The reduction of crime and the prevention of reoffending depend as much on social circumstances and individual situations, opportunities and relationships as they do on sentencing or the operation of the criminal justice services. The outcomes are to a large extent beyond the control of those services; while services may have an influence, the nature of that influence will vary from case to case and the evidence to judge or measure it is complex and often inconclusive. To make unrealistic claims or raise false expectations risks a repetition of the frustration and disillusion that existed when the coalition government came into office.

Efficiency and social values

The criminal justice process must clearly be efficient, cost-effective and well managed. Criminal justice needs institutions and services to realise and sustain it. They should operate as public services where professional skills, techniques, information and accountability are essential and business models are sometimes relevant. The process and its institutions should be thought of in the context of a larger vision of justice and of the nation's identity and social values. Criminal justice should not be seen just as a business, to be managed like any other and judged by the criteria of efficiency, effectiveness and customer satisfaction, or as a market where justice, punishment and rehabilitation can be bought and sold.

Business models based on customers, consumers and choice do not apply in criminal justice as they may do elsewhere. Whether the 'outputs' of criminal justice services and their outcomes for individuals, communities and society as a whole are 'justice', or whether they provide a sense that justice has been achieved or is being done, involves more than whether or not the individual is satisfied in the sense that a consumer is happy with a product (whether it is more value for money, longer lasting, tailored to the customer's preferences, and so forth). As a 'consumer' the victim may not be satisfied, for example, unless the offender is severely punished or permanently incarcerated, but she is not in a position to take her custom elsewhere. Other considerations, such as mitigating factors, proportionality and a wider public interest, take precedence over individual preferences of victims. The victim, and others affected by the crime, may however accept that justice has been done if communications from the police and during the court process make clear the reasons for the decisions made; if they show that the decisions are in accordance with the rule of law; if they demonstrate respect and empathy towards the victim; and if where appropriate there is provision for reparation. Insofar as the criminal justice process is fallible and wrong decisions are sometimes made, procedures must be available to allow the process or the outcome to be challenged through the courts and, in the last resort, politically.

The relationship between justice and human behaviour is not straightforward. A just society may be, but is not necessarily, a society that is free from crime or has a low crime rate. An oppressive state could restrict people's liberty and freedom of movement to such an extent that many crimes could become impossible to commit. On the other hand, a sense of being part of a just society and of sharing its social values may do more to motivate compliance with the law and prosocial behaviour than the threat of penalties or punishment. Tom Tyler (2009, p 328) has argued that instead of relying on punishment and deterrence to enforce obedience to the law, authorities could regulate behaviour by 'refocusing upon building and maintaining supportive values and then using those values as the central pillar in a strategy of regulation'. With a sense of their connection to society and the chance to benefit from mutual obligations, people are more likely to behave according to their own sense of what is fair and legitimate even if they have nothing to gain themselves.

Changes in structure and process

Changes in the structure and process of criminal justice are only as good as the effects they have on relationships and dynamics. In the complex world of criminal justice, they can too easily have perverse results. If those positive effects can be achieved by other means, structural change will be an unnecessary distraction. Describing the introduction of integrated offender management, Anne Owers, the former HM Chief Inspector of Prisons, said (2010, p 11):

> The central idea is clearly a good one. But the implementation began from entirely the wrong end. Rather than working out what offender management meant, or could realistically mean, in prisons or probation, and then creating the most effective structure to support this, it began by creating a structure (or claiming to have done so) and then trying to decide what and how it would deliver. Inevitably, this created a huge and continually changing superstructure, tweaked by passing consultants ... [and] now in its third or fourth incarnation.

A further change of structure has taken place since that time.

Implications for policy and practice

It follows from the arguments we have set out that the main focus of government policy should be on preventing crime; on reducing the suffering and the waste of lives and resources which crime and reoffending cause for victims, offenders and society as a whole; and on repairing the damage so far as it is possible to do so. In this approach, there would be a preference for social and educational rather than criminal measures as the means of preventing and reducing crime. Greater attention would be paid to understanding and acting on the social and economic contexts in which crime is experienced and committed, to finding practical means of mitigating its effects on communities and families, and to the influences and motivation which lead to criminal behaviour. Above all, there would be an emphasis on responsibility – the responsibilities of government, statutory services, voluntary organisations, companies, the media, and of offenders, their families and other citizens. It would promote a culture where harmful behaviour is censured and when necessary punished, where offenders are enabled to make reparation to victims or communities, where those affected by crime receive consideration and support, and where those who have committed crime are enabled and encouraged to develop as honest citizens and gain the dignity of a decent life.

Policy and legislation

Following this preventive, restorative and enabling approach, legislation on criminal law and sentencing would be simplified, with fewer criminal offences. Pre-emptive offences and mandatory sentences would be abolished. There would be greater clarity about the nature, purpose and legitimacy of punishment, and greater discretion for sentencers within the maximum sentences set out in legislation approved by Parliament and the Sentencing Council's guidelines. Courts, not government or Parliament, should decide on such matters as discounts for guilty pleas, taking into account the wide range of circumstances that might arise. The same sentencing structure would apply to all offences, with differences in seriousness being reflected in the maximum sentences available to the court and not in special statutory provisions relating to particular offences that have attracted public attention.

More attention would be paid to the influences on desistance from crime and to making help more accessible for problems with drugs, alcohol. Courts could be enabled to review an offender's progress and give credit for success where it is appropriate. Following the original purpose of problem-solving courts in America, they could also give local citizens a voice, for example by consulting them about sites for reparative work, and could work more closely with communities and voluntary services to help people to tackle the problems that contributed to their offending (Thomson, 2010). Penalties imposed out of court for low-level offences would no longer be recorded as a criminal conviction. Government would need to make sure that its wider social and economic policies and its priorities for public expenditure took account of their potential impact on crime and criminality, including the situations of young people at risk and of ex-offenders and their families who are trying to re-establish themselves in society.

Early-years prevention and diversion

There would be continued and increased emphasis on early-years prevention and diversion. Services would be realigned to work with offenders and potential offenders earlier in the offending cycle, where their efficacy and the long-term benefits are likely to be greatest. The age group 15-21 – in transition to adulthood[2] – is now arguably the most neglected in the penal system, and yet it is the stage in life when persistent young offenders become most prolific (T2A Alliance, 2009). There would be a more focused approach to reducing exclusions from school and on follow-up work with children who are excluded to provide effective support to those who need it. There would be similar concern for early preventive interventions for children in or leaving care, and for young adults, to support them through the various transitions they have to make and to prevent the formation of criminal gangs. An increase in the age of criminal responsibility from 10 to 12 or 14 may not be realistic in the political climate as it was at the time of writing, but there could still be a presumption that children under 14, and certainly under 12, would be dealt with by non-criminal means as far as possible, as the Independent Commission on Youth Crime and Antisocial Behaviour (2010) has proposed.

Special attention would be given to supporting the process of change so that those who committed offences in the past are no longer locked into the identity of an 'offender' by being constantly labelled as such, and so that they can establish their own identity as people capable of behaving differently and leading socially responsible and fulfilling lives. Those who have been disadvantaged or damaged by their backgrounds would be helped towards a more settled and positive way of life as citizens and members of their communities. There would be much higher expectations of what offenders and ex-offenders can do both for their own and for other offenders' rehabilitation, more emphasis on their responsibilities for their families and towards their communities, and help and support for them to carry out those responsibilities towards their families and communities. Strengths-based and solution-focused and restorative measures and procedures would be used wherever practicable and appropriate.

---

[2] The age span for transition to adulthood is necessarily imprecise, but ranges from around 16-18 to 24-25.

Discretion and bureaucracy

There would be an emphasis on 'doing things better', and on providing staff with the time and the support to 'do things properly' according to recognised standards of best practice. It is often clear what needs to be done; the more difficult task is to create the will, overcome the obstacles and mobilise the necessary resources. The police, courts, and the prison, probation and youth justice services would be enabled to 'get on with the job', with appeals and remedies available if they are needed but with less detailed direction from government. Unnecessary bureaucracy and restrictive controls would be dismantled, although it would still be necessary to retain the mechanisms necessary for accountability and the bureaucracy to support them. Information about what has been done, what it has achieved and what it has cost is important, but monitoring by central government would be much less detailed and prescriptive.[3] Special attention would be paid not just to the 'effectiveness' of the criminal justice process (whatever that means) and the criminal justice services, but also to fairness, decency and procedural justice, as discussed throughout this book. That would include proper attention to the needs and expectations of victims and witnesses and to the quality and consistency of the recognition and support they receive.

Use of imprisonment and community penalties

There is a long history of well-written and well-researched reports arguing for a reduction in the use of imprisonment and the greater use of community penalties. Important recent reports, emerging from various commissions and reviews, include: *Crime, Courts and Confidence* (The Coulsfield Report – Coulsfield, 2004); *Re-thinking Crime and Punishment* (Esmée Fairbairn Foundation, 2004); *A Review of Women with Particular Vulnerabilities in the Criminal Justice System* (The Corston Report – Corston, 2007); *Do Better Do Less* (Commission on English Prisons Today, 2009) and *Cutting Crime: The Case for Reinvestment* (House of Commons Justice Committee, 2009). They have pointed to the direct and indirect costs of imprisonment, its ineffectiveness as shown by the high rates of reconviction, and the evidence that the

---

[3] The standards, instructions and guidance for probation trusts extend to several hundred pages. The performance management system contains over 80 targets in four domains (Probation Association, 2011), although the Ministry of Justice has said they are to be reduced.

public is not as punitive in its attitude towards offenders as is usually supposed. Those arguments have not had much political traction, and criminal justice scholars have for several years expressed concern about the punitive and populist character of government policy (Bottoms, 1995; Ashworth, 2010), and about what Ian Loader and Richard Sparks (2010, pp 57-82) have called the 'hot climate' of the debate. Some have argued that the present state of affairs is too deeply embedded in British politics and in the 'late modern' character of British society to be changed without radical reform – reform that extends not only to criminal justice policy but also to the structure in which policy is formulated and put into effect. They have made various proposals for what Loader and Sparks (2010, pp 83-114) have called 'cooling devices' – for example the creation of a new institution such as Nicola Lacey (2008) has proposed with responsibilities in criminal justice with Monetary Policy in respect of the economy, or a devolution of power from central government to a more local level – which could distance criminal justice from the heat of politics and constant attention from the media.

Devolution and localisation

Most arguments for devolution and localisation come from a political perspective and relate to issues of governance and the role and size of the state. They can apply to criminal justice as they do to other services, and have important implications that have been discussed in chapters four and nine. Some reformers find the devolution of responsibility, accountability and budgets especially attractive as a means of finding a solution to the problem of capacity, particularly in prisons but for probation as well. Rob Allen (2009), the House of Commons Justice Committee (2009)[4] and the Commission on English Prisons Today (2009) have argued for a scheme for 'justice reinvestment', with the formation of local strategic partnerships that bring together the relevant local services with fully devolved budgets for prisons and probation. The Centre for Social Justice (2009) has proposed that the National Offender Management Service be abolished and replaced by a network of community prison and rehabilitation trusts, chaired by elected crime and justice commissioners.

The arguments are that local control over the allocation and use of resources would lead to more rational decision making, more effective

---

[4] The Committee argued that with justice reinvestment: 'The prison population could be safely ... reduced over a specified period to ... about two thirds of the current population.' (p 138)

coordination, and a movement away from the use of imprisonment and towards other forms of intervention based in communities. Such a development would also bring other benefits, such as a stronger sense of local ownership and responsibility and a greater capacity to take advantage of and respond to local circumstances and opportunities. The usual objection, apart from the lack of public interest and political will, has been the unsuitable geographical distribution of prison establishments and the prison population, which prevents most prisons from having any direct association with the areas from which their prisoners have come or to which they will return. Some progress might, however, be made if the prison population could first be reduced and stabilised, but a large-scale programme can only be a long-term project.

The current government's proposals

This book began by asking whether the formation of the coalition government in 2010/11 and the policies it adopted might come to be seen as a turning point in criminal justice, as it might in other aspects of government, politics and public policy. The main indications of a change in direction were in the government's green paper *Breaking the Cycle* (Ministry of Justice, 2010a), and in the accompanying *Evidence Report* (Ministry of Justice, 2010b), which summarised the evidence that was available from experience and research.[5] On policing, a consultation paper (Home Office, 2010) announced the government's proposals for elected police and crime commissioners (see chapter six), and was followed by the Police Reform and Social Responsibility Bill, which was before Parliament at the time of writing. Following the riots in August 2011, the Prime Minister, David Cameron, announced that government departments would review their domestic policies and speed up plans to improve parenting and education, and that there

---

[5] The *Evidence Report* (Ministry of Justice, 2010b, p 54) stated that:'There is a developing evidence base to inform how the aims of the criminal justice system might be delivered more efficiently and effectively. This includes:
- The potential for greater gains through prevention, early intervention, diversion and resettlement;
- Ensuring that interventions are targeted and tailored to match the characteristics of individual offenders, and improving knowledge on the best sequencing of interventions;
- Using the developing evidence base on desistance to improve understanding of how and why people stop offending and the role of practitioners in supporting this process;
- Making greater use of restorative justice and other approaches which enable greater reparation to the victim or community.'

would be an investigation into 'gang culture' in the context of the 'Big Society'.

Language and presentation

Some of the proposals in the green paper and some of the language followed a familiar pattern – better management, business models, markets, commissioning and competition, tougher community sentences, and the management of offenders, with a welcome new emphasis on rehabilitation but a continuing preoccupation with punishment and with structure and process. The government still seemed to see criminal justice in instrumental terms, to be judged by the measurable results it achieved, now including its economic return. It still followed what David Garland and Richard Sparks have called 'the rules of political speech' (Garland and Sparks, 2000, p 200; Loader and Sparks, 2010, p 78). Ministers no doubt judged that their proposals had to be presented in those terms if they were to gain public and parliamentary support. The risk is that proposals presented in this way will continue to imply unrealistic assumptions and raise expectations that may not be achieved. They are in danger of becoming discredited if they do not appear to deliver the reductions in crime and reoffending and in the prison population that the government has led the public to expect. If crime were to increase, for example, they might be represented as having 'failed' even though the reasons for any increase would undoubtedly be more complex and could just as well be attributed to the effects of the government's cuts in benefits and support for services.

Substantive proposals

The proposals in the green paper *Breaking the Cycle* were in many respects consistent with the approach favoured in this volume. The green paper set out the government's plans for reduction in the use of imprisonment, its intention to simplify legislation and administrative processes, and its readiness to allow greater freedom and discretion to judges, local managers and professional staff and greater involvement of local communities. Prisons would become 'places of hard work and industry', and there would be a new approach to the rehabilitation of offenders where rehabilitation might again become one of the principal purposes of the probation service alongside punishment and the protection of the public. Fewer defendants would be remanded in custody. The government acknowledged that criminal justice cannot succeed in reducing and controlling crime on its own, and that government departments need to work together with each other, and criminal justice services need to work with other agencies.

More ambitiously, the government looked forward to an economic return from work in prisons and from community payback (previously known as unpaid work, and before that as community service), which would help to meet the costs of the penal system and enable more funds to be made available for victims. It seemed sympathetic to 'justice reinvestment', and for young offenders it proposed that 'local authorities should share both the financial risk of young people entering custody and the financial rewards if fewer young people require a custodial sentence' (Ministry of Justice, 2010a, p 73), with a small number of pilot schemes in local areas, but any more widespread use of justice reinvestment was only on the distant horizon.

Most of the concerns that were expressed in consultation on the green paper related not so much to the proposals themselves, but to their feasibility (the expected economic returns from work in prisons); their possibly perverse effects (the arrangements for commissioning services and payment by results); funding (for example, for small voluntary organisations providing specialised services, often on a local basis); uncertainty (for example, about the dynamics and effects of the new relationships as they are formed at local level); and about the detail, much of which was still to be announced. The Legal Aid, Sentencing and Punishment of Offenders Bill, published in June, 2011, was largely irrelevant to the arguments in this book. Special concerns for our arguments, arising from the green paper, are the effects of contracting out for services where large contractors dominate the 'market' to the disadvantage of vulnerable, hard to reach and minority groups – see chapter four – and the issues of principle regarding the relative responsibilities of the state and the private sector – see chapter nine.

A framework for the future

Political and public management theorists argue that there needs to be a long-term vision which articulates the objectives of public services; provides a strategy for achieving them; motivates those who have to put it into effect; and commands the confidence of the public (2020 Public Services Trust, 2010). Any of that is exceptionally difficult in criminal justice, for two main reasons. One is the complexity of the objectives to be achieved and the tasks to be performed, and the conflict that often exists between them. The other is the deep division between those who are compassionate towards people who have offended and those who are not. Research by Roberts and Hough (2005) has shown how differences can often be softened at the level of particular individuals or situations, although in the case of more serious crimes 'opinions on the grounds of retribution are difficult to change' (Hood and Hoyle, 2008, p 240). Research by Feilzer (2009) suggests that the narrative context and emotional response holds more sway than the factual information. The different attitudes might best be reconciled by encouraging a stronger sense of social responsibility and of citizenship and common humanity so that people come to show more consideration towards one another and are less inclined to break the law because they respect it (Tyler, 2009). But that is more a task for civil society than for government.

A new style of politics?

At the time when the coalition government was formed, it seemed as if there might be a rare opportunity for a more inclusive, less confrontational politics of crime and criminal justice in which there would be fewer political obstacles to reducing the use of imprisonment and a greater emphasis on prevention, rehabilitation and restoration. During and immediately after the 2010 election, issues of criminal justice had become less politically contentious, and received less critical coverage in the media, than they had for some time. The first indications, as already described, were that the government intended to move in that direction. Because the government was a coalition and differences had to be more fully exposed and more carefully resolved, the process of policy formation leading to and following the green paper was more open and consultative than had been usual in recent times. Subsequent disagreements within the coalition and criticism of some aspects of the government's plans for sentencing, exploited by the opposition, suggest that those hopes may now be more difficult to realise. Even so, the pressures on public expenditure and the recognition, on all sides of the political spectrum, that new approaches preferably with cross-party support are needed may enable progress to be made. The riots in August 2011, and the government's and opposition's realisation that such situations cannot be prevented or resolved by criminal justice measures alone, may paradoxically provide a further impetus.

A practical way forward

The practical way forward may be for ministers to avoid promises of radical, fundamental or revolutionary change or strident criticism of the past and to seek broad, cross-party agreement to a series of incremental developments. They would present their policies not so much as a revolution, rejecting all that has gone before, but as a more rational, responsive and proportionate way of dealing with crime, the administration of justice and the rehabilitation of offenders – more rational because it builds on evidence and experience; more responsive because it takes more account of offenders', victims' and citizens' situations and expectations; and proportionate because it avoids over-reactions and unnecessary severity and takes account of what the country can afford. They would at the same time need a clear sense of direction and to communicate it to and share it with the professional leaders and managers of the criminal justice services. They will always need to respond to events and campaigns and to genuine public anxiety where it exists, for example in relation to riots or terrorism, but they should do so as far as possible without announcing sudden changes of priorities, policies or legislation.

Within the services, practitioners will need to have confidence that they can expect a reasonable degree of stability and continuity, and that programmes and projects in which they and partners have invested time and effort will not have to be abruptly abandoned. There would be greater confidence and trust in communities and civil society, and a sense among communities of their own responsibility for offenders' rehabilitation and reintegration, for example through voluntary work as mentors or in other ways with offenders or victims; or as employers, landlords or neighbours. Mechanisms and funding will be needed to ensure the survival and development of such partnerships in the new context of commissioning and payment by results.

A broader more informed understanding of 'risk' is needed, more than the usual narrow focus on the statistically identified risk of reconviction that an individual offender may be deemed to have. All risk assessments need to be time-bound if they are to make coherent scientific sense and also be linked to related management plans. But it is important to take a broader and more holistic view of risk assessment, so that it applies both to individuals and to their situations and so that it takes account not only of individuals but also of communities. For individuals it should have regard to their strengths as well as their vulnerabilities, and take account of their material and emotional resources as well as their 'criminogenic needs'. For communities, it should consider the greater risks that persist or are created in communities where those deprivations exist and nothing is done to correct them.

Professional and institutional interests will sometimes need to be challenged, especially in 'gate keeping' where services or individual practitioners may try to keep control of 'their' cases and resist involvement with cases that do not 'belong' to them, sometimes influenced by the need to meet targets and stay within budgets. The fact that a person has been taken into the criminal justice process should not mean that other services, and people generally, are then relieved of any further responsibility.

Justice and society

Adopting this preventive, reparative and enabling approach, the country would move towards a situation where it would rely less on the criminal justice process and criminal justice services as the only or principal means of preventing and of dealing with crime, and would develop other more restorative and socially inclusive means of doing so. There would be a shift of emphasis towards prevention and restoration and away from the concentration on enforcement, punishment and the criminal trial. Sentencing should not be seen as an end in itself but as the beginning of a continuing process of rehabilitation and integration. The focus would move away from institutions and the 'system', and more attention would be given to problems and situations, to the places and context in which unacceptable behaviour takes place, and to the means of resolving those situations and changing that behaviour. Criminal proceedings would always be one of the means of doing so and would remain the ultimate sanction, but it would be one among others and it might not always be the most suitable and rarely adequate on its own. As has previously been argued in this book, the focus would shift from what is claimed to work, commonly referred to as 'what works', to what helps. The state's restrictions on people's lives would be no greater than is necessary, and its interventions when they are needed would be proportionate, legitimate and openly, honestly and courteously explained. The narrative would be one of learning, not blaming; of responsibility and opportunity, not exclusion and demonisation; of trust, not fear or suspicion; and of hope and belief in the future.

References

2020 Public Services Trust (2010) *2020 Vision: A Far-Sighted Approach to Transforming Public Services*, London: 2020 Public Services Trust.

Allen, R. (2009) 'Justice reinvestment – a new paradigm?' in J. Collins and R. Siddiqui (eds) *Transforming Justice: New Approaches to the Criminal Justice System*, London: Criminal Justice Alliance, pp 57-66.

Andrews, D.A. and Bonta, J. (2010) *The Psychology of Criminal Conduct* (5th edn), New Providence, NJ: Anderson Publishing.

Annison, J., Eadie, T. and Knight, C. (2008) 'People first: probation officer perspectives on probation work', *Probation Journal*, vol 55, no 3, pp 259-71.

Appleton, C. (2010) *Life After Life Imprisonment*. Clarendon Studies in Criminology, Oxford: Oxford University Press.

Armstrong, D. (2004) 'A risky business? Research, policy, governmentality and youth offending', *Youth Justice*, vol 4, no 2, pp 100-16.

Armstrong, R. (1985, amended 1986) *The Duties and Responsibilities of Civil Servants in relation to Ministers: Note by the Head of the Home Civil Service*, London: Cabinet Office. www.civilservant.org.uk/armstrong.shtml

Arrow, K. (1963) *Social Choice and Individual Values* (2nd edn), New York, NY: Wiley.

Ashworth, A. (1996) 'Crime, community and creeping consequentialism', *Criminal Law Review*, vol 43, pp 220-30.

Ashworth, A. (2007) 'Security, terrorism and the value of human rights', in B. Goold and L. Lazarus (eds) *Security and Human Rights*, Oxford: Hart Publishing.

Ashworth, A. (2010) *Sentencing and Criminal Justice* (5th edn), Cambridge: Cambridge University Press.

Ashworth, A. and Zedner, L. (2008) 'Defending the criminal law: reflections on the changing character of crime, procedure and sanctions', *Criminal Law and Philosophy*, vol 2, no 1, pp 21-51.

Audit Commission (1989) *The Probation Service: Promoting Value for Money*, London: HMSO.

Audit Commission (1996) *Misspent Youth, Young People and Crime*, London: Audit Commission.

Baker, K. and Sutherland, A. (eds) (2009) *Multi-Agency Public Protection Arrangement and Youth Justice*, Bristol: The Policy Press.

Bason, C. (2010) *Leading Public Sector Innovation: Co-Creating for a Better Society*, Bristol: The Policy Press.

Bayley, D. and Shearing, C. (1996) 'The future of policing', *Law and Society Review*, vol 30, no 3, pp 585-606.

Beetham, D. (1991) *The Legitimation of Power*. London: Palgrave Macmillan.

Bekoff, M. and Pierce, J. (2009) *Wild Justice: The Moral Lives of Animals* (2nd edn), Chicago, IL: University of Chicago Press.

Benington, J. and Hartley, J. (2009) *Whole Systems Go! Improving Leadership Across the Whole Public Service System*, London: National School of Government.

Benington, J. and Moore, M. H. (eds) (2010) *Public Value: Theory and Practice*, Basingstoke: Palgrave Macmillan.

Benson, A. and Hedge, J. (2009) 'Criminal justice and the voluntary sector: a policy that does not compute', *Criminal Justice Matters*, no 77, pp 34-6.

Berman, G., Fox, A. and Ullman, B. (2009) *Lasting Change or Passing Fad? Problem Solving Justice in England and Wales*, London: Policy Exchange, www.policyexchange.org.uk/publications/publication.cgi?id=131.

Berry, J. (2009) *Reducing Bureaucracy in Policing: Main Report*, London: Home Office.

Better Government Initiative (2009) 'Good government: reforming Parliament and the Executive', www.bettergovernmentinitiative.co.uk.

Bichard, M. (2009) *Moving from Policy to Law: The Role of External Expertise*, London: Institute for Government.

Bingham, T. (2010) *The Rule of Law*, London: Allen Lane.

Birgden, A. (2004) 'Therapeutic jurisprudence and responsivity: finding the will and the way in offender rehabilitation', *Psychology, Crime & Law*, vol 10, no 3, pp 283-95.

Blackstone, W. (1765-69) *Commentaries on the Laws of England, Vols. 1-4*, Oxford: Clarendon Press.

Blair, I. (2009) *Policing Controversy*, London: Profile Books.

Blair, T. (2004) 'A new consensus on law and order', Speech on the Government's 5-Year Strategy for Crime, www.number10.gov.uk/page6129.

Blair, T. (2006) 'Our nation's future', Speech delivered on 23 June, www.number10.gov.uk/page9737.

Blair, T. (2010) *A Journey*, London: Hutchinson.

Blunkett, D. (2003) *Civil Renewal: A New Agenda*, London: Home Office.

Blunt, C. (2010) *Churchill Anniversary Speech on Criminal Justice Reform*, Speech given at NACRO, West Norwood Centre on 22 July 2010 (http://webarchive.nationalarchives.gov.uk/+/http://www.justice.gov.uk/news/sp220710a.htm)

Bochel, H. and Duncan, S. (eds) (2007) *Making Policy in Theory and Practice*, Bristol: The Policy Press.

Bottoms, A. (1995) 'The philosophy and politics of punishment and sentencing', in C. Clarkson and R. Morgan (eds) *The Politics of Sentencing*, Oxford: Oxford University Press.

Bottoms, A. (2001) 'Compliance and community penalties', in A. Bottoms, L. Gelsthorpe and S. Rex (eds) *Community Penalties: Change and Challenge*, Cullompton: Willan Publishing.

Bottoms, A.E. and McWilliams, W. (1979) 'A non-treatment paradigm for probation practice', *British Journal of Social Work*, vol 9, no 2, pp 159-202.

Bottoms, A., Gelsthorpe, L. and Rex, S. (2001), 'Introduction: the contemporary scene for community penalties', in A. Bottoms, L. Gelsthorpe and S. Rex (eds) *Community Penalties: Change and Challenge*, Cullompton: Willan Publishing.

Bowling, B., Parmar, A. and Phillips, C. (2008) 'Policing minority ethnic communities', in T. Newburn (ed) *Handbook of Policing* (2nd edn), Cullompton: Willan Publishing, pp 612-41.

Boyce, I., Hunter, G. and Hough, M. (2009) *St Giles Trust Peer Advice Project: An Evaluation*, London: St Giles Trust.

Bradford, B. (2011) *Police Numbers and Crime Rates: A rapid evidence review*. Report prepared for HM Inspectorate of Constabulary. www.hmic.gov.uk/media/police-numbers-and-crime-rates-rapid-evidence-review-20110721.pdf

Bradley, K. (2009) *Review of People with Mental Health Problems or Learning Disabilities in the Criminal Justice System*, London: Department of Health.

Bridges, A. (2011) 'Probation and youth offending work: a tribute to those who do it well', Valedictory Lecture given by Andrew Bridges, Chief Inspector of Probation, at the University of Oxford on 16 May 2011.

Brody, S. (1976) *The Effectiveness of Sentencing*, Home Office Research Study No 35, London: Home Office.

Burnett, R. (1996) *Fitting Supervision to Offenders: Assessment and Allocation in the Probation Service*, Home Office Research Study No 153, London: Home Office.

Burnett, R. (2004a) 'One-to-one ways of promoting desistance: in search of an evidence base', in R. Burnett and C. Roberts (eds) *What Works in Probation and Youth Justice: Developing Evidence-Based Practice*, Cullompton: Willan Publishing, pp 180-97.

Burnett, R. (2004b) 'To reoffend or not to reoffend? The ambivalence of convicted property offenders', in S. Maruna and R. Immarigeon (eds) (2004) *After Crime and Punishment: Pathways to Offender Reintegration*, Cullompton: Willan Publishing.

Burnett, R. and Appleton, C. (2004) 'Joined-up services to tackle youth crime: a case-study in England', *British Journal of Criminology*, vol 44, no 1, pp 34-54.

Burnett, R. and Hanley Santos, G. (2010) *Found in Transition? Local Inter-agency Systems for Guiding Young Adults into Better Lives. Formative Evaluation of the T2A Pilots*, Oxford: Centre for Criminology, University of Oxford.

Burnett, R. and Maruna, S. (2004) *Prisons as Citizens' Advisers: The OxCAB-Springhill Partnership and its Wider Implications?*, London: Esmée Fairbairn Foundation.

Burnett, R. and Maruna, S. (2006) 'The kindness of prisoners: strengths-based resettlement in theory and in action', *Criminology & Criminal Justice*, vol 6, no 1, pp 83-106.

Burnett, R. and McNeill, F. (2005) 'The place of the officer-offender relationship in assisting offenders to desist from offending', *Probation Journal*, vol 52, no 3, pp 221-42.

Cabinet Office (2008) *Excellence and Fairness: Achieving world class public services*, London: Cabinet Office.

Cabinet Office (2010) *The Coalition: Our Programme for Government*, London: Cabinet Office.

Cabinet Office (2011) *Open Public Services*, Cm 8145, London: The Stationery Office.

Canton, R. (2007) 'Probation and the tragedy of punishment', *Howard Journal*, vol 46, no 3, pp 236-54.

Carlen, P. (2002) 'Women's imprisonment: models of reform and change', *Probation Journal*, vol. 49, no. 2, pp 76-87.

Carter, P. (2003) *Managing Offenders, Reducing Crime: A New Approach*, London: Ministry of Justice.

Carter, P. (2007) *Securing the Future: Proposals for the Efficient and Sustainable Use of Custody in England and Wales*, London: Ministry of Justice.

Centre for Social Justice (2009) *Breakthrough Britain: Locked Up Potential – A strategy for reforming prisons and rehabilitating prisoners*, London: Centre for Social Justice.

Chakrabarti, S. (2008) 'A thinning blue line? Police independence and the rule of law (John Harris Memorial Lecture)', *Policing*, vol 2, no 3, pp 367-74.

Child, J. and Hunt, A. (2011) 'Risk, pre-emption and the limits of the criminal law', in K. Doolin, J. Child, J. Raine and A. Beech (eds) *Whose Justice? State or Community?*, Winchester: Waterside Press, pp 51-68.

Chipperfield, G. (1994) *The Civil Servant's Duty*, Essex Papers in Politics and Government, No 95, Colchester: University of Essex.

Clancy, A., Hudson, K., Maguire, M., Peake, R., Raynor, P., Vanstone, M. and Kynch, J. (2006) *Getting Out and Staying Out: Results of the Prisoner Resettlement Pathfinders*, Bristol: The Policy Press.

Clarke, R. and Hough, M. (1984) *Crime and Police Effectiveness*, London: Home Office Research Unit.

Clarke, R. and Mayhew, P. (1980) *Designing Out Crime*, London: HMSO.

Coleman, R., Whyte, D. and Tombs, S. (eds) (2008) *State, Power, Crime*, London: Sage Publications.

Collins, J. (2011) 'Payment by results in the criminal justice system: can it deliver?', *Safer Communities*, vol 10, no 2, pp 18-25.

Commission on English Prisons Today (2009) *Do Better for Less: The Report of the Commission on English Prisons Today*, London: Howard League for Penal Reform.

Corston, J. (2007) *A Review of Women with Particular Vulnerabilities in the Criminal Justice System*. (The Corston Report) London: Home Office.

Coulsfield, J. (2004) *Crime, Courts and Confidence*, London: Esmée Fairbairn Foundation.

Court of Appeal (2009) *Court of Appeal (Criminal Division) Review of the Legal Year 2007/08*, London: Judiciary of England and Wales. www.judiciary.gov.uk/NR/rdonlyres/A504FA01-E92B-4537-8C87-B01A9D45010D/0/Criminal_Division_Review_200708_web.pdf

Court of Appeal (2010) *Court of Appeal (Criminal Division) Review of the Legal Year 2009/10*, London: Judiciary of England and Wales. www.judiciary.gov.uk/Resources/JCO/Documents/News%20Release/criminal-div-review-legal-year-2010.pdf

Crawford, A. (1994) 'The partnership approach: corporatism at the local level?', *Social and Legal Studies*, vol 3, no 4, pp 497-519.

Crawford, A. (1999) 'Questioning appeals to community within crime prevention and control', *European Journal on Criminal Policy and Research*, 1999, vol 7, no 4, pp 509-30.

Crewe, B. and Liebling, A. (2011) 'Are liberal humanitarian penal values and practices exceptional?', in T. Ugelvik and J. Dullum (eds) *Penal Exceptionalism? Nordic Prison Policy and Practice*, London: Routledge, pp 175-98.

Crewe, B., Liebling, A. and Hulley, S. (2011) 'Staff culture, the use of authority, and prisoner outcomes in public and private prisons', *Australia and New Zealand Journal of Criminology*, vol 44, no 1, pp 94-115.

Crighton, D. and Towl, G. (2008) *Psychology in Prisons* (2nd edn), Oxford: Blackwell.

Crow, I. (2006) *Resettling Prisoners: A Review*, London: University of Sheffield and NOMS (National Offender Management Service).

Daicoff, S. (2006) 'Law as a healing profession: the "comprehensive law movement"', *Pepperdine Dispute Resolution Law Journal*, vol 6, no 1, pp 1-61.

DCLG (Department for Communities and Local Government) (2008) *Communities in Control: Real People, Real Power*, London: The Stationery Office.

DCLG (2010) *Evaluation of the National Strategy for Neighbourhood Renewal – Final Report*, London: DCLG.

DCSF (Department for Children, Schools and Families) (2003) *Every Child Matters*, London: DCSF.

Deakin, N. (2002) *In Search of Civil Society*, Basingstoke: Palgrave.

Dexter, P. and Towl, G. (1995) 'An investigation into suicide behaviour in prisons', in N.K. Clark and G. Stephenson (eds) *Criminal Behaviour: Perceptions, Attributions, and Rationalities*, Issues in Criminological and Legal Psychology No 22, Leicester: British Psychological Society.

Dicey, A.V. ([1885] 1915) *An Introduction to the Study of the Law of the Constitution* (8th edn), London: Macmillan.

DIUS (Department for Innovation, Universities and Skills) (2008) *Innovation Nation*, London: DIUS.

Downes, D. and Morgan, R. (2007) 'No turning back: the politics of law and order into the millenium', in M. Maguire, R. Morgan and R. Reiner (eds) *Oxford Handbook of Criminology*, Oxford: Oxford University Press.

Downes, D., Hobbs, D. and Newburn, T. (eds) (2010) *The Eternal Recurrence of Crime and Control*, Oxford: Oxford University Press.

Duff, R.A. (2001) *Punishment, Communication and Community*, Oxford: Oxford University Press.

Duff, R.A. (2007) *Answering for Crime: Responsibility and Liability in the Criminal Law*, Oxford: Hart Publishing.

Dunbar, I. and Langdon, A. (1998) *Tough Justice: Sentencing and Penal Policies in the 1990s*, London: Blackstone.

Edgar, K. and Newell, T. (2006) *Restorative Justice in Prisons: A Guide to Making it Happen*, Winchester: Waterside Press.

Edgar, K., Jacobson, J. and Biggar, K. (2011) *Time Well Spent: A Practical Guide to Active Citizenship and Volunteering in Prison*, London: Prison Reform Trust.

Ekblom, P. (1996) *Safer Cities and Domestic Burglary*, Home Office Research Study No 164, London: Home Office.

Esmée Fairbairn Foundation (2004) 'Rethinking crime and punishment: the report', www.rethinking.org.uk.

Etherington, S. (2007) *The Future of Civil Society*, The Cass Lecture 2007, on 3rd November at Cass Business School, City University London (www.cass.city.ac.uk/__data/assets/pdf_file/0008/37277/etherington.pdf).

Etzioni, A. (1996) *The New Golden Rule: Community and Morality in a Democratic Society*, New York, NY: Basic Books.

Etzioni, A. (2004) *The Common Good*, Cambridge: Polity Press.

Evans, K. and Walklate, S. (2011) 'The Corston report: reading between the lines', *Prison Service Journal*, no 194, pp 6-11.

Farrall, S. (2002) *Rethinking What Works With Offenders: Probation, Social Context and Desistance From Crime*, Cullompton: Willan Publishing.

Farrall, S., Hough, M., Maruna, S. and Sparks (eds) (2010) *Escape Routes: Contemporary Perspectives on Life after Punishment*, London: Routledge.

Farrant, F. and Levenson, J. (2002) *Barred Citizens: Volunteering and Active Citizenship by Prisoners*, London: Prison Reform Trust.

Farrington, D. and Welsh, B. (2007) *Saving Children from a Life of Crime: Early Risk Factors and Effective Interventions*, Oxford: Oxford University Press.

Faulkner, D. (2003) 'Taking citizenship seriously: social capital and criminal justice in a changing world'. *Criminal Justice*, vol 3, no 3, pp 287-316.

Faulkner, D. (2004) 'Prisoners as citizens', *Prison Service Journal*, no 143, pp 46-7.

Faulkner, D. (2006) *Crime, State and Citizen: A Field Full of Folk* (2nd edn), Winchester: Waterside Press.

Faulkner, D. (2010) 'Justice Act 1991' Paper prepared in consultation with John Halliday and presented at a Witness Seminar on 7 May at the Centre for Contemporary British History, London.

Feilzer, M. (2009) 'The importance of telling a good story: an experiment in public criminology', *Howard Journal*, vol 48, no 5, pp 472-84.

Fisher, E. (2007) *Risk Regulation and Administrative Constitutionalism*, Oxford: Hart Publishing.

Fitzgibbon, D.W. (2007) 'Risk analysis and the new practitioner: myth or reality?', *Punishment and Society*, vol 9, no 1, pp 87-97.

Flanagan, R. (2008) *The Review of Policing – Final Report*, London: Home Office.

Folkard, M., Smith, D.D. and Smith, D.E. (1976) *IMPACT: Intensive Matched Probation and After-Care Treatment*, Home Office Research Study No 36, London: Home Office.

Frank, J.D. (1961) *Persuasion and Healing*, Baltimore, MD: John Hopkins University Press.

Fulton, J.S. (1968) *The Civil Service: Report of the Committee*, London: HMSO.

Garland, D. (2001) *The Culture of Control: Crime and Social Order in Contemporary Society*, Oxford: Oxford University Press.

Garland, D. (2011) 'Criminology's place in the academic field' in Bosworth, M. and Hoyle, C. (eds) *What is Criminology?*, Oxford: Oxford University Press, pp 17-34.

Garland, D. and Sparks, R. (2000) 'Criminology, social theory and the challenge of our times', *British Journal of Criminology*, vol 40, no 2, pp 189-204.

Garside, R. (2009) *Risky People or Risky Societies? Rethinking Interventions for Young Adults in Transition*, London: Centre for Crime and Justice Studies.

Genders, E. and Player, E. (1995) *Grendon: A Study of a Therapeutic Prison*, Oxford: Clarendon Press.

Gilling, D. (2007) *Crime Reduction and Community Safety: Labour and the Politics of Local Crime Control*, Cullompton: Willan Publishing.

Giordano, P.C., Cernkovich, S.A. and Rudolph, J.L. (2002) 'Gender, crime, and desistance: toward a theory of cognitive transformation', *American Journal of Sociology*, vol 107, no 4, pp 990-1064.

Goldsmith, P.H. (2006) 'Government and the rule of law in the modern age', Lecture to the London School of Economics, 22 February.

Goldson, B. and Muncie, J. (2006) 'Rethinking youth justice: comparative analysis, international human rights and research evidence', *Youth Justice*, vol 6, no 2, pp 91-106.

Guilfoyle, M. (2010) '"Twenty year stretch": a probation officer's view from the front line', *Criminal Justice Matters*, no 81, pp 10-11.

Hall, N., Grieve, J. and Savage, S. (2009) ' Introduction: the legacies of Lawrence', in N. Hall, J. Grieve and S. Savage (eds) *Policing and the Legacies of Lawrence*, Cullompton: Willan Publishing, p 1021.

Halliday, J. (2001) *Making Punishments Work: Report of a Review of the Sentencing Framework for England and Wale*, London: Home Office.

Hayek. F.A. ([1960] 2010) *The Constitution of Liberty*. London and New York: Routledge.

Hazel, N., Liddle, M. and Gordon, F. (2008) *Evaluation of RESET programme – Final report*, London: Catch22, www.catch-22.org.uk/publications.

Hedderman, C. and Hough, M. (2004) 'Getting tough or being effective: what matters?', in G. Mair (ed.) *What Matters in Probation*, Cullompton: Willan, pp 34-52.

Herbert, N. (2010) Speech to the Policy Exchange, www.homeoffice.gov.uk/media-centre/speeches/nick-herbert-policy-exchange.

Hickman, M., Thomas, L., Silvestri, S. and Nickels, H. (2011) *Suspect Communities'? Counter-terrorism policy, the press, and the impact on Irish and Muslim communities in Britain*, London: London Metropolitan University.

Hinsch, W. (2010) 'Justice, legitimacy, and constitutional rights', *Critical Review of International Social and Political Philosophy*, vol 13, no 1, pp 39-54.

HM Chief Inspector of Prisons in England and Wales (2010) *Annual Report, 2008-2009*, HC 323, London: The Stationery Office.

HM Chief Inspectors of Prison and Probation (2008) *The Indeterminate Sentence for Public Protection: A Thematic Review*, London: Ministry of Justice.

HM Inspectorate of Constabulary (2010a) *Valuing the Police*, London: HM Inspectorate of Constabulary.

HM Inspectorate of Constabulary (2010b) *Anti-Social Behaviour: Stop the Rot*, London: HM Inspectorate of Constabulary.

HM Treasury (2009) *Operational Efficiency Programme*, London, HM Treasury.

Hollin, C., Palmer, E., McGuire, J., Hounsome, J., Hatcher, R., Bilby, C. and Clark, C. (2004) *Pathfinder Programmes in the Probation Service: A Retrospective Analysis*, Home Office Online Report 66/04, London: Home Office.

Home Office (1959) *Penal Practice in a Changing Society*, Cmnd 645, London, HMSO.

Home Office (1962) *Report of the Departmental Committee on the Work of the Probation Service* (Morison report), Cmnd 1650, London: HMSO.

Home Office (1966) *Report of the Inquiry into Prison Escapes and Security* (The Mountbatten Report), Cmnd 3175. London: HMSO.

Home Office (1977) *A Review of Criminal Justice Policy 1976*, London, HMSO.

Home Office (1979) *Committee of Inquiry into the United Kingdom Prison Services* (the May Committee), Cmnd 7673, London: HMSO.

Home Office (1984) *Probation Service in England and Wales: Statement of National Objectives and Priorities*, London: Home Office.

Home Office (1988a) *The Parole System in England and Wales. Report of the Review Committee* (Carlisle Committee), Cm 532, London: HMSO.

Home Office (1988b) *Punishment, Custody and the Community*, Cm 424, London: HMSO.

Home Office (1990a) *Crime, Justice and Protecting the Public*, Cm 965, London: HMSO.

Home Office (1990b) *Supervision and Punishment in the Community: A Framework for Action*, Cm 966, London: HMSO.

Home Office (1990c) *Partnership in Dealing with Offenders in the Community*, London: Home Office.

Home Office (1995) *Review of Police Core and Ancillary Tasks* (Posen review), London: Home Office.

Home Office (1995b) *Review of Prison Service Security in England and Wales and the Escape from Parkhurst Prison on Tuesday 3rd January 1995* (Report of the Learmont Inquiry), Cmnd 3020, London: HMSO.

Home Office (1997) *No More Excuses: A New Approach to Tackling Youth Crime in England and Wales*, Cm 3809, London: The Stationery Office.

Home Office (2002) *Justice for All*, Cm 5563, London: The Stationery Office.

Home Office (2004) *Reducing Re-Offending: National Action Plan*, London: Home Office.

Home Office (2007a) *Crime in England Wales 2006/07*, Home Office Statistical Bulletin, London: Home Office.

Home Office (2007b) *National Community Safety Plan, 2008-2011*, London: Home Office.

Home Office (2008) *From the Neighbourhood to the National: Policing our Communities Together*, Cm 7448, London: The Stationery Office.

Home Office (2009) *Protecting the Public: Supporting the Police to Succeed*, Cm 7749, London: The Stationery Office.

Home Office (2010) *Policing in the Twenty-first Century: Reconnecting Police and the People*, Consultation Document, London: Home Office.

Home Office (2011) *A National Crime Agency: A Plan for the Creation of a National Crime-fighting Capability*, Cm 8027, London: Home Office.

Hood, C. (1991) 'A public management for all seasons?', *Public Administration*, vol 69, no 1, pp 3-19.

Hood, C. and Lodge, M. (2006) *The Politics of Public Service Bargains: Reward, Competency, Loyalty – and Blame*, Oxford: Oxford University Press.

Hood, R. and Hoyle, C. (2008) *The Death Penalty. A Worldwide Perspective* (4th edn), Oxford: Oxford University Press.

Hood, R., Shute, S., Feilzer, M, and Wilcox, A. (2002) 'Sex offenders emerging from long-term imprisonment: a study of their long-term reconviction rates and of Parole Board members' judgements of their risk', *British Journal of Criminology*, vol 42, no 2, pp 371-94.

Hope, T. (2008) 'A firing squad to shoot the messenger: Home Office peer review of research', in W. McMahon (ed) *Critical Thinking about Uses of Research*, London: Centre for Crime and Justice Studies.

Hough, M. (2010) 'Gold standard or fool's gold? The pursuit of certainty in experimental criminology', *Criminal Justice*, vol 10, no 1, pp 11-22.

Hough, M., Allen, R. and Padel, U. (2006) *Reshaping Probation and Prisons: The New Offender Management Framework*, Bristol: The Policy Press.

Hough, M., Allen, R. and Solomon, E. (eds) (2008) *Tackling Prison Overcrowding: Build More Prisons? Sentence Fewer Offenders?*, Bristol: The Policy Press.

House of Commons Community and Local Government Committee (2011) *Localism*. Third Report of Session 2010–12, HC547. London: The Stationery Office.

House of Commons Home Affairs Committee (2005) *Rehabilitation of Prisoners*, First Report of Session 2004-2005, Volume I, London: The Stationery Office.

House of Commons Home Affairs Committee (2007) *Police Funding*, Fourth Report of Session 2006-2007, London: The Stationery Office.

House of Commons Justice Committee (2008) *Towards Effective Sentencing*, Fifth Report of Session 2007 2008, HC184, London: The Stationery Office.

House of Commons Justice Committee (2009) *Cutting Crime: The Case for Justice Re-investment*, First Report of Session 2009-2010, HC 94, London: The Stationery Office.

House of Commons Justice Committee (2011) *The Role of the Probation Service*. Eighth Report of Session 2010-12. Vols I-II, HC 519-I and HC 519-II. London: The Stationery Office.

Howard League for Penal Reform (2011) *Business Behind Bars: Making Real Work in Prison Work*, London: Howard League for Penal Reform, www.howardleague.org/fileadmin/howard_league/user/online_publications/Business_behind_bars.pdf.

Howard, M. (2010) 'More prisons equals less crime. It's a fact', *The Times*, 14 December, p 20.

Hoyle, C. (ed) (2009) *Restorative Justice*, London: Routledge.

Hubble, M., Duncan, B. and Miller, S. (eds) (1999) *The Heart and Soul of Change: What Works in Therapy*, Washington, DC: American Psychological Association.

Hucklesby, A. and Hagley-Dickinson, L. (eds) (2007) *Prisoner Resettlement: Policy and Practice*, Cullompton: Willan Publishing.

Hudson, B. (2003) *Justice in the Risk Society*, London: Sage Publications.

Independent Commission on Youth Crime and Anti-social Behaviour (2010) *Time for a Fresh Start*, London: Police Foundation.

Ipsos Mori (2010) 'Evaluation of the London Youth Reducing Reoffending Programme (Daedalus)', http://lcjb.cjsonline.gov.uk/area23/library/Publications/2010_06_02_LYRRPEmergingFindingsRpt.pdf.

Jackson, J. and Bradford, B. (2009) 'Crime, policing and social order: on the expressive nature of public confidence in policing', *British Journal of Sociology*, vol 60, no 3, pp 493-521.

Jackson, J., Bradford, B., Hough, M., Kuha, J., Stares, S., Widdop, S., Fitzgerald, R., Yordanova, M. and Galev, T. (2011) 'Developing European indicators of trust in justice', *European Journal of Criminology*, vol 8, no 4, pp 267-85.

Jacobs, J. (1962) *The Life and Death of American Cities*, London: Jonathan Cape.

Jacobson, J. and Hough, M. (2010) *Unjust Deserts: Imprisonment for Public Protection*, London: Prison Reform Trust.

Jahanbegloo, R. and Parekh, B. (2011) *Talking Politics: Bhikhu Parekh in Conversation with Ramin Jahanbegloo*, New Delhi: Oxford University Press India.

James, A. and Raine, J. (1998) *The New Politics of Criminal Justice*, London: Longman.

James, E. (2011) 'Foreword', in K. Edgar, J. Jacobson and K. Biggar (2011) *Time Well Spent: A Practical Guide to Active Citizenship and Volunteering in Prison*, London: Prison Reform Trust.

James, O. (2009) 'Evaluating the expectations disconfirmation and expectations anchoring approaches to citizen satisfaction with local public services', *Journal of Public Administration Research and Theory*, vol 19, no 1, pp 107-23.

Johnston, L. and Shearing, C. (2003) *Governing Security: Explorations in Policing and Justice*, London: Routledge.

Jones, T. (2008) 'The accountability of policing', in T. Newburn (ed) *Handbook of Policing* (2nd edn), Cullompton: Willan Publishing, pp 693-724.

JUSTICE (1980) *Breaking the Rules*, London: JUSTICE.

Kaariainen, J. (2007) 'Trust in the police in 16 European countries', *European Journal of Criminology*, vol 4, no 4, pp 409-35.

Kant, I. ([1785] 1907) *Fundamental Principles of the Metaphysic of Morals*, translated by T. K. Abbott (3rd edn), London: Longmans.

Kemshall, H., Canton, R. and Bailey, R. (2004) 'Dimensions of difference', in A. Bottoms, S. Rex and G. Robinson (eds) *Alternatives to Prison: Options for an Insecure Society*, Cullompton: Willan Publishing.

King, R. and Morgan, R. (1980) *The Future of the Prison System*, Farnborough: Gower.

Lacey, N. (1994) 'Government as manager, citizen as consumer: the case of the Criminal Justice Act, 1991', *Modern Law Review*, vol 57 no 4, pp 534-54.

Lacey, N. (2008) *The Prisoners' Dilemma: Political Economy and Punishment in Contemporary Democracies*, Cambridge: Cambridge University Press.

Lakoff, G. (2002) *Moral Politics: How Liberals and Conservatives Think* (2nd edn), Chicago, IL and London: University of Chicago Press.

Lambert, M.J. and Barley, D.E. (2002) 'Research summary on the therapeutic relationship and psychotherapy outcome', in J.C. Norcross (ed) *Psychotherapy Relationships that Work*, New York, NY: Oxford University Press, pp 17-32.

Lambert, R. (2009) John Harris Memorial Lecture given to the Police Foundation on 2 June, www.police-foundation.org.uk.

Lanning, T., Loader, I. and Muir, R. (2011) *Redesigning Justice: Reducing Crime through Justice Reinvestment*, London: Institute for Public Policy Research.

Lappi-Seppälä, T. (2011) 'Explaining imprisonment in Europe', *European Journal of Criminology*, vol 8, no 4, pp 303-28.

Laub, J. and Sampson, R. (2003). *Shared Beginnings, Divergent Lives: Delinquent Boys to Age 70*, Cambridge, MA: Harvard University Press.

Law Commission for England and Wales (2010) *Criminal Liability in Regulatory Contexts*, Consultation Paper 195 (Overview), London: Law Commission for England and Wales.

Liddle, M. and Gelsthorpe, L. (1994) *Crime Prevention and Inter-agency Co-operation*, Crime Prevention Unit Paper 53, London: Home Office.

Liebling, A. (2004) *Prisons and their Moral Performance: A Study of Values, Quality and Prison Life*, Oxford: Oxford University Press.

Liebling, A., Crewe, B. and Hulley, S. (2011) 'Values and practices in public and private sector prisons: a summary of key findings from an evaluation', *Prison Service Journal*, no 196, pp 55-8.

Lipsey, M.W. and Cullen, F.T. (2007) 'The effectiveness of correctional rehabilitation: a review of systematic reviews', *Annual Review of Law and Social Science*, vol 3, pp 297-320.

Loader, I. (2006) 'Fall of the "Platonic guardians": liberalism, criminology and political responses to crime in England and Wales', *British Journal of Criminology*, vol 46, no 4, pp 561-86.

Loader, I. and Sparks, R. (2010) *Public Criminology?*, London: Routledge.

Loader, I. and Sparks, R. (2011) 'Criminology's public roles: a drama in six acts', in Bosworth, M. and Hoyle, C. (eds) *What is Criminology?*, Oxford: Oxford University Press, pp 17–34.

Loader, I. and Walker, N. (2007) *Civilising Security*, Cambridge: Cambridge University Press.

Loftus, B. (2008) 'Dominant culture interrupted: recognition, resentment and the politics of change in an English police force', *British Journal of Criminology*, vol 48, no 6, pp 756–77.

Loftus, B. (2010) 'Police occupational culture: classic themes, altered times', *Policing and Society*, vol 20, no 1, pp 1–20.

Longstaff, A. (2010) *Policing Drugs and Alcohol: Is Harm Reduction the Way Forward?*, Report of the Eighth Oxford Policing Policy Forum, London: Police Foundation.

Longstaff, A. (2011) *Are Young People Over-policed and Under-protected?*, Report of the Ninth Oxford Policing Policy Forum, London: Police Foundation.

MacIntyre, A. ([1981] 2007) *After Virtue: A Study in Moral Theory* (3rd edn), London: Duckworth.

MacIntyre, A. (1999) *Dependent Rational Animals*, London: Duckworth.

Macpherson, W. (1999) *The Stephen Lawrence Inquiry*, Cm 4262, London: The Stationery Office.

Mair, G. (2004) 'The origins of What Works in England and Wales: a house built on sand?', in G. Mair (ed) *What Matters in Probation?*, Cullompton: Willan Publishing.

Mannheim, H. and Wilkins, L. (1955) *Prediction Methods in Relation to Borstal Training*, Studies in the Causes of Delinquency and the Treatment of Offenders, London: HMSO.

Marshall, W.L. and Serran, G.A. (2004) 'The role of the therapist in offender treatment', *Psychology, Crime and Law*, vol 10, no 3, pp 309–20.

Martinson, R. (1974) 'What works? Questions and answers about penal reform', *Public Interest*, no 35, pp 22–54.

Maruna, S. (2001) *Making Good: How Ex-convicts Reform and Rebuild their Lives*, Washington, DC: American Psychological Association.

Maruna, S. (2011) 'Reentry as a rite of passage', *Punishment & Society*, 13(1), 3–28.

Maruna, S. and Immarigeon, R. (eds) (2004) *After Crime and Punishment: Pathways to Offender Reintegration*, Cullompton: Willan.

Maruna, S., LeBel, T., Mitchell, N. and Naples, M. (2004) 'Pygmalion in the reintegration process: desistance from crime through the looking glass', *Psychology, Crime and Law*, vol 10, no 3, pp 271–81.

Matthews, R. (2005) 'The myth of punitiveness', *Theoretical Criminology*, vol 9, no 2, pp 175–201.

Matthews, R. (2009)'Beyond "so what?" Criminology: rediscovering realism', *Theoretical Criminology*, vol 13, no 3, pp 341-62.

May, J. (1979) *Committee of Inquiry into the United Kingdom Prison Services: Report*, Cmnd 7673, London: HMSO.

McAra, L. (2004) 'The cultural and institutional dynamics of transformation: youth justice in Scotland, England and Wales', *Cambrian Law Review*, vol 35, pp 23-54.

McAra, L. and McVie, S. (2007) 'Youth justice? The impact of system contact on patterns of desistance from offending', *European Journal of Criminology*, vol 4, no 3, pp 315-45.

McGuire, J. (ed) (1995) *What Works: Effective Methods to Reduce Re-offending*, Chichester: Wiley.

McGuire, J. (2002) 'Integrating findings from research reviews', in J. McGuire (ed) *Offender Rehabilitation and Treatment: Effective Programmes and Policies to Reduce Re-offending*, Chichester: Wiley.

McGuire, J. (2003) 'Maintaining change: converging legal and psychological initiatives in a therapeutic jurisprudence framework', *Western Criminology Review*, vol 4, no 2, pp 108-123.

McIvor, G. (2009) 'Therapeutic jurisprudence and procedural justice in Scottish drug courts', *Criminology & Criminal Justice*, vol 9, no 1, pp 29-49.

McKnight, J. (2009) 'Speaking up for probation', *Howard Journal*, vol 48, no 4, pp 327-43.

McNeill, F. (2006) 'A desistance paradigm for offender management', *Criminology & Criminal Justice*, vol 6, no 1, pp 39-62.

McNeill, F. and Weaver, B. (2007) *Giving Up Crime: Directions for Policy*, Glasgow: Scottish Centre for Crime and Justice Research.

McNeill, F., Bachelor, S., Burnett, R. and Knox, J. (2005) *21st Century Social Work. Reducing Re-offending: Key Practice Skills*, Edinburgh: Scottish Executive.

Merrington, S. and Stanley, S. (2000) 'Doubts about the What Works initiative', *Probation Journal*, vol 47, no 4, pp 272-5.

Mills, H., Silvestri, A. and Grimshaw, R. (2010) *Police Expenditure, 1999-2009*, London: Centre for Crime and Justice Studies.

Ministry of Justice (2007) *Evaluation of the North Liverpool Community Justice Centre*, Ministry of Justice Research Series 12/07, London: Ministry of Justice.

Ministry of Justice (2008a) *Punishment and Reform: Our Approach to Managing Offenders*, London: Ministry of Justice.

Ministry of Justice (2008b) *NOMS Third Sector Strategy: Improving Policies and Securing Better Public Services through Effective Partnerships*, London: Ministry of Justice.

Ministry of Justice (2008c) *Working with the Third Sector to Reduce Re-offending: Securing Effective Partnerships*, London: Ministry of Justice.

Ministry of Justice (2008d) *Delivering the Government Response to the Corston Report. A Progress Report on Meeting the needs of Women with Particular Vulnerabilities in the Criminal Justice System*, London: Ministry of Justice, http://webarchive.nationalarchives.gov.uk/+/http://www.justice.gov.uk/docs/corston-progress-report.pdf .

Ministry of Justice (2010a) *Breaking the Cycle: Effective Punishment, Rehabilitation and Sentencing Offenders*, Cm 7972, London: Ministry of Justice.

Ministry of Justice (2010b) *Green Paper Evidence Report*, London: Ministry of Justice.

Ministry of Justice (2011a) *Criminal Justice Statistics Quarterly Update to December 2010.* Ministry of Justice Statistics bulletin, May 2011. Online publication: www.justice.gov.uk/downloads/publications/statistics-and-data/criminal-justice-stats/criminal-stats-quarterly-dec10.pdf

Ministry of Justice (2011b) *Business Plan, 2011-2015, May 2011*, London: Ministry of Justice.

Morgan, R. (2003) 'Foreword', in *HMIP Annual Report 2002/2003*, London: Home Office.

Morgan, R. (2008) 'The risk of risk preoccupation: criminal justice policy in England', in *Risk and Public Services*, ESRC Public Services Programme, www2.lse.ac.uk/researchAndExpertise/units/CARR/publications/specialReports.aspx

Morgan, R. and Newburn, T. (2007) 'Youth justice', in M. Maguire, R. Morgan and R. Reiner (eds) *The Oxford Handbook of Criminology* (4th edn), pp 1024-60, Oxford: Oxford University Press.

Muncie, J. (2005) 'The globalisation of crime control: the case of youth and juvenile justice', *Theoretical Criminology*, vol 9, no 1, pp 35-64.

Muncie, J. (2008) 'The "punitive turn" in juvenile justice: cultures of control and rights compliance in Western Europe and the USA', *Youth Justice*, vol 8, no 2, pp 107-21.

Muncie, J. and Hughes, G. (2002) 'Modes of youth governance: political rationalities, criminalisation and resistance', in J. Muncie, G. Hughes and E. McLaughlin (eds) *Youth Justice: Critical Readings*, London: Sage Publications, pp 1-18.

Napo (2007) *Changing Lives: An Oral History of Probation*, London: Napo.

National Audit Office (2003) *The Operational Performance of PFI Prisons: Report by the Comptroller and Auditor General*, HC700 Session 2002-2003, London: Stationery Office.

National Audit Office (2009) *Innovation across Central Government*, London: National Audit Office.

Nellis, M. (2004) '"Into the Field of Corrections": the end of English Probation in the early 21st century', *The Cambrian Law Review*, 35, pp 115–33.

Nellis, M. (2006) 'NOMS, contestability and the process of technocorrectional innovation', in M. Hough, R. Allen and U. Padel (eds) *Reshaping Probation and Prisons: The New Offender Management Framework*, Bristol: The Policy Press.

Nellis, M (2009) 'Circles of support and accountability for sex offenders in England and Wales: their origins and implementation between 1999-2005', *British Journal of Community Justice*, vol 7, no 1, pp 23-44.

Newburn, T. and Reiner, R. (2007) 'Policing and the police', in M. Maguire, R. Morgan and R. Reiner (eds) *The Oxford Handbook of Criminology* (4th edn), Oxford: Oxford University Press, pp 910-52.

Newman, O. (1972) *Defensible Space: People and Design in the Violent City*, London: Architectural Press.

Neyroud, P. (2011) *Review of Police Leadership and Training*, London: Home Office, www.homeoffice.gov.uk/publications/consultations/rev-police-leadership-training/appendices?view=Binary.

Nolan, J.L. (2009) *Legal Accents, Legal Borrowing: The International Problem-Solving Court Movement*, Princeton, NJ: Princeton University Press.

Nozick, R. (1974) *Anarchy, State, and Utopia*, Oxford: Blackwell.

Nussbaum, M.C. and Sen, A.K. (eds) (1993) *The Quality of Life*, Oxford: Clarendon Press.

Obama, B. (2006) *The Audacity of Hope: Thoughts on Reclaiming the American Dream*, Edinburgh: Canongate Books.

Oborne, P. (2007) *The Triumph of the Political Class*, London: Simon and Schuster.

Oldfield, M. (1994) 'Talking quality, meaning control: McDonalds, the market and the probation service', *Probation Journal*, vol 41, no 4, pp 186-92.

O'Mahony, P. (2000) *Prison Policy in Ireland: Criminal Justice Versus Social Justice*, Cork: Cork University Press.

Omand, D., Starkey, K. and Adebowale, V. (2009) *Engagement and Aspiration: Reconnecting Policy Making with Front Line Professionals*, London: Cabinet Office.

Orwell, G. (1951) *Nineteen Eighty-Four*, London: Secker and Warburg.

Osborne, S. (ed) (2010) *The New Public Governance: Emerging Perspectives on the History and Practice of Public Governance*, London: Routledge.

Osborne, S. and Brown, L. (2011) 'Innovation, public policy and public services delivery in the UK: the word that would be king?', *Public Administration*, Online pre-publication version, May 2011. http://onlinelibrary.wiley.com/doi/10.1111/j.1467-9299.2011.01932.x/abstract

Osborne, S., Chew, C. and McLaughlin, K. (2008) 'The innovative capacity of voluntary and community organisations and the provision of public services: a longitudinal approach', *Public Management Review*, vol 10, no 1, pp 51-70.

Owers, A. (2010) *Valedictory Lecture to the Prison Reform Trust*, London: Prison Reform Trust.

Packer, H.L. (1968) *The Limits of the Criminal Sanction*, Stanford: Stanford University Press.

Parekh, B. (2000) *The Future of Multi-ethnic Britain: Report of the Commission on the Future of Multi-ethnic Britain*, London: Profile Books.

Pease, K. (2010) *Prison, Community Sentences and Crime: The Social Cost of Fewer Custodial Sentences*, London: Civitas.

Phillips, N. (2000) *The BSE Inquiry: The Report*, London: The Stationery Office, www.bseinquiry.gov.uk.

Pinker, S. (2002) *The Blank Slate: The Modern Denial of Human Nature*, London: Penguin.

Pitts, J. (2001) 'Korrectional karaoke: New Labour and the zombification of youth justice', *Youth Justice*, vol 1, no 2, pp 3-16

Player, E. (2010) 'Prisons' policy: the redevelopment of Holloway Prison', in D. Downes, D. Hobbs and T. Newburn (eds) *The Eternal Recurrence of Crime and Control*, Oxford: Oxford University Press, pp 95-114.

Prime Minister's Strategy Unit (2006) *The Government's Approach to Public Service Reform*, London: Cabinet Office.

Prior, D. (2011) 'Safer communities and community justice', in K. Doolin, J. Child, J. Raine and A. Beech (eds) *Whose Criminal Justice? State or Community?*, Winchester: Waterside Press, pp 159-72.

Probation Association (2011) *Hitting the Target, Missing the Point. A Constructive Critique of the Regulatory Framework for Probation Trusts*, London: Probation Association.

Pryor, S. (2001) *The Responsible Prisoner*, London: Her Majesty's Inspectorate of Prisons.

Putnam, R. (2000) *Bowling Alone: The Collapse and Revival of American Community*, New York, NY: Simon and Schuster.

Pycroft, A. and Gough, D. (2010) (eds) *Multiagency Working in Criminal Justice: Control and Care in Contemporary Correctional Practice*, Bristol: The Policy Press.

Radzinowicz, L. (1999) *Adventures in Criminology*, London: Routledge.

Raine, J. (2011) 'Community justice and the courts – a step forwards, backwards or sideways?', in K. Doolin, J. Child, J. Raine and A. Beech (eds) *Whose Criminal Justice? State or Community?*, Winchester: Waterside Press, pp 173–86.

Raine, J. and Willson, M. (1993) *Managing Criminal Justice*, Hemel Hempstead: Harvester Wheatsheaf.

Rawls, J. (1971) *A Theory of Justice*, Cambridge, MS: Belknap Press.

Rawls, J. (2001) *Justice as Fairness: A Restatement*, Cambridge, MA: Harvard University Press.

Raynor, P. (1985) *Social Work, Justice and Control*, Oxford: Blackwell.

Raynor, P. (2004) 'Opportunity, motivation and change: some findings from research on resettlement', in R. Burnett and C. Roberts (eds) *What Works in Probation and Youth Justice*, Cullompton: Willan Publishing, pp 217–33.

Raynor, P. and Robinson, G. (2005) *Rehabilitation, Crime and Justice*, Basingstoke: Palgrave Macmillan.

Raynor, P. and Vanstone, M. (2007) 'Towards a correctional service', in L. Gelsthorpe and R. Morgan (eds) *Handbook of Probation*, Cullompton: Willan Publishing, pp 59–89.

Raynor, P., Smith, D. and Vanstone, M. (1994) *Effective Probation Practice*, London: Macmillan.

Reiner, R. (2010) 'New theories of policing: a social democratic critique', in D. Downes, D. Hobbs and T. Newburn (eds) *The Eternal Recurrence of Crime and Control*, Oxford: Oxford University Press, pp 141–82.

Rex, S. (1999) 'Desistance from offending: experiences of probation', *Howard Journal*, vol 38, no 4, pp 366–83.

Rex, S. (2005). *Reforming Community Penalties*. Cullompton: Willan Publishing.

Rix, A., Joshua, F., Maguire, M. and Morton, S. (2009) *Improving Public Confidence in the Police: A Review of the Evidence*, Research Report 28, London: Home Office.

Roberts, C. (2004) 'Offending behaviour programmes: emerging evidence and implications for practice', in R. Burnett and C. Roberts (eds) *What Works in Probation and Youth Justice: Developing Evidence-based Practice*, Cullompton: Willan Publishing, pp 134–58.

Roberts, C., Burnett, R., Kirby, A. and Hamill, H. (1996) *A System for Evaluating Probation Practice: A Method Devised and Piloted by the Oxford Probation Studies Unit and Warwickshire Probation Service*, Probation Studies Unit Report No 1, Oxford: Centre for Criminological Research, University of Oxford.

Roberts, J. (2010) 'Women offenders: more troubled than troublesome?', in J. Brayford, F. Cowe and J. Deering (eds) *What Else Works? Creative Work with Offenders*, Cullompton: Willan Publishing.

Roberts, J.V. (2009) *Listening to the Victim: Evaluating Victim Input at Sentencing and Parole*, Chicago, IL: University of Chicago.

Roberts, J.V. and Hough, M. (2005) *Understanding Public Attitudes to Criminal Justice*, Maidenhead: Open University Press.

Roberts, R., Crook, F., Simon, J., Nellis, M., Seal, L., Pemberton, S. and Christie, N. (2010) 'Debating bad language in criminal justice', *Criminal Justice Matters*, no 81, pp 29-34.

Robinson, G. and Burnett, R. (2007) 'Experiencing modernization: frontline probation perspectives on the transition to a National Offender Management Service', *Probation Journal*, vol 54, no 4, pp 318-37.

Rock, P. (1996) *Reconstructing a Women's Prison: The Holloway Redevelopment Project, 1968-1988*, Oxford: Oxford University Press.

Royal Commission on Criminal Justice (1993) *Report*, Cm 2263, London, HMSO.

Royal Commission on Criminal Procedure (1981) *Report*, Cmnd 8092, London: HMSO.

Rutherford, A. (1993) *Criminal Justice and the Pursuit of Decency*, Oxford: Oxford University Press.

Ryan, M. (1999) 'Penal policy making towards the millennium: elites and populists; New Labour and the new criminology', *International Journal of the Sociology of Law*, vol 27, no 1, pp 1-22.

Ryan, M. (2003) *Penal Policy and Political Culture in England and Wales*, Winchester: Waterside Press.

Sandel, M. (2009) *Justice: What's the Right Thing To Do?*, London: Penguin.

Sanders, A. and Young, R. (2007) *Criminal Justice* (3rd edn), Oxford: Oxford University Press.

Scarman, L. (1981) *The Brixton Disorders 10-12 April 1981: Report of the Inquiry*, Cmnd 8427, London: HMSO.

Scottish Prisons Commission (2008) *Scotland's Choice: Report of the Scottish Prisons Commission* (McLeish Report), Edinburgh: Scottish Prisons Commission.

Scraton, P. (2008) 'Demonization', in B. Goldson (ed) *Dictionary of Youth Justice*, Cullompton: Willan Publishing.

Sen, A. (2009) *The Idea of Justice*, London: Allen Lane.

SEU (Social Exclusion Unit) (2002) *Reducing Re-offending by Ex-prisoners*, London: SEU.

Shapland, J., Atkinson, A., Atkinson, H., Dignan, J., Edwards, L., Hibbert, J., Howes, M., Johnstone, J., Robinson, G. and Sorsby, A. (2008) *Does Restorative Justice Affect Reconviction? The Fourth Report from the Evaluation of Three Schemes*, Ministry of Justice Research Series 10/08, London: Ministry of Justice.

Sheehy, P. (1993) *Inquiry into Police Responsibilities and Rewards*, London: Home Office.

Shewan, G. (2010) 'Evidence to the All Party Parliamentary Local Government Group Inquiry into Justice in Communities', www. restorativejustice.org.uk.

Skogan, W. (1994) *Contacts between Police and Public: Findings from the 1992 British Crime Survey*, Home Office Research Study No 134, London: HMSO.

Smith, D (1983) *Police and People in London*, London: Policy Studies Institute.

Snow, C.P. (1959) *The Two Cultures and the Scientific Revolution*, Cambridge: Cambridge University Press.

Solomon, E. and Garside, R. (2008) *Ten Years of Labour's Youth Justice Reforms: An Independent Audit*, London: Centre for Crime and Justice Studies.

Sowell, T. (2007) *A Conflict of Visions: Ideological Origins of Political Struggles*, New York, NY: Basic Books.

Sparks, R., Bottoms, A. and Hay, W. (1996) *Prisons and the Problem of Order*, Oxford: Oxford University Press.

Squires, P. and Stephen, D. (2010) 'Pre-crime and precautionary criminalisation', *Criminal Justice Matters*, no 81, pp 28-9.

Stanley, S. (2009) 'What works in 2009: progress or stagnation?', *Probation Journal*, vol 56, no 2, pp 153-74.

Stevens, A.W. (2011) 'Telling policy stories: an ethnographic study of the use of evidence in policy-making in the UK', *Journal of Social Policy*, vol 40, no 2, pp 237-55.

Stevens, A. (forthcoming) *Offender Rehabilitation and Therapeutic Communities: Enabling Change the TC Way*, London: Routledge.

Sunningdale Institute (2009) *Engagement and Aspiration: Reconnecting Policy Making with Front Line Professionals*, London: National School of Government.

T2A Alliance (2009) *A New Start: Young Adults in the Criminal Justice System*, London: Barrow Cadbury Trust, www.t2a.org.uk/publications.

Tam, E. (2003) 'The taming of desert: why Rawls' deontological liberalism is unfriendly to desert', Paper presented to the 2003 Canadian Political Science Association Conference held at Dalhousie University, Halifax, Canada. www.cpsa-acsp.ca/paper-2003/tam.pdf.

Thaler, R.H. and Sunstein, C.R. (2008) *Nudge: Improving Decisions about Health, Wealth, and Happiness*, New Haven, CT: Yale University Press.

Thomson, M. (2010) *Big Judges and Community Justice Courts*, Clinks Briefing, October London: Clinks, www.clinks.org/publications/briefings.

Towl, G. (2004) 'Applied psychological services in HM Prison Service and the National Probation Service', in A. Needs and G.J. Towl (eds) *Applying Psychology to Forensic Practice*, Oxford: BPS Blackwell.

Towl, G. (2010) 'Ethical issues in forensic psychological policy and practice', in Towl, G. and Crighton, D. (eds) *Forensic Psychology*. Oxford: BPS Blackwell.

Tyler, T. (2006a) *Why People Obey the Law: Procedural Justice, Legitimacy and Compliance*, Princeton, NJ: Princeton University Press.

Tyler, T. (2006b) 'Psychological perspectives on legitimacy and legitimation', *Annual Review of Psychology*, vol 57, pp 375-400.

Tyler, T. (2009) 'Legitimacy and criminal justice: the benefits of self-regulation', *Ohio State Journal Of Criminal Law*, vol 7, no 1, pp 307-59.

Tyler, T. and Huo, Y. (2002) *Trust in the Law: Encouraging Public Cooperation with the Police and Courts*, New York, NY: Russell Sage Foundation.

Vanstone, M. (2004) *Supervising Offenders in the Community: A History of Probation Theory and Practice*, Aldershot: Ashgate.

Victim Support (2010) *Victims' Justice? What Victims and Witnesses Really Want from Sentencing*, London: Victim Support.

von Hirsch, A., Garland, D. and Wakefield, A. (eds) (2000) *Ethical and Social Perspectives on Situational Crime Prevention*, Oxford: Hart Publishing.

von Hirsch, A. Bottoms, A., Burney, E. and Wikström, P.-O. (1999) *Criminal Deterrence and Sentence Severity: An Analysis of Recent Research*, Oxford: Hart Publishing.

Wacquant, L. (2009) *Prisons of Poverty*, Minneapolis, MN: University of Minnesota Press.

Waddington, P. (2010) 'A virtuous exception: the Macpherson inquiry and report into the murder of Stephen Lawrence and its investigation', in D. Downes, D. Hobbs and T. Newburn (eds) *The Eternal Recurrence of Crime and Control*, Oxford: Oxford University Press, pp 183-210.

Walden, G. (2000) *The New Elites: Making a Career in the Masses*, London: Penguin.

Walker, A. (2009) 'Primary justice – negotiating the narrow path', in *Transforming Justice: New Approaches to the Criminal Justice System*, London: Criminal Justice Alliance, pp 47-56.

Walklate, S. (2011) 'Victims policy: 1997-2010', in A, Silvestri (ed) *Lessons for the Coalition: New Labour and Criminal Justice: An End of Term Report*, London: Centre for Crime and Justice Studies.

Wallis, E. (2001) *A New Choreography: An Integrated Strategy for the National Probation Service for England and Wales*, London: Home Office.

Walters, R. (2008) 'Government manipulation of criminological knowledge and policies of deceit', in W. McMahon (ed) *Critical Thinking about Uses of Research*, London: Centre for Crime and Justice Studies.

Wampold, B.E. (2001) *The Great Psychotherapy Debate*, Mahwah, NJ: Erlbaum.

Ward, T. and Maruna, S. (2007) *Rehabilitation: Beyond the Risk Paradigm*, London and New York, NY: Routledge.

Ward, T. and Stewart, C.A. (2003) 'Criminogenic needs and human needs: a theoretical model', *Psychology, Crime, and Law*, vol 9, no 2, pp 125-43.

Westmarland, L. (2008) 'Police cultures' policing', in T. Newburn (ed) *Handbook of Policing* (2nd edn), Cullompton: Willan Publishing, pp 253-80.

Wexler, D.B. (2001) 'Robes and rehabilitation: how judges can help offenders "make good"', *Court Review*, vol 38, no 1, pp 18-23.

Wexler, D.B. and Winick, B.J. (eds) (1996) *Law in a Therapeutic Key: Developments in Therapeutic Jurisprudence*, Durham, NC: Carolina Academic Press.

Wheatley, P. (2010) 'The importance of purpose, vision and values in improving offender management performance', *Euro Vista*, vol 1, no 1, pp 32-7.

Whitehead, P. and Stratham, R. (2007) *The History of Probation: Politics, Power and Cultural Change, 1876-2005*, London: Sweet and Maxwell.

Whyte, D. (ed) (2009) *Crimes of the Powerful: A Reader*, Maidenhead: Open University Press.

Wilkinson, R. and Pickett, K. (2009) *The Spirit Level: Why More Equal Societies Almost Always Do Better*, London: Allen Lane.

Wilson, A. (2008) *Punching Our Weight: The Humanities and Social Sciences in Public Policy Making*, London: British Academy.

Wilson, J. and Kelling, G. (1982) 'Broken windows: the police and community safety', *Atlantic Monthly*, March, pp 29-38.

Windlesham, D. (1993) *Responses to Crime: Penal Policy in the Making, Vol 2*, Oxford: Oxford University Press.

Windlesham, D. (1996) *Responses to Crime: Legislating with the Tide, Vol 3*, Oxford: Oxford University Press.

Woolf, H. (1991) *Report of an Inquiry into the Prison Disturbances of April 1990* (The Woolf Report), Cmnd 1456, London: HMSO.

Young, J. (1999) *The Exclusive Society: Social Exclusion, Crime and Difference in Late Modernity*, London: Sage Publications.

Young, R. and Hoyle, C. (2003) 'New improved restorative justice? Action-research and the Thames Valley initiative in restorative cautioning', in A. von Hirsch, A. Bottoms, J. Roberts, J. Roach and M. Schiff (eds) *Restorative Justice and Criminal Justice: Competing or Complementary Paradigms?*, Oxford: Hart Publishing.

Zedner, L. (2007a) 'Seeking security by eroding rights', in B. Goold and L. Lazarus (eds) *Security and Human Rights*, Oxford: Hart Publishing.

Zedner, L. (2007b) 'Pre-crime and post-criminology?', *Theoretical Criminology*, vol 11, no 2, pp 261-81.

Zedner, L. (2010) 'Reflections on criminal justice as a social institution', in D. Downes, D. Hobbs and T. Newburn (eds) *The Eternal Recurrence of Crime and Control*, Oxford: Oxford University Press, pp 69-94.

Zedner, L. (2011) 'Putting crime back on the criminological agenda', in M. Bosworth and C. Hoyle (eds) *What is Criminology?*, Oxford: Oxford University Press, pp 271-85.

Index

Note: Page numbers followed by *n* refer to information in a footnote.

J

James, Erwin 160-1
jobs *see* employment
joined-up working 33-4, 131, 174
  see also inter-agency working
Judge, Lord 98
judgements: impossibility of
  perfection 4
judicial independence principle of
  47, 50
judiciary
  and community justice
    community justice centres 77, 90
    lay magistracy 76, 78
  discretion in sentencing 191, 196
  involvement after sentencing 186
  relations with Conservative
    government 42-50, 98-9
    with Labour government 58
  see also courts; sentencing
juries: trials without juries 87, 88
'just deserts' *see* proportionality
justice
  community and local justice 76-80,
    191, 194-5
  meanings, concepts and theories of
    15, 16-22
  due process and legitimacy 15, 22-9,
    137-8, 189, 193
  quality improvement and
    Conservative policy in 1980s 38
  quality under threat from Labour
    reforms 88
  and relations between state and
    citizens 15, 29-32
  and society 200
  see also *theories of justice*
JUSTICE (all-party reform
  organisation) 89, 90
Justice for All (white paper) 58-9, 114
'justice reinvestment' 65, 185-6, 194,
  197
juvenile justice
  doli incapax 128-9, 192
  devolution of responsibility for 197
  and Labour policy in 1990s 55, 56
  and restorative justice 102, 103
  transition to adulthood programmes
    140-2, 192
  see also borstal institutions; youth
    justice system; youth offending
    services

K

Kant, Immanuel 17, 29
  categorical imperative 17
  Kantian ethic 17
  universal law 17
Khan, Sadiq 6
kindness 3*n*
  kind treatment 138
  see also humanity, decency
King, R. 152
knives 95 *see also* violence
knowledge of effectiveness 125, 195*n*
  academic knowledge 7, 181-2
  see also evidence-based policy; 'what
    works'

L

Labour governments 8-9, 54
  and innovation 178
  language of managerialism 35
  in 1990s and 2000s 55-68
    complexity and volume of new
      legislation 61-2
    and court proceedings reform
      87-8
    managerialism and criminal justice
      'system' 34, 35, 62-3
    police and policing 113-14
    punitive approach to sentencing
      95-6
    role of civil society and
      communities 70-2
    victims as focus of 55, 60, 100
    'what works' policy approach 57,
      66-8, 127, 129-30
  and research evidence 180, 181
  and role of civil society and
    communities 70-2, 73
  community justice centres 77
  debasing of community service 76-7
  voluntary sector and service delivery
    81, 83
Lambert, M.J. 134, 135
Lacey, Nicola 65, 194
Lane, Lord 42-3
language
  coalition and instrumental language
    196
  and Conservative policy in 1980s
    45-6
  debasing usage 34, 76-7
  political slogans 35
  and power relations in prison 149